Praise for
The American Longbow

Pope, Young, and the Thompson brothers were lonely voices when they began to write about bows and bowhunting in America, but we now enjoy a wealth of literature on these subjects. Some tell readers how to make a bow, while others focus on how to use one. In this lucid volume, Stephen Graf takes the process one step further by addressing what may be the most important question of all: Why? Make no mistake, this book will provide both novice and experienced bowyers plenty of practical, perhaps even inspired, information about how to build an American Semi-Longbow, and he does this as well as I've ever seen it done. But his ability to integrate the goal of his labor into the environment he inhabits—reminiscent of Aldo Leopold—makes this book stand out from all the rest. You heard it here first: Graf has written a classic.

E. Donnall Thomas, Jr.
Co-editor of *Traditional Bowhunter Magazine* and author of many books including *How Sportsmen Saved the World*

At last! A real treasure for us who are enamored with the simple longbow. As a professional bowyer for over 50 years, I can happily testify that Steve's book will give you a complete, accurate, thorough and pleasant examination of the hows and whys of the modern American Semi-Longbow.

Fred Anderson
Maker of Skookum bows and author of several books including *The Traditional Way*

I have built several wood bows, but the specialized skills required to craft a fiberglass-backed bow have always remained to me a mystery. Until now. Here, In *The American Longbow. How to Make One and Its Place in A Good Life*, former NASA space engineer Stephen Graf provides detailed building instructions that leave nothing to chance, further clarified by meaningful illustrations. And icing on the cake, in Stephen we find an exceptionally thoughtful outdoorsman, a devoted family man and self-reliance advocate with something worth saying and the skills to say it well. Even if, like me, you never plan to build a glass-backed bow, this book is surprisingly thought-provoking and a joy to read. Thank you, Mr. Graf.

David Petersen
Conservationist, founding member of Back Country
Hunters and Anglers, and author of many books including
On the Wild Edge and *Hunting for the Natural Life*

The American Longbow

How to make one,
and its place in a good life

Stephen Graf

Raven's Eye Press
Durango, Colorado

Raven's Eye Press
Durango, Colorado
www.ravenseyepress.com

Graf, Stephen.
    The American Longbow: How to make one, and its place in a good
    life / Stephen Graf
    p. cm.

1. Bowhunting
2. Woodworking
3. Ecology
4. Philosophy
I. Title

ISBN 978-0-9907826-6-7
LCCN 2017941306

Cover and interior design by Lindsay J. Nyquist, elle jay design

Printed in the United States of America
1 3 5 7 9 10 8 6 4 2

This book is for my children.

Any proceeds from the sale of this book are hereby assigned to the Theodore Roosevelt Conservation Partnership. The Partnership works to preserve wild places, whether public or private, so that we may always have somewhere to hunt.

An investment in the land is an investment in the good life.

Contents

Thank You

As I began to write this book, I had no idea how much effort it would take, or how it would affect me. In truth, I never expected to finish it. But here I am at the end of the process, thinking of those who helped me. I should have kept a list.

Since I didn't, I will keep it short.

I'd like to thank Nate Steen for his guidance in learning the swing draw. When I contacted him, it was with the intent of buying one of his famous bows. While he has so far, and steadfastly, refused to add me to his mile long list of waiting archers, he has spent countless hours schooling me in the way of the swing draw at no charge (in the highest tradition of archers). Thank you my friend.

I'd like to thank my mom for wading through the rough draft and helping to make it a better book. My sister-in-law Shannon McConnell deserves thanks too for giving what was supposed to be the final draft a really careful reading (not quite the final draft, as it turned out). My thanks to both of you.

I'd like to thank Zach Watkins for editing this book (he never saw this part, so he can't be held responsible) and Lindsay Nyquist for doing the layout. Without their work this book would never have been published. Still, they meant well.

Finally, I'd like to thank my wife. Jacqueline was the first to read these chapters as they were written, and she read them too many times to count. Her patience, critique, and support glued this book together. Thank you my wife.

Nomenclature

Nomenclature is the naming of things, particularly as they apply to science or other disciplines. It is also a source of controversy.

A longbow has always been just that, a longbow. It had been unchanged in Europe for a thousand years until John Smith and his band from the Virginia Company founded Jamestown and a new country was born. In that new country, archery again took root and by the early 20th century those inventive Americans had applied their new perspectives and needs to the bow, and made the first significant changes to this venerable weapon since its invention so long ago.

The need to distinguish between the new and the old predictably arose.

The old longbow, a device used by all those in Europe, was nevertheless referred to as an English Longbow. Its design has been static for untold generations.

The new bow, a device born in the United States with deep roots in the European bow, has seen many variations in its design. Herein lie the foundations of the controversy over its defining characteristics. Herein lie the challenges of nomenclature.

The English Longbow, made of a single piece of yew, was necessarily at least 6 feet long to preserve its integrity. The American versions, made of other woods and made by laminating several pieces together, could be shorter, wider, and thinner. Where to draw the line?

Those that started this experimentation were familiar with bows 6 feet long. To them anything less than 6 feet was not a longbow, but a semi-longbow. For those of us familiar with shorter bows, we are comfortable calling bows 5 feet, or 5 1/2 feet, or 4 1/2 feet, a longbow. Is this a problem?

I used the phrase "American Longbow" in the title of this book to distinguish what I have studied from its European ancestor, while attempting to avoid a thorny debate on the cover. In truth, I feel the phrase "American Semi-Longbow" is a more accurate name and will use it in the remainder of the book.

For those of us new to shooting and making these bows, this nomenclature discussion may seem odd, unnecessary, even irrelevant. The word "semi" just clutters up the title and begs more questions than it answers.

For those of us practiced in shooting and making bows, this nomenclature is familiar and may hold special meaning and be dear to our hearts. Thus, adding the word "semi" could raise the hackles of those whose ideas about the American Semi-Longbow diverge from my own.

There is no definitive way to know if I am correct in my nomenclature. There is no absolute authority we can consult on the matter.

There are those that may feel that what I have described in this book is nothing more than a flat bow. There are those that agree with me, that it meets the definition of an American Semi-Longbow.

As you read this book, you will have to decide for yourself what to call it. You will have to decide if it really matters.

Hopefully, in the end, what we call it is not as important to us as what we learn from making and shooting it, and what it has to teach us about living the good life.

Foreword

My intention in writing this book was simply to outline how I make my version of the American Semi-Longbow. As I started to put it down in writing, I realized that it is hard to separate the "how-to" from the "why-to."

Additionally, I came to realize that even just recording the "how-to" was hard to do. Learning how to make bows is a process that never seems to stop. Trying to determine when to start such a book is like trying to decide when to buy a computer.

Computer technology is continually improving, and prices are continually falling. A person in the market to buy a new computer soon discovers that there is no ideal time to commit to the purchase. If we wait for the next innovation or price drop, we end up never buying the computer at all.

It is best to simply buy a computer when we need it and when it is convenient. It is best not to fret over getting the best deal, or the best machine.

I found the same to be true of writing this book. If I were to wait until I had finally nailed it down, finally arrived at the best design, finally made the best bow possible, I would never have started.

Thus this book doesn't represent the last word in my bow making adventure, but merely a fuzzy line in the sand.

If you read this book, you will see that I never outline, in so many words, how to make the best bow. You will notice that sometimes I call out one quality of the bow as good, while later on putting another, seemingly opposite, quality in the limelight.

If this book has value to you in your journey to make an American Semi-Longbow, it may simply be in that it outlines the various features such a bow can have and why they might be important. It is up to you to decide what is right for you.

There are no secrets revealed in this book. I have simply tried to put the nature of the American Semi-Longbow in context with the work required to make one, and with the mindset I had to develop to appreciate it.

If you read this book, with notebook and pen at hand, you should be able to outline, for yourself, what you want to build and how you plan on doing it. If this proves true, then I have succeeded in my purpose.

Additionally, it must be realized that I am strictly a hobbyist. No one in their right mind would hand over money in exchange for one of my bows. The perspective I bring to this book, and the message I want most to convey to you, is simply: Hey, if I can do it, you can too!

Chapter 1
By Way of Introduction

What is it about the American Semi-Longbow, hereafter referred to as ASL, that has me so dedicated to it? I don't have a simple answer to that. I grew up as most other country kids of my generation did, which included making bows from bent saplings and arrows from straight sticks. These of course proved less effective than my imagination had predicted. As I grew past my boyhood days, bent sapling archery got left behind. I took up deer hunting with a rifle and was happy. Then I saw a compound bow in the Best Buy store and, as they say, got hooked.

I am now in midlife, far enough along that I can look back and there is something to see. What I see is that the trajectory of my interest in hunting has taken the typical track. At the beginning I was googly-eyed to kill deer with guns, scopes, and gadgets. Further along, I moved to compound bows, what I saw at the time as more of a challenge. And now, presumably half way along my curve, I have taken to traditional bows.

Here I see a curve within a curve, almost a fractal construct. I started with curvy, scxy recurves promising speed, technology, and forgiveness. And now I have taken to the ASL: simple, straight, reliable, but still laminated back and belly with fiberglass. Having the experience of middle age and the ability to extrapolate my life trajectory into the future, do I see myself moving on to self bows with no hint of modern technology? I don't know. I can't say. And I don't really care. There are those that feel like the introduction of fiberglass to the sport of archery spelled its demise as a primitive sport as Paul Comstock laments in his excellent book *The Bent*

Stick. At this time, I am not in that camp.

But I do feel the need to make and keep hunting and archery traditional. Not necessarily primitive, but traditional. The difference between primitive archery and traditional archery balances on the point of view of the hunter. To me, primitive archery is about understanding, duplicating, and using archery tack as it would have been made during the Pleistocene epoch. Traditional archery is about using a simple bow, without the aid of sights or other gadgets, to kill game. It focuses on the skill required to hunt successfully with such gear, and the social and ecological value of such hunting. Others may disagree with me, but I believe the skill required to shoot a self bow and a fiberglass backed traditional bow are about the same. So I think of primitive archery as a subset of traditional archery.

At one time, the ASL could have been called a primitive bow, as it was made without the advantage of fiberglass. But for the most part, bows made today include this wonderful material. Thus, I think of the ASL, with its back and belly of fiberglass, as a traditional bow.

And I think of it as traditional not just in terms of its construction, but also in terms of its function and use. It is part of a metaphor for how we should think about and interact with the land. There are those who recognized this metaphor long before I did. Here is how Dave Sigurslid puts it in *An Archer's Inner Life*:

> *My conscience has begun to bother me because I am a hunter. Those who paint with too broad a stroke will come to false conclusions about me because I am a hunter. I am, against all my wishes, prayer, arguments to the contrary, grouped by the majority of Americans with the techno-hunter. But I am seeking less blood and steel, less warfare with nature, more poetry. We are not at war, we are predators. Natural predators use piercing teeth and scratching claws. Our remote ancestors use the piercing tooth of a stone tipped arrow. To again become predators ourselves, we do not need the implements of modern warfare. We are sentient beings with the gift of metaphor, with the ability to use links that stand us closer to what we seek: nature, our nature.*

Here lies my love of the ASL. As I get older, I have become as concerned with how I acquire my meat as I am with the meat itself. Just as wild meat is better for the mind and body than industrial meat, the act of hunting works to improve the mind and body too. A quick trip to the woods with rifle or compound makes for a more surely successful hunt. But it also makes for less work. Many days spent going afield are surely better for the body and mind than one trip.

Aside from this obviously more challenging and rigorous aspect to hunting with a traditional bow, the bow itself contains within it all the ingredients of a more rigorous effort. A quick trip to the sporting goods store to purchase a rifle does not require much physical effort, compared to the effort required to fashion a bow from wood and glass, to whittle and scrape it to adjust its behavior, and to practice during the off-season to perfect, or at least try to perfect, its use.

Muscle and mind benefit from the effort.

The simplicity of a stick and string speaks to the merits of living a simple and cooperative life with nature and serves to constantly remind me that I am here for but a short time and I have a responsibility to leave this place at least as alive as I found it. While many of the qualities of the ASL are the qualities of any traditional bow, they are maybe easier to appreciate as there are few other qualities to cloud the issue and interfere with my observations. There are no fancy curves to the limbs, no oversized handle with lots of colors and contrasts to steer my eye away from the big picture. Just the fundamentals. A straight limb, a small riser (or handle) that allows me to hold the bow, and simple string nocks at the ends of slender tapered limbs.

The power, durability, forgiveness, and quiet performance of an ASL are not immediately obvious. They have to be experienced by the bowhunter. And they can only be experienced if the bowhunter is willing to learn how to handle such a bow.

A recurve, or a compound for that matter, is designed in such a way that there is no hand shock when the arrow is loosed. Hand shock is the result of energy, left in the bow after the arrow has left on its mission, looking for a way to expend itself. Recurves are designed with short limbs and a big riser. These short limbs efficiently deliver energy to the arrow, the remainder being absorbed by the overly large and massive riser. But to my mind, they serve as a step to separate us from what is happening, from nature.

An ASL, by contrast, has longer limbs and a smaller riser incapable of absorbing this surplus energy. But still, it can be a sweet shooter. It is up to the bowhunter, not the engineer, to deal with the surplus. In this fact is the first lesson the observant bowhunter learns. We all too often ask our engineers or politicians to deal with our surpluses or wastes that harm our land. We drive our big cars and buy our gadgets made from complex materials shaped in complex ways and leave it to others to deal with the consequences. We are all too comfortable in the false expectation that politicians, businessmen, and engineers can negate the consequences of such inharmonious contraptions and actions.

If we commit ourselves to a simpler weapon, we learn that there are ways of shooting the bow, ways of changing the arrow and the string, that will result in a forgiving and gentle shot. Through this commitment to a simpler weapon, we can learn that there are ways of living that will result in a forgiving and robust ecology, and a gentle and satisfying life.

This lesson leads to a further observation, if we are patient and learn from our lessons. We discover that we are part of the system. The way I was raised and schooled led me to the perspective that we humans are apart from nature. Nature's overseer. Zookeeper. This perspective led me, and I suspect most people, to believe that my actions are somehow apart from nature, an overlay. Sort of like the top-down block diagram mentality of corporate management. This made me blind to the truth that I am part of the biotic system. My actions are no more important or separate than the yearly migrations of robins, or the eager mating rituals of spring peepers. The real distinction is my ability to judge my actions. To add moral weight to them.

So I can shoot a recurve or compound that has been designed to damp out the hand shock of a poorly tuned bow, oblivious to the pain the bow is experiencing and eternally frustrated that my arrow never seems to fly true. No doubt I'll be surprised and disappointed when one day the bow splits apart, unable to handle its hidden strain any longer.

While this example is admittedly extreme, it serves to show me a correlation in nature. How many times have I poured some offensive material down the drain, designed to relieve me of my waste products without a second thought? Or taken a load of garbage to the dump? Out of sight, out of mind.

But now, shooting my ASL, it continually reminds me when I am doing something that hurts the system. It reminds me if I am not heeling the grip as I should, or canting the bow too much, or failing to align my string arm with the arrow. Natural systems, left to their own devices, tend toward complexity and health. Humans, by their curiosity and intellect, tend to disrupt these natural systems. My ASL constantly reminds me that if I want to be happy in my shooting, I have to work with it. And by extension, if I want to be happy in my life, I need to work with nature. I am a part of the system. Not apart from it.

For me, this is probably the biggest lesson my ASL has taught me. I am a mechanical engineer by trade. It seems I have been hardwired since birth with the idea that I can fix anything, make it better, simply by designing a suitable mechanism. While superficially this is true in many circumstances, the bigger truth is that for most things that are important to a good life, nature already has suitable mechanisms in place. I just need to learn to see and understand them.

I don't mean to disparage recurves and compounds by my comments. I just mean to explain what it is that draws me to the ASL. The reader may get the impression that I hold a negative opinion of other bows. I do not. In fact, I see these other bows as stepping stones in my journey to understand the world we live in and its ecological systems. Without them, I wouldn't be where I am today.

I mentioned before that nature tends toward complexity and health. By "complex" I don't mean "complicated." A complicated mechanism is one that performs a task, but it has superfluous elements that don't contribute to the task. They simply exist. Whereas a complex mechanism is one that performs a complex task. It can do so because it is capable of performing complex operations, and is robust in that disruptions to its operation are tolerated and don't affect the outcome... much.

An example of a complicated mechanism is the old Mousetrap board game. Players add components to the mousetrap until at some point it can perform a series of operations that ultimately results in the mouse being captured. The fun is in watching this complicated mechanism rattle along with only a marginal chance of completing its task. A simpler example may be dominos set up so that one can be tipped over, setting off a cascade of falling dominos. Again, almost any disruption to the system can stop the cascade.

Luckily for us, nature, or the land, is not so susceptible to disruption.

I used the word "land" in this context already in this chapter. By land I do not mean only that which we stand on, I mean the new context of the word that Aldo Leopold gave us in *A Sand County Almanac*:

> *The land ethic simply enlarges the boundaries of the community to include soils, waters, plants, and animals, or collectively: the land.*

Man can and does constantly disturb the land's systems and so far, at least, humans have not had to face any major consequences.

We can see this same dynamic when we look at the ASL and compare it to a compound. An ASL consists of an elastic member (bow) and a string. And that's it. The string communicates with the bow via grooves filed into the tips of the limbs. How much more simple could it be? And yet it performs its task perfectly every time it is shot. Compare this to a compound bow. It consists of a metal riser, limbs rigidly attached to the ends of the riser, pulleys affixed to the ends of the limbs, and a series of cables that connects the pulleys on both ends of the bow together.

The compound bow is so short that it cannot be reliably loosed with the hand. It must be triggered by a mechanical release. Together with sights, stabilizers, cable guards, bearings, and vibration dampers, this makes the basic compound system. As such, it is a very accurate weapon. In fact, should a compound shooter and an ASL shooter stand side by side, the compound shooter will most always shoot more accurately.

But let's perturb the system. Let's move the target to an unknown distance. Let's make the target move while the archers try to shoot it. Let's make the archers stand on one foot and shoot behind their backs. Now the outcome is not so sure. In fact, I would go so far as to say that the ASL shooter now has the advantage and will likely be the better shooter.

Another perturbation is to actually shoot the bows. Traditional archers love to shoot their bows and do so at every opportunity. The more the bows are shot, the better they shoot. This is not the case with compounds. Ask a compound shooter the last time he practiced with his bow and he is likely to say he shot it 10 times before the season to make sure it was "dialed in." And that's it. Why? While I won't attempt to debate whether shooting compound bows is fun, I will say that they can be finicky if shot too much. The sight can move from vibration. The arrow rest can move in a similar way, and a cable can stretch, putting the cams out of timing. Any of these things, and more, will make the system fail to perform its job.

The more we separate ourselves from the basic function of the bow, the less we can count on that which separates us. The compound was designed and built to relieve us of the necessity to build our physical fitness and our eye-hand coordination. Instead of time and effort separating us from our goal of hitting the mark or killing a deer, it is only money. But the true price we pay is in poorer health, less time spent enjoying the flight of the arrow, and when the moment of truth arrives, some doubt as to the outcome.

And so we look back to the ASL and see a simple machine. Can it fail? Oh yes. But if it is not abused by underweight arrows, overly high temperatures in the attic, or some other avoidable disaster, it will serve for many, many decades. Look around and you will see traditional bows built 60 years ago still in service, being shot every day. I doubt you will find many compounds even five years old still being used. Most traditional bows will shoot more arrows in a year than a compound will loose in its lifetime.

And for some reason, maybe it's just the simple joy of it, owners of ASLs seem to lead the traditional pack in arrows shot. I have no empirical data to support this statement. Just my personal observations. It is my experience that no other design of bow can give the same joy to the archer as loosing an arrow from an ASL and watching it arc through the air and drop into the target.

As we add layers of complication between us and the land we are a part of, I wonder if we are not robbing ourselves of the simple joy of living. We pulled the plug on the hunter-gatherer life 10,000 years ago when we planted spelt in the ground and stopped to watch it grow. We can never go back to the way it was. Cities are the natural outcome of the transition to an agricultural species. But living in large communities as we do, oblivious, mostly, to the vagaries of weather, it becomes harder and harder to remember what makes a joyful life. For me, the ASL serves to connect me, through its simple form and elegant function, to the land.

So what makes an ASL an ASL? And what makes a good ASL a good ASL? The first question is pretty easy to answer. The answers to the second question may invite debate.

Archery has survived in Western culture in fits and spurts ever since its heyday in the Middle Ages as a weapon of war. As its use as a weapon (for war and hunting) was made obsolete by black powder and the invention of the gun, it gained recognition as a tool for sport and leisure time.

In Europe, archery has pretty much stayed a recreational target sport. In the United States, with its bounty of wild game, not only was archery enjoyed as a target sport, but the bow was embraced, once again, as a hunting weapon. Maurice Thompson and his brother Will were the first in modern times to employ it for hunting. Maurice and Will were veterans of the Confederacy and as such were prohibited from owning or using guns. They naturally turned to the bow to answer their need to hunt.

Maurice chronicled their adventures in his ever-famous book, *The Witchery of Archery*. As they gained experience in using the bow for hunting, they stuck with the European design of the long bow. Their bows were long, 70 inches or more, worked through the handle, and had a round belly.

While I am sure many Americans before and after the Thompson brothers used bows for hunting, history has no record of it. The next recorded turn in bow hunting was taken by Saxton Pope, Art Young, and Will Compton. Their adventures were recorded in Pope's book *Hunting with the Bow and Arrow*. In it, Pope records his early experiences with Ishi, the last wild Indian of the Yahi tribe who left his wilderness home when he became ill. Ishi made acquaintance with Saxton Pope, his doctor, in a hospital in California.

While Pope, Young, and Compton had the advantage of studying and using Indian bows, they again chose to remain with the tried-and-true English Longbow design. Pope records the results of his testing of various bow designs which, to his mind, showed the superiority of the English Longbow in power and cast as compared to the Indian designs:

> *The following is a partial list of those [bows] weighted and shot. They are, of course, all genuine bows and represent the strongest. Each was shot at least six times ... In fact we spared no bows because of their age, and consequently broke two in the testing. It will be seen from these tests that no existing aboriginal bow is very powerful when compared to those in use in the days of robust archery in old England.*

Much can be said about the merits of different designs based on materials and usage. And indeed many books have been written on the subject. Suffice it to say that with the available materials, an English Longbow made from Pacific yew provided the most durable bow with the best cast. And so the design of the longbow remained static even into the early 20th century.

The next, and most important, historical reference in the evolution of the longbow is from Howard Hill. Hill started shooting the longbow as it was shown to him in its English War Bow configuration. I do not know, and cannot say, what drove his development of this bow. But his motivation was, I imagine, the same as all of ours: to tinker with the thing we love the most.

While it may not be deserved, I give credit to Howard Hill for the development of the American Semi-Longbow, if for no other reason than he is the one who coined the name in his book *Hunting the Hard Way*:

> *Of all the varying designs and combinations of features there has been only one bow developed in modern times that makes a better hunting bow than the conventional English longbow, and that is the American semi-longbow.*

The ASL differs from its ancestor in a number of significant ways. It is a somewhat shorter bow than the English Longbow, which makes it easier to take through the woods. It does not bend through the handle, which makes it more forgiving of poor shooting and easier on the archer's arms. It is flat on both the back and the belly, which gives it better cast and more durability.

At the time Hill began his development of the ASL, there were no real technological improvements to materials and adhesives available to him that were not already available to earlier bowyers. He did, however, explore ways of designing and building bows that others had not.

Hill settled on bamboo as the finest material from which to make a longbow. Since bamboo does not grow in a solid trunk, but rather in a hollow colm, Hill had to experiment with laminating many layers of bamboo together to achieve the necessary blank from which to form his bow. In addition to making his bow blank from laminated bamboo, he added a small handle, or riser, to the center of the bow. This allowed him to stiffen the bow and improve its performance while also adding an arrow shelf to get the arrow off the hand. The use of bamboo in place of yew allowed him to make the bow shorter, as bamboo can tolerate greater compression forces.

And so was born the American Semi-Longbow.

The ASL continued to evolve with the explosion of material science that accompanied the Second World War. Fiberglass was adopted as the best material to use for the back and belly of the bow. Adhesives were developed that allowed more durable and weatherproof bows to be made. Coatings were developed to apply to the exterior of the bow to make them even more weatherproof.

But the basic design requirements, and the function and feel of the bow, have changed little since Hill's time. Maybe that's what attracts me to it. I find myself constantly balancing my need to make things better with my desire to keep life simple. I find a perfection of this balancing act in the ASL.

The ASL limbs bend in a single arch from the handle to the string nock. What more is needed? The limbs are thick enough to provide good cast, but thin enough that they will endure many decades of shooting. Who wants to put all that effort into a bow just to watch it fail while the memory of its construction is still fresh in the mind? It has a small riser that provides the necessary stiffness to enhance the bow's performance and ergonomics, yet doesn't take away from the beauty of the limbs by its overbearing presence.

Life is a yin-yang struggle for balance. There is no free lunch, as they say. We are always struggling to find a balance in our lives between what we need to do, and what we want to do. This struggle takes expression in the things we make and buy to make our lives better. All too often we acquire things with the intent to make our lives better, when in fact they serve only to remove us one step farther from truly experiencing life.

We get into hunting because we want to reconnect with nature and our ancestral selves, or we want to improve the quality of the food we eat, or we want to develop a tradition in our family that binds us together. Most likely all three. This is a good start. But then we apply our modern-day algorithms (designed to help us cope with our ever more complex world) to our newfound desire to hunt. And the result is too often unnecessary complication of the hobby. I find that my ASL is a good anchor. It keeps me honest and focused on what's important.

You can't get too far out of whack if your starting point is an ASL. It has no holes for mounting accessories, so stabilizers, arrow rests, sights, slings, etc. are not an option. Think of the money saved! The arrow shelf is shallow, which means an arrow with a weaker spine will fly best. No worries about the most expensive carbon arrows or chasing that ever elusive "fast setup."

The ASL is a true "point and shoot" bow. It works best with a relaxed style, an easy low wrist hold on the bow, a comfortably canted posture to get the eye over the arrow. All these things come more naturally than the Olympic posture taken to shoot high-strung recurves at target butts 90 yards away. The American Semi-Longbow is a true pleasure to shoot. Howard Hill said in his book *Hunting the Hard Way* that the reason he shot the American Semi-Longbow was because he was not a good enough shot to shoot anything else:

I have been asked why I don't shoot a recurve. I can answer that query simply and to the point, without hesitation: I am not skilled enough to shoot a short recurved bow accurately. This simple statement is not meant to be a jest; it is the straight truth, and I am not ashamed of it.

I think what he meant to convey by this statement is the sentiment that we need to keep it simple to do our best. I have found this true. Every time I pick up my ASL, I am reminded of it.

Speaking of picking up an ASL, the first thing you will notice about it is how light it is. I doubt you will find one over 18 ounces. Compare this to a typical recurve weight of 3-4 pounds, or a compound weight of 4-5 pounds. It is light in the hand, truly easy to point and shoot.

The next thing you will notice is the shape of the grip. Since the riser is small, there is no room for experimentation with fancy, deep, high-wristed constructs. It must, by necessity, be simple. There are very few variations you will find in the design of the grip, but they are important.

The simplest and most common grip design is the straight grip. The line on the palm side of the handle runs straight down from the bottom of the arrow shelf into the fade on the lower limb. It may be thinner or thicker, it can be rounded over and blended into the lower limb. By its simple nature it causes no muss, no fuss.

Another design option is called a dished grip. Instead of a straight line down the palm side, the grip is slightly curved, with the bottom of the curve occurring in the center of the handle.

A less popular design option is called the bulbous grip. It is the opposite of the dished grip in that the curve extends outward with its high point occurring in the center of the handle.

As simple as the ASL is, it still offers infinite opportunities to tweak its form and encourage the uniquely human desire to make an ever more perfect tool.

So why is it that I want to design and build my own bow when there are plenty of good bows built by good bowyers for sale? I could justify it by saying that I don't want to spend any more money than I have to, which sounds good. But if you build your own bow, you will soon learn that the cost of doing it yourself far exceeds the cost of simply buying one. I could justify it by saying that I think I can come up with a better design than anyone else has, but that hubris is soon proven unjustified by the performance comparison of my bow to any quality bow on the market.

I think the answer is to be found in that uniquely human desire to understand. When people come to traditional archery and the ASL, their immediate thought is not "I want to build one." It is more likely: "I want to learn to shoot one." Learning to shoot a traditional bow is an adventure in and of itself. As one learns to shoot a bow, one learns the personality of the bow. How to grip it, how to pull the string, what kind of arrows to feed it, and so on. As one learns the personality of the bow, one naturally wants to learn what is responsible for that personality, and how one can best "communicate" with it.

This exercise of learning about the bow becomes a lifelong endeavor. It can be compared to a Buddha exercise or even meditation. It is a simple exercise with infinite possibilities. How is it that it can take a lifetime to learn to pull a string back and send an arrow into a bullseye, which may be only 15 yards from the archer? I can only answer this question with another question: How is it that it can take a lifetime to perfect the act of meditation? The act of sitting still and clearing one's mind. Of building a mental discipline that allows one to control one's mental state to benefit the mind and body. It becomes an end in itself.

The perfect shot requires a Zen-like concentration and clarity of purpose which are hard to achieve and even harder to repeat. While we may get lucky and hit the bullseye every now and again, being able to do it every time or even regularly is a whole new world.

Complicating this journey by building our own bows is a tricky proposition. I call it the bowyers curse. The clarity required to make a perfect shot requires that we clear our minds of all thought and focus our entire consciousness on the bullseye. This clarity must be perfected to the point that everything else in the world blurs, darkens, or fades out. The world does not reappear until the arrow has hit its mark.

This alone is hard enough. When we add the additional challenge of building our bows and arrows, we add additional layers of thought to our minds that we must scrape away to make the perfect shot. This is doubly hard.

I know from personal experience, and from watching others go through it too, that when we start to build our own bows, our conscious, and unconscious minds get distracted when we shoot. Instead of focusing entirely on the shot, I am struggling to stop thinking about how the limbs of the bow are bending, how the grip feels in my hand, what that sound was during the last shot, if the arrow shelf is rounded correctly, and on and on. It makes the execution of the perfect shot a challenge, to be sure.

You won't find any Olympic archers building their own bows. Doesn't happen. In fact, I would wager that the winners at every level of competition do not build their own bows.

It is a well known fact, often stated by archery coaches, that the mind cannot focus on more than one thing at a time. Al Henderson clearly makes this point in his book *Understanding Winning Archery*:

> *Aiming is the amount of concentration you put into melting that sight pin into the gold and burning a hole through that 10 ring for the arrow to enter. That, my friends, is aiming. That is concentration... the shot explodes and you must not falter one iota in your concentration on aiming until the arrow has arrived in the 10 ring. Then and only then, may you become aware that the world is still around you.*

In the pursuit of better shooting, students are taught to perfect their shooting form without regard to where the arrow goes. Then when it comes time to make a perfect shot, they are advised to completely clear their mind of any thoughts of shooting form and simply focus on the center of the target.

When we decide to build our first bow, we are, in a sense, neglecting to pay heed to this wise and proven advice. We are adding a layer of complication into our effort to become the best shot we can be. But if we pursue the perfection of the bow with the same zeal with which we pursue the perfection of the shot, I believe that we can achieve both. And in doing so we add a layer of complexity to our consciousness that will make us better shooters, bowyers, and people.

Intuition is built from experience. And I believe that the experience gained by learning the nature of the bow and training our minds to perfect its use helps each of us to become a better, more complete person. This end result can be achieved by any number of activities we may challenge ourselves with. But I think the pursuit of archery, bowhunting, and the art of the bowyer give us unique insights into the nature of ourselves and the natural world that benefit not just ourselves, but our families and communities. The knowledge we build as we increase our understanding of the system of archery, from bow to archer, gives us an intuition into the inner workings of all things. It helps us realize that just like the deer we hunt, we too are wild.

So let us begin this journey to build our own American Semi-Longbow and, as we do, to understand what makes an American Semi-Longbow what it is. Maybe even, if we are lucky, we will begin to understand a little bit more what it is that makes us who we are.

Chapter 2
Design Considerations

Whenever a person sets out to design something, whether it is a house, a tool, software, whatever, it is always best to set down a list of design considerations. Design considerations are those requirements designers have in mind that they wish to incorporate into the work. The objective of these considerations is to make the work fit its purpose as best it can, by anticipating as many characteristics and features as possible that will contribute to the best performance.

Another phrase which needs defining in this context of design considerations is "best performance". Best performance is where things go from the objective to the subjective, and where the opportunities for design variation become infinite, even in something so apparently simple as an American Semi-Longbow.

In this chapter I will attempt to identify those features of the ASL that, in my experience, seem to have an effect on the performance of the bow (as I define it), and how they can be modified to affect the way the bow behaves. In the following chapters, these features will be addressed again in the context of building a bow and where decisions have to be made.

All archers and all bowyers are different and see the world and their bows from different points of view. If it were otherwise, there would be only one bow design and not much need to discuss it. If you are reading this book, I think we can at least agree that the fundamental qualities of the ASL are attractive to us.

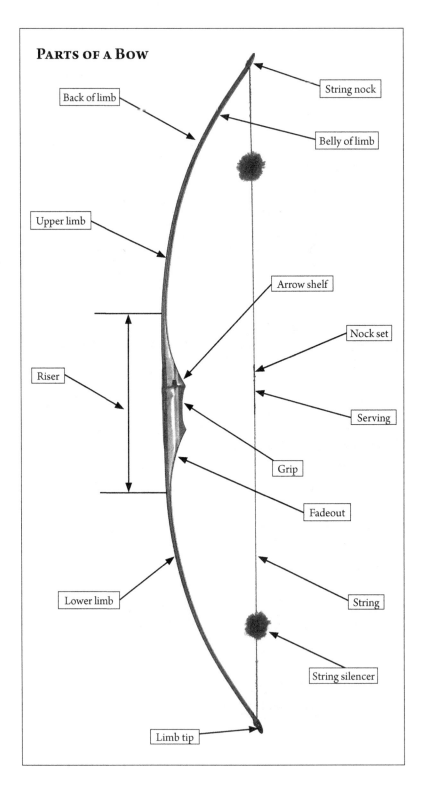

PARTS OF A BOW

Back of limb

String nock

Belly of limb

Upper limb

Arrow shelf

Nock set

Riser

Serving

Grip

Fadeout

Lower limb

String

String silencer

Limb tip

So let's outline those characteristics of the ASL that make it an ASL. We will accept the characteristics as immutable and leave it at that. Once identified, these characteristics will help inform the design choices we make as we explore how we can craft the "perfect" ASL.

Limb Profile

While there is much dispute among target archers about what constitutes a longbow limb, about the only thing that they can agree on is that the string cannot touch the belly of the limb when the bow is at brace. Those who embrace the ASL avoid this tedious debate entirely. In regard to the limb profile, all other "longbows" attempt to simulate the ASL while grasping for improved performance.

The limbs of an ASL can show backset, meaning that their unstrung profile arcs or bends toward the bow back (away from the archer). Or the limbs of an ASL can show string follow, meaning that their unstrung profile arcs or bends toward the bow belly (toward the archer). Or finally the limbs of an ASL can be straight and true, bending towards neither the back nor the belly of the bow.

Regardless of what the limbs of an ASL show when unstrung, once the bow has been strung and braced, the limbs will grace the eye with a gentle steady curve that begins at the riser fadeouts and ends at the string nocks. The shape of this curve is determined by stresses built into the limb that contribute to its unstrung profile.

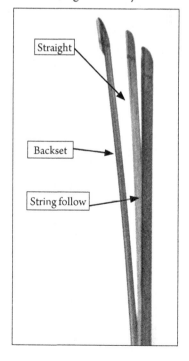

Straight

Backset

String follow

Limb Width

The limbs of an ASL are thicker and more narrow than other bow designs. The limbs will taper from their widest point at the fadeouts to their narrowest point at the string nock. That part of the limb that extends past the string nocks does no work, and it is better understood to be part of the limb tips.

Riser Shape

I bring this up because life is full of slippery slopes. While philosophers agree that the slippery slope argument is a logical fallacy, in the practice of living, it nevertheless proves true as often as not. We must be careful to avoid depending on this fallacy when making decisions, but we must nonetheless be aware of the tendency of things to go downhill. The profile of the back of the bow must be perfectly straight from one fade out to the other when the bow is unstrung. Any deviation from this benchmark begins the slide.

This characteristic might be controversial to some, but I define it this way for several reasons. The shape of the riser has a significant effect on the performance and feel of a bow. It can also complicate or simplify the appearance of the bow. Just compare the unstrung look of an ASL to a recurve or hybrid (deflex/reflex) bow. The shape of the riser can lead to complication in the profile of the limbs, which then need to compensate for this nonlinear shape, and which take away from the simple beauty seen in an ASL. Finally, if the riser is not kept arrow-straight it provides the opportunity to sneak in design aspects that throw the bow into the hybrid category and subtly take away from its shooting character.

Arrow Shelf

This is the single most important characteristic that separates the ASL from its more primitive ancestors. Self bows, which are made from ex-

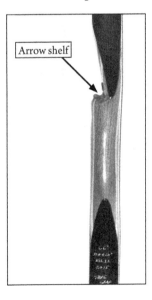

Arrow shelf

actly one piece of wood, have no riser as we have come to know it. The self bow can have a thickened middle and can be tillered (see Chapter 10 for explanation of this word) so that there is an upper limb. However, the upper limb is not identified by an arrow shelf, but rather by a mark of some kind in the form of ink, brand, leather, or thread.

Some human technological advancements have resulted in more trouble than might have been anticipated when they were made. Some advancements have allowed us to make great strides in civilization but have also had some unforeseen consequences.

Take for example the combustion engine and the resulting carbon dioxide emissions that destroy our marble buildings and monuments in the short term and our ecological stability in the long term. Happily, there appears to be no such downside to the arrow shelf.

The arrow shelf has been so successful in eliminating injury to the bow hand and improving accuracy that it has been adapted into a variety of bow designs. So while it is not unique to the ASL, I believe it is an important and defining characteristic.

The Grip

The bow hand holds the ASL differently than any other bow. In my opinion, it is more ergonomic in that it doesn't require the wrist to hold the hand high and take the weight on a small area of the thumb. Instead, the wrist is relaxed and the weight of the bow is taken against the heel of the thumb. This allows the elbow of the bow arm to bend slightly, keeping the string away from the arm.

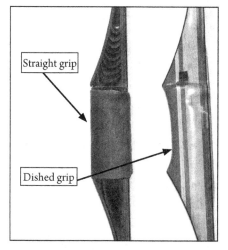

The shape of the grip is simple and can vary from a simple straight line down the back of the grip, to a dished shape that cradles the hand and allows it to sink into the grip.

String Nocks

The string nocks of an ASL are cut into the side of the limb and require only subtle overlays to protect the limb from shock in cases where modern string materials like Fast Flight are used. A thin piece of linen phenolic used as an overlay, with maybe a piece of matching wood, is all that is required.

Alternatively, the phenolic, in the form of a wedge, can be placed within the laminations of the bow to serve both as protection from shock and to stiffen the tips of the bow. This leaves a smooth limb tip that looks similar to the limb tip of a self bow.

I prefer to separate the functions of tip overlays from tip wedges by placing a thin phenolic overlay on the limb tips and a subtle wedge within the limb. When we try to design a device that serves two purposes, I find that it performs neither one very well.

If you see a bow with a thick overbearing tip overlay where the string groove spreads from the sides of the bow over and through the overlay, it is a clear sign that the bow you are looking at is not an American Semi-Longbow.

There are other characteristics of the bow that may be modified and have tremendous effect on the performance, forgiveness, and appearance of the bow. These characteristics are not unique to the ASL, but they must be addressed in order to make the best bow we can.

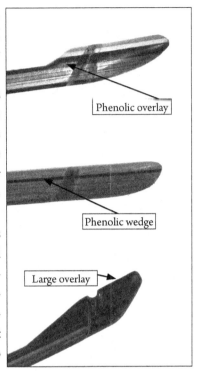

Phenolic overlay

Phenolic wedge

Large overlay

As I address these items, I will make mention of engineering terms that have specific meanings to an engineer and can be used to mathematically describe and predict the function of a bow. I prefer a more experimental approach to bow design because it is more accessible to most of us, and more fun.

The analytical approach to understanding bow performance has been handled in detail by other authors more qualified than myself (for example: Hickman et al. in Archery, the Technical Side and Hamm et al. in Traditional Bowyers Bible series) and there is no need for me to repeat it. I would encourage you to explore those other books because an understanding of what is happening in the bow informs good experimentation.

Core Materials

There are many materials from which the core of a bow may be made. Some are natural, some artificial. I will limit my discussion to natural materials, namely wood and bamboo.

Because we are applying fiberglass to both the back and belly of the bow, we are not dependent upon the core material to provide much elasticity to the bow. The core material serves but three purposes: it must separate the back and belly glass by a prescribed distance, thus instilling the required elasticity; it must not inhibit the action of the fiberglass; and it should look good.

The elasticity of a limb based on its profile and thickness can be predicted by applying the equations of a cantilever beam and the second moment of inertia of the cross section. But the results obtained do not justify the effort involved. It is best to simply observe what others have done and proceed empirically to find what works best for you.

I have found that the most important qualities of a good core material are durability, low mass, and low hysteresis.

Durability is self-explanatory.

Low mass is important because, as the string is released at full draw and the limbs relax to brace, it is desirable that the majority of the energy stored in the limbs goes into the arrow. The heavier the limbs, the less energy is transferred to the arrow, and thus more of it stays in the bow and gets expressed as noise and hand shock.

Low hysteresis means that the limbs have the ability to transfer the majority of the energy stored in them to the arrow. Different woods have varying levels of internal friction when bent. It is hard to predict which woods have the lowest internal friction (and thus lowest hysteresis) from looking at their physical properties. Experimentation is required. We will come back to this again in the section on stack.

Limb Cross Section

Most materials are stronger in tension than compression. Concrete and stone are obvious exceptions. In the world of bow making, we have been limited by the strength of wood for the last 30,000 years or so. In the 1940s, things changed with the development of fiberglass. Fiberglass is almost as strong in compression as it is in tension, and for our purposes we will assume it is equally as strong.

That being said, the core material is not. There is another engineering term that we need to be familiar with: neutral plane. In order to understand what the neutral plane is, and where it is, we need to consider the forces in the limb when it is drawn.

As the limb is taken from its unstrung position to its braced position, it begins to strain. The back of the bow comes under tension while the bel-

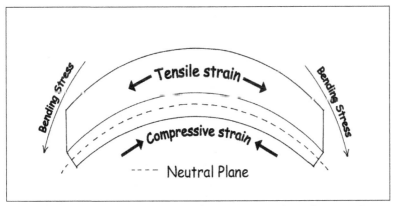

ly comes under compression. As the bow is drawn, these forces increase. Logically, if the back is under tension, and the belly is under compression, there must be some point (and thus plane) within the limb that is under neither tension nor compression.

I have found that since the fiberglass takes most of the strain of bending, only minor precautions are necessary to protect the core from failure. If we move the neutral plane but a small ways toward the belly of the bow, we can ensure that the core material will not fail from repeated compression cycles. We do this by slightly reducing the width of the back as compared to the belly. The traditional term for this is trapping. This word is derived from the trapezoid geometric shape. In the extreme, the corners can be taken off so that the cross section does indeed look exactly like a trapezoid.

Trapping will ensure that the neutral plane moves toward the belly of the bow. The closer the neutral plane is to the belly, the smaller are the compression forces it is subjected to. It will also lighten the limb, provide a faster response, and reduce hand shock. All good things.

Limb Taper

Limb taper refers to the rate at which the limb thickness changes from fadeouts to string nock. A limb can vary from a parallel taper, meaning that the thickness is constant, to something in the neighborhood of 0.004 to 0.006 of an inch per inch. The unit inch per

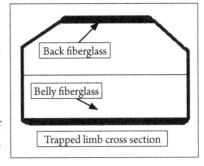

inch specifies how many thousandths of an inch the limb decreases in thickness per inch of travel down the limb.

The taper of a limb has great effect on the performance and feel of a bow, particularly in the case of the ASL.

The use of a parallel taper in the ASL is tricky business. It will result in a bow with a pleasing curve to the limbs when the bow is braced, but it can be accompanied by a tortured wood core and hand shock that cannot be ignored. It is usually accompanied by some unintended string follow, which results from the core taking set in response to the excessive stress it must endure.

It can be made to work, but care must be taken to narrow the limbs at a rate that results in something close to a pin nock, and to trap the back a little more.

As we add more taper to the limb, it breathes a sigh of relief and feels better in the hand. But we notice that some cast is lost as compared to the parallel limb bow we made before.

A bow, like life, is an exercise in balance. We are always shifting from here to there, looking for that perfect balance between doing what we need to do to survive and doing what we want to do to thrive. We need to balance how we want the bow to perform against what the bow must do to survive. As is the case with most things, bows that live fast die young.

The word "cast" is used to describe how well a bow can shoot an arrow. This is not the same thing as how fast it can shoot in absolute terms, but rather how fast it can shoot an arrow with respect to the bow's draw force and the arrow's mass weight. So we would say that a low draw weight bow that can shoot a heavy arrow at the same speed as a heavier draw weight bow has better cast, even though they shoot the same arrow at the same speed.

When we talk about relative

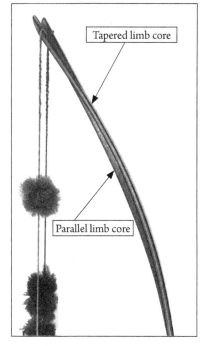

Tapered limb core

Parallel limb core

relationships, we often use ratios. Cast is no different. In order to judge one bow's cast against another, we use the ratio (arrow weight) / (bow draw force). This gives us a term with the units of grains per pound (gpp).

We can now speak of the relative speed of a bow and compare it to another. We can say this bow shoots a 10 gpp arrow at 155 feet per second (fps) and that bow shoots a 10 gpp arrow at 160 fps. Without knowing the absolute weight of the arrow or the bow, we can now judge one to have better cast than the other.

The cast that a bow will achieve can, in part, be predicted from the profile of the limbs seen during the draw. It can be understood by comparing this profile to what we know about throwing rocks.

When a young boy picks up a small rock and wishes to see how far he can throw it, he instinctively knows that he needs to whip his arm around using his wrist and outer arm to sling the rock on its way. When that same young boy picks up a heavy river rock that barely fits in his hand, he knows too that he must now keep his arm stiff and use his shoulder muscles to hurl the rock.

A bow is no different.

The reasons behind these different strategies for getting the most distance to the throw have to do with the ratio of the mass of the projectile to that of the arm, and the elastic rate of recovery of the arm. Whether his hand is empty or full, a boy can move his arm only so fast.

When the equations of motion are balanced and solved in our young boy's brain, it unerringly determines that the best solution for a light projectile is to use the whippy wrist to hurl the rock as its low inertia is best handled by the delicate muscles of the forearm.

In the same way, it determines that the stronger, slower muscles of the shoulder give a greater advantage to the cast than the forearm muscles would, overburdened as they would be by the inertia of a heavy projectile.

When we watch a bow bend, we can tell where it is working by where it is bending. If the bow limb is stiff in the tips and bends mostly near the riser, it will cast a heavy arrow. If the bow limb is stiff in the first third of its length and bends mostly at the tips, it will cast a light arrow. If the bow limb bends throughout its length, with maybe just a touch of stiffness in the last few inches it will shoot a pretty heavy arrow pretty fast.

As the action in the limb moves toward the tips, the hand shock decreases. As the action in the limb moves toward the riser, the hand shock increases.

Now that we understand that the same bow cannot be made to shoot heavy arrows and light arrows with equal efficiency, we must decide, do we want to shoot a lighter arrow, or a heavier arrow?

If your intention is to hunt, then you will want to shoot a heavier arrow. If your intention is to target shoot, then you will want to shoot a lighter arrow.

Stack

The stack refers to the number and character of the separate laminations used to build up the thickness of the limb. In the case of our ASL, it will have a back and belly lamination of fiberglass, and then the possibilities open up.

How many laminations of wood do we need?

Using several laminations of wood accomplishes several things. By using several laminations, we can build pre-stress into the glue lines between laminations. This pre-stress will be greater if the bow is built on a form that has backset built into it. This pre-stress contributes to greater cast.

By using several laminations, we can build a more homogeneous limb. Why this is important is understood through observing the character of wood. Wood is a natural material and thus has natural variations in stiffness, strength, and grain. By using several laminations, we hope to even out the strength and divide the weakness, resulting in a predictable and reliable bow.

At this point, a self bow bowyer is surely snickering at me. He takes another strategy to making his wooden bow which he feels is more in touch with this glorious material nature has given us. And he may be right.

He surely feels that it takes greater skill and shows greater wisdom to work with wood alone. To leave a limb thick around a pin knot. To follow a single growth ring when shaping the back. And, ultimately, to make a bow from a single stave, no need for fiberglass.

In this line of reasoning, I have no defense. But I prefer another line of reasoning. My argument is based on the observation that man is, for better or worse, a creative animal. And, for better or worse, we need to express that creativity.

Chasing the growth rings and grain in a stave to reveal the self bow

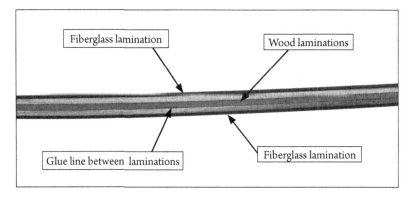

within is an admirable exercise in craftsmanship for which I have only the highest respect. But I need to instill something of myself into my bows, something of my own creativity.

When building ASLs as I describe, it doesn't take long to realize that a lifetime can be spent exploring the possibilities and applying one's creativity to the design and construction of such a bow. Every morning I wake up, the first words to come to my mind are: "What if..." And therein lies the joy.

What wood should we use?

Here is another opportunity for infinite variety. There are many woods that qualify as good core materials. But first we should consider the trend to use clear glass on bows and to put a thin lamination of wood (that some might think attractive) under the glass. It doesn't really contribute much to the function of the bow other than appearance. And it is usually a wood with lots of "character": figured grain with lots of color. A wood like this would not otherwise be used in a bow as it would not be strong enough to provide durability or uniform enough to offer good cast.

If we are to make the best bow we can, I would propose we leave any wood with character on the drawing board where it can do no harm. As we design our core, we need to take account of what contribution each lamination and glue line makes.

Glue lines have two main effects. First, each glue line locks in some of the backset (or string follow) we build into the bow. We call this prestress. If we build no backset in, then the glue line at least locks in the memory of the bow profile and limits set, or string follow. And the glue line adds mass to the limb.

While I have done no empirical experiment to determine exactly how much mass is added, I have made some laminated arrows and compared them to arrows made of the same wood without glue lines. What I have learned is that a glue line that runs the length of the arrow will add about 50 grains to that arrow. Extrapolating this observation to the area of a bow limb glue line yields the expectation that each glue line will add somewhere between 150 and 200 grains to the limb.

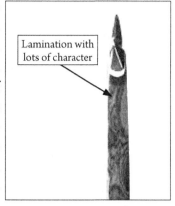

Lamination with lots of character

Using a figured lamination under clear glass adds an additional glue line and thus additional mass. Because the figured lamination is so thin, the two glue lines associated with it are so close together that very little pre-stress is locked in. The only reason to use a figured lamination is so that we can look at it. To me, this is a shallow reason for using it and gives moral authority to the idea that beauty is just skin deep. It ignores the truth that simplicity is the greater beauty.

It also keeps us from realizing the full strength and durability that fiberglass can give to the bow. How is this? By adding the additional figured wood and clear glass to the bow, we are tempted to separate the glass from the riser fadeouts. If we allow the belly fiberglass to communicate directly with the riser, we gain the full strength of the glass on the belly and the strong woods of the riser. This bond will most reliably resist the compressive forces exerted on the bow during the draw.

There is another benefit to this configuration. By keeping all the core woods running together along the back of the riser, we allow them to experience the same stress profile. This allows the core woods to work together most predictably.

To understand this, we must consider the alternative, which is to have the figured lamination (or the figured lamination and one core lamination) run up the fades on the belly. With your mind's eye, follow these laminations down the fades to where they meet up with the rest of the core that took the path along the back of the riser. Where they meet, you will see that the belly laminations must bend overly much to join the curve that has been defined by the form, even for a straight bow. This pre-stress locked into the belly laminations makes them stiffer and less likely to work in harmony with the rest of the core laminations. And it causes them to do more work on each draw. The fiberglass cares not, but the wood remembers and suffers for it.

This observation came to me, not in an "ah ha!" moment of intellectual bliss, but as the result of standing there holding a bow that was once a fine mate to my arrows, but was now a collection of shards, blown apart after it could take the stress no longer.

Armed with this newfound knowledge, I began to notice that the really old (50 years or more) examples of American Semi-Longbows that I had seen all shared these same traits: the belly fiberglass was bonded directly to the fadeouts of the riser and all core woods were laid against its back. We shall remember and respect this lesson.

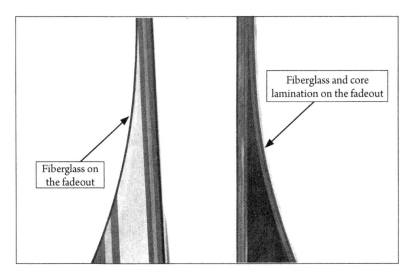

Fiberglass and core lamination on the fadeout

Fiberglass on the fadeout

Back to the question of what woods to use in the core. Here again, there are many possibilities to consider. But first we must observe, either through direct experience, or through the experiences of others, that the core material has very little positive effect on the cast of the bow. This is because wood, of any type, cannot compare to fiberglass for its ability to withstand compressive or tensile stress, or for the elasticity it brings to the bow.

Material	Modulus of Elasticity	Compressive Rupture	Tensile Rupture
Fiberglass	5,600,000 psi	77,700 psi	130,000 psi
Bamboo	2,610,000 psi	8,990 psi	11,020 psi
Yew	1,350,000 psi	8,100 psi	15,200 psi
Osage	1,689,000 psi	9,380 psi	18,650 psi
Eastern cedar	880,000 psi	6,020 psi	8,800 psi
Data from Gordon Composites and www.wood-database.com			

The core wood's job is a simple three-part task: It must separate the belly glass from the back glass so that the limb can act as a cantilever beam with lots of spring; it must be durable; and it must not inhibit the action of the limb through hysteresis.

With these qualities in mind, we can eliminate many potential candidates. Any wood that is overly heavy, stiff, brittle, or soft can be discarded. Any wood that is overly expensive, hard to come by, or hard to work with can be similarly discounted.

That leaves us with a handful of tried and true woods, and a large number of woods that will probably work just fine too. Since no one person would have the time to test and compare all potential candidates in order to provide a complete picture, they remain to be discovered.

I have tried a small variety of woods including: eastern red cedar, red elm, black walnut, osage orange, bamboo, laminated bamboo, and laminated birch. Other woods that have been used by other bowyers include: a variety of tropical woods, yew, sugar berry, and sugar maple (hard rock maple).

When I speak of things like laminated birch, and laminated bamboo, I am speaking of what is commonly called action wood. Action wood consists of vertically laminated pieces of wood that are then cut perpendicular to the lamination lines. This results in a limb lamination consisting of strips of wood laminated together. What this wood is, and how to make it, is covered in chapter 7.

The choices I made in core woods were based on availability, cost, and popularity with other bowyers. I have settled on two for my bow making efforts.

Eastern red cedar: I have made many bows with eastern red cedar and laminated eastern red cedar. In my area, it is a commonly available

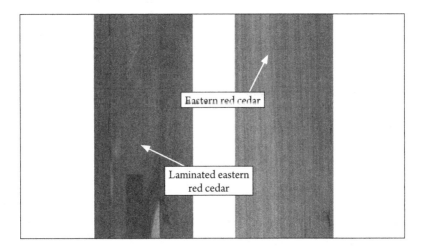

Eastern red cedar

Laminated eastern red cedar

wood which I only have to go behind the house to acquire. Aside from its thrifty qualities, I find it an outstanding wood in that it meets all three of the criteria for a core lamination just discussed. In fact, its use resulted in the fastest and most gentle bows I have made. The trick with eastern red cedar is to come up with a piece of wood that is 36 inches long and has no knots. It is doable, but results in a lot of waste. This is what led me to make laminated eastern red cedar. See the section in chapter 7 on making action cedar for further discussion.

Laminated bamboo: Actually, laminated bamboo and black walnut are about even in my mind. They perform about the same and are about as easy to work with. I say "about." Black walnut, being a natural material, still results in waste due to knots and unacceptable grain. Laminated bamboo, on the other hand, being a homogeneous lamination, is perfect through and through. No waste. Easy.

So where does this leave us? With the usual balancing act.

I will tell you the compromise that I came to with core design. It is up to you to balance it for yourself. I use three laminations of eastern red cedar or laminated eastern red cedar on most bows. The use of three laminations balances out, on the one hand, the need to make a homogenous core with enough pre-stress captured in the glue lines to give the bow good cast with, on the other hand, the need to minimize the mass of glue used and the effort and expense of fabricating each lamination.

So that leaves just the back and belly fiberglass to work out. There are a few variables here to consider: thickness, color, and cross weave. The term used by fiberglass manufacturers for cross weave is scrim. We will

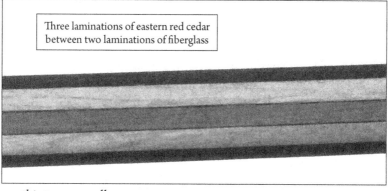

Three laminations of eastern red cedar between two laminations of fiberglass

use this term as well.

Thickness will be determined in part by what force you want your bow to pull. I have found that for bows of 50 pounds or more, a thickness of 0.050 inch works well. You can use thinner glass for lighter bows. I have found that for a set core thickness, varying the fiberglass thickness by 0.001 inch will result in a 1-pound variation in draw force. Similarly, for a set fiberglass thickness, varying the core thickness by 0.003 inch will result in a 1-pound variation in draw force.

It has been observed that since fiberglass is so much heavier than the core wood, tweaking the design for a set bow force so that the core thickness is maximized and the fiberglass thickness is minimized will result in the best cast. I believe this to be true, but I haven't gone down this road for two reasons. Fiberglass for longbows is available in just a few standard thicknesses of 0.030, 0.040, 0.050, and 0.060 inch. So I try to match my core to those available thicknesses. And keeping a bunch of different thicknesses of fiberglass on hand would be expensive, especially for a hobbyist like myself.

Scrim in fiberglass is simply a layer of glass that runs perpendicular to

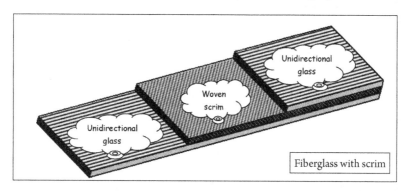

Unidirectional glass

Woven scrim

Unidirectional glass

Fiberglass with scrim

the length of the glass. This cross-weave layer helps to keep longitudinal cracks from forming in the glass. It also adds 0.010 inch to the thickness of the lamination that does not help cast. I go back and forth on this. It is nice to have glass that will not develop longitudinal cracks, but the cracks do not affect the cast or durability of the bow. What is the aesthetic value of a bow without cracks compared to a bow that could have a wee bit more cast if not for the scrim? You will have to decide for yourself.

Which leaves us with color. Fiberglass is available in a small variety of colors, including clear, black, brown, tan, green, and white. Color is of little consequence, except to the eye.

Tip Wedges

A tip wedge is a wedge of core material, usually in the neighborhood of 2 to 6 inches long or so, that tapers from some thickness to zero. I make mine about twice the thickness of the thin end of a core lamination, or 0.050 inch, whichever is less. It is placed in the end of the limb.

The purpose of the tip wedge is to change the bending profile of the limb, and thus affect its draw curve in a positive way. To explain why requires the introduction of two more concepts: string angle and stack.

String angle is the angle that the string makes with the limb as the bow is drawn. As the angle increases, the force required to pull the string back increases. The angle should never reach 90 degrees, as this would re-

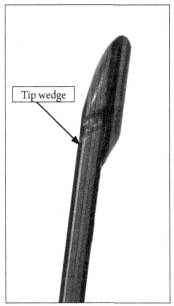

Tip wedge

sult in the greatest force to pull the string back, and it should never exceed 90 degrees, as then the string will be in danger of pulling off the end of the limb.

Stack has two meanings in bow construction. In the previous section, we discussed the meaning as it applies to the number and character of laminations used to make the bow. Its second meaning relates to drawing the bow.

Stack is simply the word used to describe the feel of the tension in the bow as it is being drawn. As the string angle increases toward 90 degrees and the draw force increases in the string, it feels as though you will hit a wall and not be able to draw the bow further. The draw force has stacked up, as they say.

Discussions about string angle usually involve a recurve, and I see no better way to illustrate its affect. The recurve tip arcs forward so much that, at brace, the string lays on the limb. As the bow is drawn, the string lifts off the limb but is still close. Compare this to an ASL where the string is well off the limb at brace and quickly moves farther away from it as the bow is drawn. It can be seen, then, that the profile of the limb determines string angle.

So the purpose of a tip wedge in an ASL is twofold. First, it will alter the profile of the bow as it is being drawn so that the string angle is re-

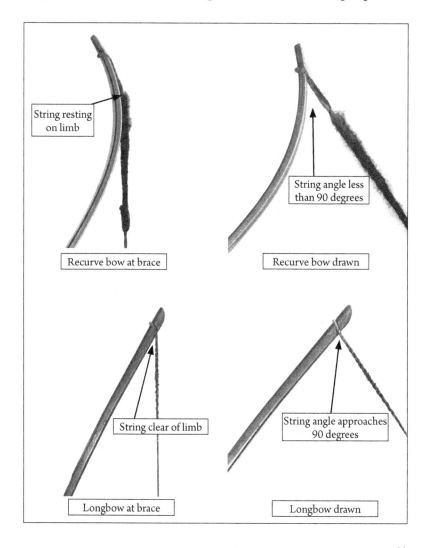

String resting on limb

Recurve bow at brace

String angle less than 90 degrees

Recurve bow drawn

String clear of limb

Longbow at brace

String angle approaches 90 degrees

Longbow drawn

duced and the sense that the bow is stacking is minimized. Secondly, the cast can be improved.

Implicit in the use of a tip wedge in an ASL is that the limb must have a taper to its thickness. Again we find ourselves in a balancing act.

An ASL can be made with parallel limbs, meaning that the core thickness is constant from fadeout to tip. This will produce a profile that is pleasing to the eye when braced, but the bow will develop set in the limbs and lose cast over time. There are those that prefer this design, often called a string follow bow. They believe that the cast lost is offset by the forgiveness gained by virtue of a gentler bow.

An ASL can be made with tapered limbs, meaning that the core thickness decreases from fade out to tip. This will also produce a profile that is pleasing to the eye when braced. Comparing these two bows at brace, side by side, you will notice that the tapered bow has a string angle that is already moved back from the limb. It will cast an arrow well, though maybe not quite so well as the parallel bow. The one thing it won't do is lose cast over time. It will not take the set seen in the parallel bow. Another thing the shooter might notice is that the tapered bow will shoot a light arrow with more speed than a parallel limb bow.

So we see virtues that we like in both these bows. Is there some way to marry these desired virtues into a single bow? As we know, the universe of possibilities is infinite, but one solution that seems to work well is the tip wedge.

A tip wedge stiffens the last few inches of the limb, which results in a lower string angle. This allows the use of a tapered limb, which reduces the stress at the base of the limb and which would normally result in a whippy tip, but for the effect of the tip wedge.

And so the balancing act begins. What limb taper should be used? What wedge thickness should be used? What length wedge should be used?

As we race ahead with our newfound opportunity to use our creativity to make a better bow, we can feel that sensation coming on in the back of our heads that makes us ask an existential question: If I add a tip wedge, can I still call this bow an American Semi-Longbow?

I think one of the greatest dangers to our happiness is the creation and adherence to arbitrary and rigid rules. So in the spirit of the pursuit of happiness, which in my case at least in part involves shooting a simple bow that performs well and is durable, I won't worry about it. In truth, I don't think adding tip wedges harms the aesthetic of an ASL, and it surely helps its performance and durability. And so I feel comfortable adding the wedges and still calling the bow an ASL. I think Howard Hill would approve.

Limb Length

A bow, arrow, and archer are like an ecosystem. There are forces in effect, both internal and external, that interplay to make the system behave in a healthy manner (the bow and arrow shoot for the archer in a forgiving, predictable, and reliable manner for many years) or unhealthy manner (the bow and arrow shoot for the archer in a harsh, unpredictable, and unreliable manner that may result in lost arrows, broken strings, forearm rashes, or even broken bows).

These forces are linked and interconnected in ways we cannot imagine the first time we pick up a bow and shoot it. As we gain experience shooting, we begin to see the cause and effect relationships that exist between the various parts of the system (bow, bowstring, arrow, etc.) and the various ways that we as the archers apply our forces to the bow, and finally loose the string.

As we gain shooting experience, we build wisdom. This wisdom leads us to improve our archery skills and ultimately to ask ourselves, what more can be done? For some, the desire to answer this question leads them to building their own bows.

When we look at a bow with the critical eye of a budding bowyer, we may first assume that the limbs of a bow should be of equal length and strength. This symmetry would seem to provide balance.

But if we take a breath and think about it again, we will note that we can't hold the bow at its exact center while at the same time allowing the arrow to rest at the bow's exact center. Two objects cannot occupy the same space at the same time.

And so again, we must make a compromise in our desire to build a balanced system.

The grip of an ASL is traditionally kept at 4 inches in length. If the limbs of the bow are of equal length, and the riser fadeouts are also of equal length, then the center of the bow is in the center of the handle, and the arrow rests about 2 inches above center. This sets the stage for trouble.

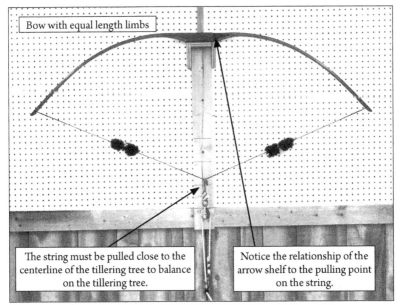

Bow with equal length limbs

The string must be pulled close to the centerline of the tillering tree to balance on the tillering tree.

Notice the relationship of the arrow shelf to the pulling point on the string.

An ASL of this design will surely shoot. But will it shoot to its full potential, and will it behave in the healthy manner previously mentioned? In my experience, the answers are no.

This design will lure the new bowyer to it like a fly to honey. And if not careful and aware, the new bowyer may get stuck in it. This bow design is symmetrical and will produce a lovely curve when placed upon the tillering tree, assuming the string is pulled from its middle.

This should be our first clue that something is not right. If we stop to consider that the string is not pulled from the center by the archer, but instead is pulled 2 inches up the string toward the upper limb, we begin to recognize the problem. If we test our hypothesis by moving the tillering tree rope up the string and pulling again, we will come face to face with confirmation that all is not right as the bow rocks toward the upper limb and threatens to launch out of the tillering tree altogether.

This experiment should lead us to think about the hints that have been dropped in plain sight for us to see. As we hold the bow in our hand level to the ground, we feel torque in our fingers as the bow answers to gravity and tries to align itself to the earth, lower limb down. We remember shooting this bow, or another with equal limbs, and remember too how finicky it was. We have found the imbalance.

These same experiments will inform us how to regain balance. If we can move the center of the bow toward the arrow shelf, then we can more closely honor Newton's law of motion, which warns us that for every action there is an equal and opposite reaction. If the force applied to the bow handle can be put more closely in line with the force that pulls on the string, then the torque caused by the eccentricity between them can be minimized. And the small discrepancy that remains can be nullified by making one limb weaker than the other.

To put it simply, the upper limb should be 1-2 inches longer than the lower limb, 2 inches being half the length of the grip. The astute observer will notice that making the upper limb 2 inches longer moves the center of the bow up the limb by 1 inch, leaving it still an inch below the arrow shelf.

This brings us back to the question of balance. If we make the upper limb much more than 2 inches longer than the lower limb, it gets clumsy and hard to time to the lower limb. It also gets heavier and less efficient at casting an arrow.

Tradition, determined by all those bowyers better than I who have come before me, has settled on a 1- to 2- inch difference in limb length. I am happy to leave it at that.

And so that brings us back to consider the implications of limbs of different length. Pros and cons, as they say. There are very few cons, so let's get them out of the way first. By having different length limbs, they will bend differently. This makes tillering the bow more of a challenge and

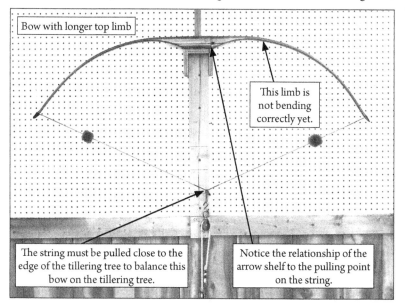

Bow with longer top limb

This limb is not bending correctly yet.

The string must be pulled close to the edge of the tillering tree to balance this bow on the tillering tree.

Notice the relationship of the arrow shelf to the pulling point on the string.

requires us to see past the simple symmetry of equal length limbs. We will have to measure the behavior of the bow instead of its geometry. We will need to make the lower limb slightly thinner than the upper limb to compensate for its shorter and stiffer character. And we will have to make peace with the fact that nothing we can do will make the two limbs look exactly the same.

Once we have made peace with the idea of unequal limb length, we can benefit from the multiple advantages of a bow balanced with unequal limbs. The bow will sit in the hand without twisting. The bow will shoot from different positions, say on the ground and in a tree stand, more consistently. The bow will come to full draw and point more naturally. And the bow will shoot more quietly and with less hand shock. Finally, it will be noticed by the observant shooter that the heel of the hand can be pressed more firmly into the grip, allowing a more comfortable stance. To sum up, the bow will be a better hunting bow.

Riser Construction

The riser of our ASL is arguably the most important component of the bow with regard to accuracy. It represents half of our union to the bow through which we, as the archers, communicate directly. (The other half being the string). In order to produce consistent and reliable accuracy, we need to make sure there is no miscommunication.

In order to ensure that our desired point of impact is communicated to the bow without error, we must ensure that nothing is lost in translation. Since we communicate with the bow through the simple application of force, we must ensure that this force is not misapplied.

The responsibility for accurate communication falls mainly on us, as the archers. We must be consistent in our message from shot to shot. This is the bottom line. But as the bowyer of said bow, we have an additional advantage in that we can construct the riser so that it is attuned to our ergonomic needs.

There are a few simple features we can build into the riser to maximize our chances of making a good shot. First, we can make the riser heavy. This provides inertia, which will help to damp out the wavering nature of our outstretched bow arm and reduce the recoil felt as the arrow leaves the bow. (This feature accommodates less-than-perfect bow tillering and shooting. As you get better at tillering an ASL and shooting it, a light riser, in the end, is better.) Second, we should make the riser long enough to push the working part of the limb away from our hand, which also contributes to the stability of our hold. Third, we can shape the grip to help ensure a consistent hand placement that augments our natural tendency to heel the bow for stability, and minimizes the variation in the resultant reactive force the bow exerts back on us. And finally, we should make the riser strong enough to resist the stresses of repeated shooting while absorbing the energy that remains in the bow after the shot is completed.

The first consideration is materials. A popular approach is to use heavy tropical woods to make the riser. These woods serve our purposes well in that they are strong, heavy, attractive, and easy to work with. They meet all of our design requirements and make a good riser. If you wish to stop your appraisal of materials here, tropical woods will serve you well.

But I would encourage you to take your appraisal a little further. Consider where these woods come from, and what the implications are for the rain forests to which they are native. I think, as traditional bowhunters, we have developed a more sensitive appreciation for how we are connected to the webs of life that make up this biome we call Earth.

We want not only to successfully hunt our deer, we want our deer to be successful. We know that in order for deer to thrive, they need a sustainable environment in which to live. As my world view has expanded, I have come to realize that this environment includes not only the back forty, but also the air and water that flow through it. And finally I realized that that air and water are citizens not only of my neck of the woods, but of the entire planet.

If I care about my back forty, I must care about all the back forties around the world and do what I can to protect and enhance them. One way I can do this is to not use tropical woods. It is a small gesture, to be sure, my bow having but a short piece of wood in it. But when you add all the small gestures of all the traditional bowhunters together, it becomes meaningful.

So I choose to make my riser with local woods that are in no danger of extinction and are soon replaced by new trees that keep our local forests sustainable.

In fact, taking an old sugar maple tree out of the woods opens them up and allows the understory to flourish for a few years, providing habitat for some deer I will likely never meet. It is likely, though, that some other lucky hunter will. And so my choice to use local woods not only reduces the stress on tropical rain forests, it may add to the hunting stories a man tells his son or daughter in years to come.

Making the decision to use local woods, which are lighter in mass, puts me at a design disadvantage, but only for a moment. The mass lost in my decision to avoid tropical woods is soon made up by adding other materials, like paper phenolic and lead.

Paper phenolic is a man-made composite of epoxy and paper. It is strong, heavy, easy to work, and available in a limited number of colors.

Lead is more worrisome. I have used it and told myself: "It's just this once, for this experiment..." But that excuse gets old, even when kept private. It is easy to work with and adds good mass to the riser at low cost. It does, however, present its own health and environmental issues. I use old lead from abandoned duck decoys, tire weights, and old fishing weights. While this does little to assuage my guilt, at least it doesn't contribute to new demand. It also doesn't change the health effects of working with it. On the whole, I would encourage you to pursue phenolic as your device to increase riser mass.

I hesitated to include this option of adding lead, but in the end I decided that showing how I made up for my lack of tillering skill was important to telling the whole story.

In the end though, making the riser heavy is most helpful to a new bowyer. As you get better and better at making bows, they will become sweeter and sweeter to shoot. Eventually you will not need a heavy handle. But to start out, this mass helps to make a less-than-perfect bow more fun to shoot by absorbing unspent energy.

Now you must select your wood.

Since woods available from North American forests are usually not as homogeneous as tropical woods, we must accommodate this through the use of glue lines.

Some woods, like maple, osage, red oak, and dogwood, are strong enough that they can hold their own without added glue lines. Other woods, like walnut and cherry need glue lines.

While I have used all the aforementioned woods and then some, I have settled on using walnut, cherry, and maple in combination. These woods are attractive in their color contrast and are easily accessible to

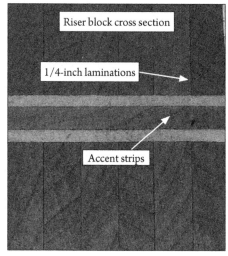

Riser block cross section

1/4-inch laminations

Accent strips

me. If I lived where osage was common, I would definitely use it more. A riser made with dogwood and osage would have no need for added weight and would be as durable and attractive as any riser made from tropical woods.

After deciding what woods to use, the next consideration is strength of construction. The woods I use and the look I want determine how I will assemble the riser.

If I am making a simple riser with no accent strips or other design complexities, I will usually laminate 6(ea) 1/4-inch thick pieces together, oriented so the glue lines run back to belly. This forms a riser blank of 1 1/2 inches.

If I am adding an accent strip, I may or may not go to the trouble of first laminating the 6(ea) 1/4-inch pieces together. If I were using walnut as the main wood, I would. If I were using maple or osage (which are stronger woods), I wouldn't.

Finally, the length of the riser must be determined. I have found through experimentation (confirmed by others: see Hamm, et al. Traditional Bowyers Bible volume one, page 69) that a 66-inch bow provides the best overall performance for a 28-inch draw. I have not made this a topic of discussion as there are too many variables to say explicitly that a 66-inch bow is best. But with this 66-inch bow in mind, I have found that a riser of 16 or 17 inches provides the best balance of durability, forgiveness, and cast for the beginning American Semi-Longbow bowyer.

If you stick with making these bows, you will soon learn that longer limbs and shorter risers make a better bow, if the bow is properly tillered. Properly tillering a bow is the biggest challenge a new bowyer faces. I started with short risers and my elbow paid the price for my lack of tillering skills.

Chapter 3
In Defense of Hunting

Before I get too deep into the makings of the American Semi-Long-bow, I feel the need to dwell a moment on why I would even care about bows.

What we do, what we take interest in, is all connected somehow. We don't do anything in a vacuum, as they say. Every time we sit down to eat, we should be reminded of our connection to the earth. Our food comes from the earth, nowhere else. And the ability of the earth to provide our food is the result of myriad connections both on the planet and off. For if our earth did not orbit our sun, there would be no light to power life.

It is my need to eat that connects me to this world. This connection is made, at least partly, by the way we collect our food. If we go to the store and buy our food mostly prepared for us, our connection to the earth is weak. We can strengthen this connection by collecting our own food.

The bow was invented by man to allow us to collect our food directly. With the invention of the bow, and the spear before it, man developed the ability to collect his meat when he desired it. Humans were no longer dependent on scavenging an irregular meal of meat from already dead animals. We could now hunt.

Some argue that hunting animals is what caused man to evolve an adaptive thinking brain. They argue that we owe our prey thanks for the development of our intellect. Not only do I believe this is true, I believe that by learning to hunt, we have acquired (whether we want it or not) a responsibility to our prey and the entire biome of the planet. Our responsibility is unique among all the animals that live or have lived in this world. With our power to kill at will comes the obligation to live in a sustainable way that acknowledges the rights of all life on this planet to live. If we don't acknowledge this obligation, our species will surely pay the ultimate price.

Hunting with an American Semi-Longbow helps me acknowledge this responsibility, even celebrate it. When I move slowly through the trees, looking for a deer or a squirrel, I am fully connected to my planet. I hunt with my simple American Semi-Longbow to live and to celebrate life.

So what does hunting mean?

Hunting is a word that, for better or worse, broadly defines the killing of a wild animal. The context in which this killing happens seems to hold very little authority over the definition of the word.

I think this is where the problem starts, and maybe where I should begin in building a defense for the act of hunting. It seems odd to me that hunting should need to be defended within the larger context of humanity's relationship to the world in which we live. As a society, we have given very little thought to the act of dumping untold quantities of pollution into the air and water and onto the land. We give equally little thought to scraping the oceans clean of things we want to eat.

As I write these words and read over the first few paragraphs I have written, it occurs to me that the implication that hunting needs to be defended, and my personal experience, are at odds. While very few people I know actually hunt, almost none with a bow, I have rarely encountered negative attitudes toward me and my hunting. In fact, most people are somewhat amazed by the whole idea.

So maybe what I imply by these words is not that a person's privilege to hunt needs to be defended, but rather that the biome that is our earth, "the land" as Aldo Leopold framed it, must be protected. It must be protected so that there is a place suitable for wild animals to live, and wild animals living in it to hunt.

As the market hunters of the 19th century were systematically cleaning the land of animals, we came very close to losing everything in this country that was fit to eat, or to be used to make fur coats and feather hats. As luck would have it, we also had a cadre of naturalists that saw this impending doom and stepped up to stop it. The list of names is long, but suffice it to say, it is topped off by Theodore Roosevelt, our conservation president.

Roosevelt firmly believed that the strenuous life of hunting built character and physical health. His perspective on conservation and preservation of game species came from his belief, as expressed in *The Wilderness Hunter*, that their loss would diminish our lives:

> *In hunting, the finding and killing of the game is after all but a part of the whole. The free, self-reliant, adventurous life, with its rugged and stalwart democracy; the wild surroundings, the grand beauty of the scenery, the chance to study the ways and habits of the woodland creatures—all these unite to give to the career of the wilderness hunter its peculiar charm. The chase is among the best of all national pastimes; it cultivates that vigorous manliness for the lack of which in a nation, as in an individual, the possession of no other qualities can possibly atone.*

Thankfully his convictions led him, as president, to protect many millions of acres of wild lands and establish policies that helped to stop the wholesale slaughter that market hunters had wrought upon the land and to save countless species from extinction.

A young man was growing up at that time who would take this thinking further yet. He was a member of the first graduating class of forestry students in this country, and he spent his formative early adult years in the Arizona territory of the southwest. There he saw firsthand how agricultural practices and a careless attitude toward the land were causing degradation of the environment and the loss of its animals. This young man's name was Aldo Leopold. He would take these observations and combine them with his inherent love of the natural world and hunting to form what he called the "Land Ethic."

The Land Ethic that Leopold proposed in his book, *A Sand County Almanac*, is really the first major change in human attitudes toward the land since we stood up and killed that first animal so many eons ago.

Our relationship to the land has changed in fits and spurts, for better or worse, since we gave up the hunter-gatherer life and picked up the hoe 10,000 years ago. While our relationship with the land has changed, I believe our attitude toward it has not. We steadfastly believe that the land is there for us to do with as we like. While it is no doubt presumptuous of me to make any conclusions about what motivated Roosevelt, I believe that he too lived by this belief, as expressed in his state of the union speech in 1900:

> *To waste, to destroy our natural resources, to skin and exhaust the land instead of using it so as to increase its usefulness, will result in undermining in the days of our children the very prosperity which we ought by right to hand down to them amplified and developed.*

Key words in this statement can tell us about the relationship of man to land. "Natural resources" is a catch-all phrase that defines everything in nature as a resource. Resource, a supply, an asset. Resources are property. Property can be disposed of however we see fit. No need to dwell on it, simply use it as required.

"Increase its usefulness." Here is the key to Roosevelt's motivation. He recognized that the greed of our newly industrialized world would soon wipe out our "natural resources." In this, he felt an ethical obligation to provide for future generations of humans. I think this profound obligation Roosevelt felt to future generations is what motivated his great work to preserve the wild lands of this country. But the obligation he felt was to people, not the land.

Just as this belief limited our understanding of the land, it has limited our understanding of hunting. Hunting has always been seen as an activity that would "make a man out of you." It was not seen as part of a larger experience, or a broader purpose, or a moral obligation.

Leopold changed that. He changed it by introducing the idea that we have an ethical obligation to the land. Having an ethical obligation to the land raises the land from simple property to an entity with rights. He illustrated this idea of extending rights to that which we once considered mere property with the story of Odysseus and his return from the wars in Troy, chronicled in *The Odyssey*:

> *When God-like Odysseus returned from the wars in Troy, he hanged all on one rope a dozen slave-girls of his household whom he suspected of misbehavior during his absence. This hanging involved no question of propriety. The girls were property. The disposal of prop-*

erty was then, as now, a matter of expediency, not of right and wrong. Concepts of right and wrong were not lacking from Odysseus' Greece: witness the fidelity of his wife through the long years before at last his black-prowed galleys clove the wine-dark seas for home. The ethical structure of that day covered wives, but had not yet been extended to human chattels. During the three thousand years which have since elapsed, ethical criteria have been extended to many fields of conduct, with corresponding shrinkages in those judged by expediency only.

Which brings me back to my point. Hunting can no longer be seen simply as an activity which will provide us with something. It is an activity that has consequences not only for the hunter, but for the hunted, and for the land. It is an expression of our relationship with the land, and we need to acknowledge it in an ethical context.

As our modern life gets more complicated and thus more compartmentalized, we are in danger of drifting yet farther away from our obligation and relationship to the land. We allow others to do our killing for us. This has resulted in the industrialization of our food. This industrialization is worrisome because our food is a principle way in which our relationship with the land is expressed. The less we nurture our relationship to the land, the more strained it becomes.

Getting and maintaining a clear perspective on this relationship is a challenge, to say the least. The older I get, the more clearly I see that everything in the universe is connected.

Take quantum physics and astronomy for example. They stand in for all science disciplines in this argument. Astronomers have been astronomers since ancient times. But even in ancient times there was a hint to the interwoven nature of the cosmos as our ancestors recognized a connection between star patterns in the sky and seasons on the earth. The fact that they misinterpreted those patterns and attributed the seasons to gods and not to the orbit of the earth around the sun does not diminish the observation of a connection.

Just as astronomers were astronomers, physicists were physicists. What both disciplines shared in common were the scientific method and mathematics, but not much more. In recent times, with the advent of yet another discipline, computer science, these same scientists have discovered through observation, prediction, and experimentation (on huge sums of data, made possible by computers) that the forces that control the smallest particles of matter are the very same forces that dictate the nature of the cosmos. This realization has been so profound that these two fields of study have come together and are now called cosmology, the study of everything.

Everything but life, that is. We still don't know what makes life tick. But I am confident that, at some point in our journey as a species, we will figure it out. And when we do, I am just as confident that we will discover that life is not apart from the rest of the cosmos. It is a part of it.

Carl Sagan observed that we are nothing but star dust. Every molecule within our bodies was formed in the core of some long-dead star. In fact, our atoms necessarily have spent time in at least two stars, for some stars make light atoms and others make heavy atoms. The magnitude of the time that has passed, and the serendipity of the events that have unfolded, to make all this come together into the person that is me or you, are just almost beyond comprehension.

The magnitude of this serendipity could cause agitation if a person were to demand an answer to why this has happened. It could also cause a person to misinterpret the patterns and misattribute the reasons.

We are the universe made manifest. We are the universe attempting to know itself. The first statement is fact, the second conjecture. I am comfortable with the second statement because it contains not a judgment, but a challenge. A challenge to come to know the universe around us and in us as fully as we can in the span of a human life, and to share what we learn.

If there is such a thing as a miracle, I think the miracle is that a series of inanimate events starting with the Big Bang (an arbitrary point in time and space I admit), and proceeding through the lifespan of several stars, the coalescing of a cloud of dust into our solar system, the beginnings of life on our planet, and finally the evolution of a primate into what is a *homo sapien* has resulted in a chunk of the cosmos that is self-aware, philosophical, and occasionally moral.

The path from demanding answers to things we cannot yet know to developing a habit of self-righteousness is pretty straight and short. Carl Sagan warns us against the habit of a self-absorbed perspective in his narrative to the *Cosmos* television series He spoke these words as the image of the earth, "a pale blue dot" (as seen from the Voyager spacecraft as it left the solar system), was shown:

> *Look again at that dot. That's here. That's home. That's us. On it everyone you love, everyone you know, everyone you ever heard of, every human being who ever was, lived out their lives. The aggregate of our joy and suffering, thousands of confident religions, ideologies, and economic doctrines, every hunter and forager, every hero and coward, every creator and destroyer of civilization, every king and peasant, every young couple in love, every mother and father, hopeful child, inventor and explorer, every teacher of morals, every corrupt politician, every "superstar," every "supreme leader," every saint and sinner in the history of our species lived there - on a mote of dust suspended in a sunbeam...*
>
> *Our posturings, our imagined self-importance, the delusion that we have some privileged position in the Universe, are challenged by this point of pale light. Our planet is a lonely speck in the great enveloping cosmic dark. In our obscurity, in all this vastness, there is no hint that help will come from elsewhere to save us from ourselves...*
>
> *It has been said that astronomy is a humbling and character-building experience. There is perhaps no better demonstration of the folly of human conceits than this distant image of our tiny world. To me, it underscores our responsibility to deal more kindly with one another, and to preserve and cherish the pale blue dot, the only home we've ever known.*

And there it is, in the first paragraph of Sagan's speech. The word "hunter." It sits right next to words like "civilization," "hero," "explorer," "love," "inventor," and "teacher of morals." All powerful words that describe important aspects of a good life (the word "coward" notwithstanding).

We can't all be great scientists, inventors, kings, or explorers. But some of us can be hunters and, in so doing, develop the knowledge, wisdom, and humility to become good "teachers of morals".

Hunting provides an opportunity for us to experience the interconnected nature of the cosmos. It gives us the opportunity to learn that what we do has consequences not only for us, but for everyone and everything on our pale blue dot.

But it also provides a measure we can use to objectively determine if what we are doing to the earth as self-aware creatures, as a society, is right.

What is right? In this larger context of our belonging to the cosmos, I think Leopold's definition still applies:

A thing is right when it tends to preserve the integrity, stability, and beauty of the biotic community. It is wrong when it tends otherwise.

If there are no animals to hunt, then by definition the integrity of the biotic community has been disrupted. If there is no place to hunt, then again the biotic community has been compromised.

Hunting serves as the proverbial canary in the coal mine.

Yet I think it is better than a canary. A canary can tell you if the air is safe to breath in the space around the canary, but it cannot tell you anything about the air around the next bend. Hunting, on the other hand, serves to warn us not only if the air goes bad, but if the water and soil are failing too. In short, it tells us if the land as a whole is healthy or not.

Why can't we just keep tabs on the land? Measure pollution, animal populations, erosion, etc.? I expect in an ideal world, that might work. But the land is dynamic, and as much as we know about it, there is still more we don't know. We cannot get the whole picture just by taking measurements. And we must be reminded yet again that we have taken most of the predators out of the system.

By combining a watchful presence with the dynamic interaction of hunting both to replace the lost predators and to take stock of the fitness of the land, we can hope to manage our effect on the land.

I would like to encourage a different perspective on what "management" means. Up to this point in human history, we have thought of the land as a resource we manage for our own benefit. This perspective, sloppy with hubris, has led us to narrowly define what is and is not important to manage. The result is that our management has not been good for the land, and by extension it has not been good for us.

For example, we manage sport fish and table fish without regard to the underlying layers of fish that serve to feed the higher predators. As a result, we now face the collapse of the entire marine food chain as the "economically unimportant" fish have been wholesale scooped up to feed farmed salmon, shrimp, and other species.

For another example, we managed deer for increasing populations to the point that many native plant species could no longer endure the browsing pressure of these newly overabundant deer. These native plant species have been replaced by invasive species that the very same deer, whose population we wanted to maximize, cannot feed on. This effort to increase the deer herd has, ironically, resulted in a diminished and less healthy herd. A quick search of the internet will yield many studies and examples that confirm this observation.

We live on this planet, as a part of the land, every day of our lives. Thus it is hard for us to see how very unique and important the land is to us. And thus, we take it for granted. Not only do we take it for granted, we get angry and indignant when the land cannot endure our abuses, and we suffer for them.

How many news stories talk about the "victims" being displaced from their homes by some unforeseen and apparently unpredictable flood?

How many of these same stories talk about how the rivers have been straightened, levies built upstream, fields left bare all winter to lose their topsoil to the river with every rain and snow? Almost none. Are we victims not so much of nature's vagaries, but rather more of our own thoughtlessness?

As Sagan has observed, this earth is our only home. We can have no other. We must learn to live gently upon it.

As hunters, we have a unique opportunity to appreciate the beauty in the land and how fundamental it is to our very existence. We can renew our relationship with it. When I go outside in the crisp predawn of the day, holding my strung bow at my side, I look up at the stars. No matter where I am, I can always find Orion chasing the Seven Sisters known collectively as the Pleiades. Just as Orion will likely not catch the sisters today, I am unlikely to kill a deer. But the act of hunting has value all the same.

In fact, the act of hunting is where most of the value is. While taking a deer (or other game) is the stated purpose of hunting, we hunters know it runs deeper than that. Aside from the known benefits of hunting to ourselves and our children in terms of food, physical fitness, mental alertness, and a family story stitched over time, I think we can now add the additional benefit of acknowledging our place in the land and our ethical obligation to live gently upon it. We can remember too, that hunting helps to measure the health of the land.

Hunting is, and always will be, the most fundamental expression of our connection to the land. Through it, we can acknowledge our well-earned place in the cosmos. And by it, we can understand our duty to conserve the land so it flourishes long after our need of it has passed.

Chapter 4
Building a Form

The first step out of the theoretical and into the practical, in regard to building our ASL, is the task of building a form. The shape of the form will determine the profile of the bow and thus establish the maximum potential character of the bow.

The form is the thing wherein we commit ourselves to building a bow that reflects our understanding of what makes a good one. We can talk all we want about how important backset is, or string follow, or whatever our pet quality is this week. But when we finally build a form that incorporates our theories and experiences, it shows commitment. The form is where the rubber meets the road.

That said, I've built lots of forms. They hang vertically, each suspended by a wire hung over a nail in my tractor shed. Covered in dust, side by side like so many forgotten shoes in the bottom of the closet. They are shadows of past excitement, now obsolete. By all rights, they should be cut up for kindling or in some other way recycled. But they represent too much work and thought for me to destroy them. Maybe some day.

The form is like the foundation of a house. It determines the quality of everything that sits upon it. If your foundation is crooked, so will your house be. For a good bow to be built, it is important that it is built on a good form.

While these instructions are long, the task of building a good form will take no more than a couple days, and it is an enjoyable process. A prelude of things to come.

Material

Just as how I make bows has evolved, how I make forms has evolved too. I started making forms in the conventional way, gluing and screwing two pieces of "three-quarter" plywood together and hoping for the best. What's wrong with plywood forms? Where to start...

Plywood, even good cabinet-quality plywood, just doesn't measure up. What I mean is that you can't actually get a piece of 3/4-inch plywood. The idea is that a longbow blank is made using standard 1 1/2-inch wide fiberglass and wood laminations. Therefore, the form should also be 1 1/2-inch wide. What you will find is that plywood marked "three quarters" is actually 1/16-inch shy. Compound this discrepancy by gluing two pieces together and you have a form that is 1/8 inch too narrow. Here the trouble begins.

What's wrong with using a form that is 1/8 inch shy? There are several problems that creep up. First, after the form surface has been sufficiently prepared (we'll talk about that later), a strip of old fiberglass or formica must be glued down. This material will arrive at your doorstep exactly 1 1/2 inchs wide. If you glue it on as is, you have created a lip around which the laminating epoxy can creep and cure and which makes removing the bow from the form nearly impossible. You may wonder how I know this to be true. I leave it to your imagination to figure out. Thus you will need to sand the strip down to meet the width of the form. Sanding 1/8 inch of fiberglass away is a lot of work.

Let's assume that you are really enthusiastic and ready to do this sanding, as I was after finally removing my first bow from the form, happy I hadn't destroyed either the form or the new bow. Once the chore is behind you, the sailing ahead looks smooth. Except now you will discover that you will have a hard time keeping all the laminations and the riser lined up correctly, as there is no longer an edge to which they can be aligned.

Now that we see the wisdom of making a form exactly the same width as our work materials, can some 1/8-inch thick material be found to sandwich between the plywood? I'm sure somewhere, somehow, some material can be found. But now you are talking additional cost and effort.

Another problem with plywood is that, while it is more homogenous than lumber, it doesn't have the rigidity of wood and tends to warp as humidity changes. Even under the best circumstances, it is never really straight.

Additionally, good quality plywood is expensive.

Once you decide to abandon plywood as a form material, it becomes obvious that there are many other options to provide a form that is exactly 1 1/2 inches wide. This is a relief. But then the question of structural integrity comes up. What is as strong and reliable as plywood? Strength is important.

People have made forms from MDA, pine two-by-eights, and even aluminum I-beams. What I have found works the best, and is the cheapest, is just plain old 1 inch (actual measurement is 3/4 inch) by 12 inch pine boards from a wood supply store. At the time of this writing, a 6-foot board of this type can be had for 13 dollars. Two boards are required for a form, resulting in a 26 dollar expenditure, which is less than half of what a piece of plywood will cost. An additional benefit is that you don't have all that unused plywood to store or dispose of.

Here we come to another fork in our decision tree. Do we want to build a form that uses elastic bands or bungee cords to hold the bow to it (an open form), or do we want to build a form that takes advantage of the uniform pressure provided by the air hose setup (a closed form)? Either option is acceptable. I have made many bows each way.

Open Form

Let's consider the open form first. Building a form in this manner will require about half the wood and maybe two-thirds the labor of building a closed form. It will also be substantially cheaper to make, as the hardware, including the air hose section and plugs, of a closed form is not required.

That's where the pros end and the cons start. There are chiefly three problems I have experienced with open forms. The first is structural.

I say the problem is structural, but that implies that the integrity of a bow made in this way can be questioned. In fact, I have not had a bow that was made on an open form fail due to the fact that it was made on an open form. The integrity of a bow made on this type of form is as good as that made in a closed form. I say the problem is structural because (and it will be obvious to you if you see it in a bow) it is a result of how the bow was made. The problem is that the force applied to the bow (by bungee cords or elastic bands) as it cures is concentrated under the cord or band. The result is that the belly glass will be deformed along the lines of force

Open form

Open form with bungee cords

applied by the bungees. To see it, simply hold the belly of the bow up to the light and watch it reflect off.

While I have no experience or empirical evidence to suggest that these deformations in any way affect the quality or character of the bow, I don't like them.

The second con with open forms is the amount of effort required to affix a bow to it. Once the bow is laid onto the form, the bungees must be tightly wrapped around the bow. This requires a great amount of effort to ensure the bungees are evenly tight. I usually break a sweat before getting the entire bow bound down. You will also notice that the hydraulic pressure of the glue against the plastic wrap used to protect the form from the glue will cause it to leak through and get on the bungee cords. It happens every time.

The third con with open forms is the trouble it takes to make sure that the fiberglass running up the fades is evenly bound down, and that the various parts of the bow stay where they are intended to be. As you tighten the bow down in one area, it is prone to squish out in another. Sometimes right away, sometimes over the several hours it takes the glue to start setting up. The result can be heartache when you discover an otherwise perfect bow has to be scrapped because something slipped.

If you intend to build only one bow, then I would encourage you to use an open form. It is the cheapest and easiest first bow option. But I would caution you that almost no one can build just one bow. If you intend to build more than one bow, or even think you might, I would encourage you to consider the closed form.

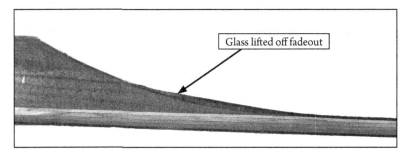

Glass lifted off fadeout

Closed Form

A closed form consists of the wooden form discussed above, metal hardware to hold the form top and bottom together, and an air hose, which is placed on top of the bow within the form. The air hose, when pressurized, serves to compress the laminations together during the curing process. The hardware and air hose for this form can be purchased from Bingham Projects, Inc. I have not found a better system for the hobbyist bowyer than the one they sell.

A form that is 6 feet long and 1 1/2 inches wide, exposed to a pressure of 60 psi (manufacturer's recommended pressure), will experience a total

Closed form

force of 6480 pounds. This force will be distributed across the four bolts that hold the form together. Thus each bolt will see 1620 pounds. These numbers should be kept in mind when contemplating shortcuts.

Despite these impressive numbers, a well-made closed form is very safe and easy to use. I also believe that the bow produced from this type of closed form is superior to what can be produced in an open form, simply due to the pressure available to press the laminations together while the epoxy sets.

We can't possibly appreciate how much of an improvement the use of a closed form is until we have struggled through a few bows on an open form. In fact, I might even encourage you to build a few bows on an open form just so you can really appreciate what a pleasure it is to "upgrade" to a closed form. But I shan't.

The instructions that follow are specifically intended to aid in the construction of a closed form using the hardware available from Bingham Projects. But if you would like to build an open form, the information you will need is there, in the instructions, for you to pick and choose from.

So let's get started.

Construction of the Form

The first thing you will need to do is to determine what sort of ASL bow you want to build: straight, straight with "ears," string follow, or simply backset. I have built all four and find that the simple backset design is the overall best for me. When I make a statement like this, I do it with hesitation. I ask myself whether my experiences and preferences are going to rob the reader of the process of discovery. Maybe, if I didn't suggest what works for me, you would find something that works even better for you. I believe I am right, and so I will risk it.

For the purposes of these instructions, the profile I use is for illustration only. The profile you choose is entirely up to you.

One of the dangers in life is to think that things are the way they are and cannot be otherwise. Every step you take on your adventure of shooting and maybe even building an ASL is fraught with this danger. As you read these instructions, please feel free to think of other, better ways of doing it. I present them to you in the spirit that they are the best I have arrived at, but they surely could be better.

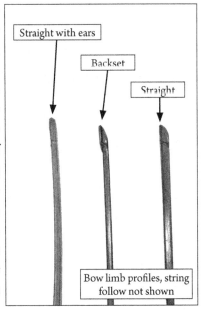

Straight with ears

Backset

Straight

Bow limb profiles, string follow not shown

Once you have settled upon your design, the next steps are to think about how you will construct your form, and what your shopping list will look like.

I need to pause again. Getting started can be like that. Before we get too far into this process, I would like to recommend that you begin a notebook. I know what you are thinking: "I will only build this one bow, and I can keep it in my head." Nope and nope.

If you are reading this book and seriously considering building an ASL, I can tell you that, likely as not, it will not be your first and only. Do yourself a favor and keep track of your design process and construction process. And do yourself another favor by making the notebook your first acquisition.

Be brutally honest in your notebook. The purpose of your notebook is to help you make a better bow. It will help you by recording your current thoughts and by keeping a record of the results. If you fudge a speed reading or a draw force so that your notes look impressive, you will be defeating the purpose. You will have a good looking notebook, but no bow to show for it.

My notebook entries have evolved over time. Leafing through these pages, I see I have recorded the construction of some 60 bows over the last nine years or so. There were a half dozen that were constructed without the benefit of a notebook before that time. If you look at the image (on the following page) of my notebook entry for a bow I made, you will see what I have come to find important:

- In the upper left corner you will find a table listing the lamination thickness measurements for four positions along the lamination (I have since moved on to use seven measuring points). There is a column for both the upper and lower limb, as well as for measuring the stack of laminations.

- Below that are construction notes used during the fabrication of the bow.

- In the upper margin of the right page is what amounts to serial number information for a bow. I found that even if I had written the information down in a notebook, if I couldn't match it to a bow, it was useless. After a while I forget which bow is which. This bow is part of the eleventh series of "Hill Bow" designs, and it is the 11th bow in the group called "ASL."

- The first half of the right page defines the characteristics of the bow: length, core material, laminations used, riser design, limb length, etc.

- Below the first half are notes I take as I finish the bow out. Sometimes I also include notes about what finish I applied to the bow.

- I add the pencil check marks as I collect and/or make the various parts.

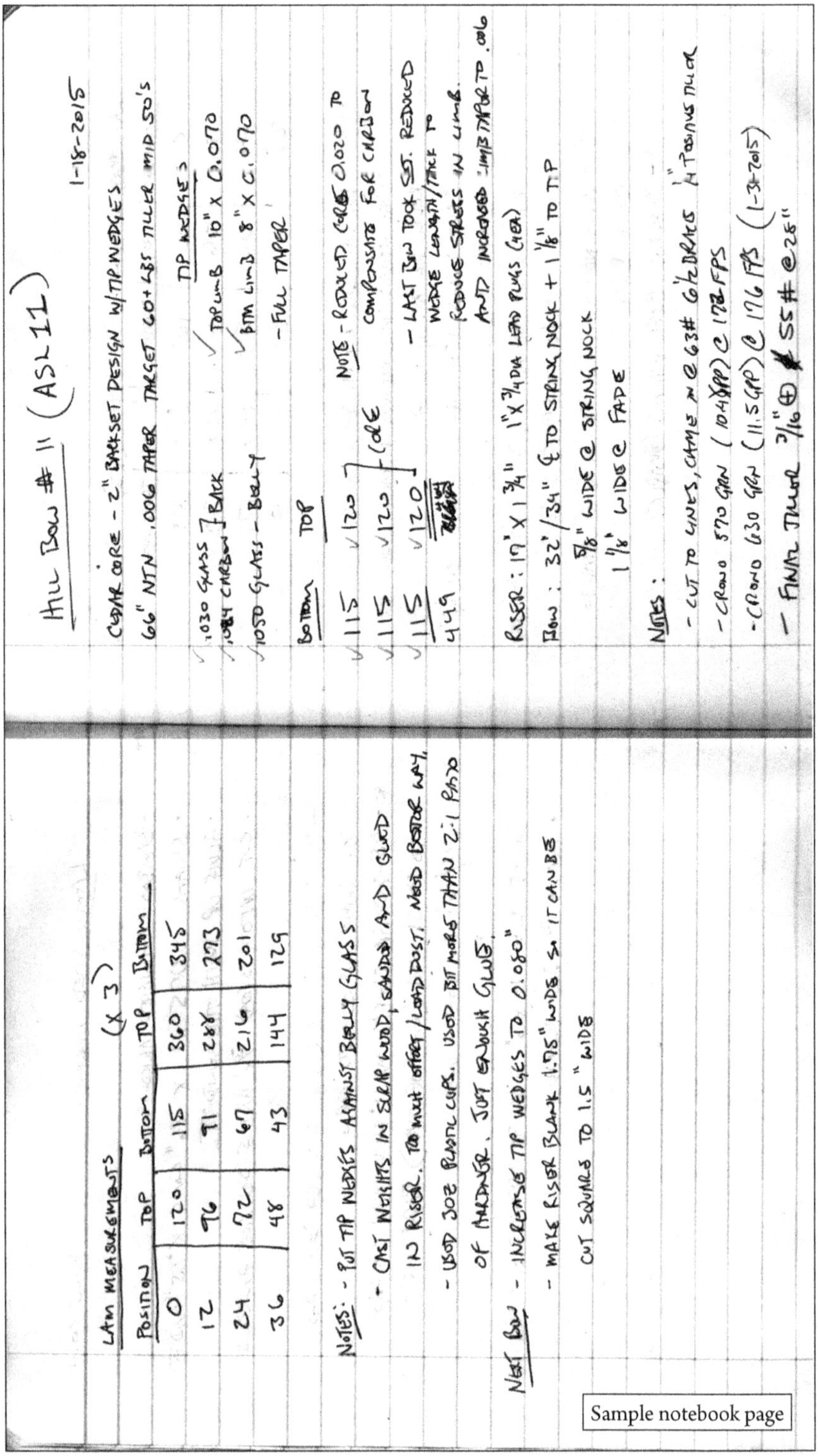

HILL BOW #11 (ASL 11)   1-18-2015

CEDAR CORE - 2" BAKSET DESIGN W/TIP WEDGES
66" NTN .006 TAPER TARGET 60+ LBS TILLER MID SO's

TIP WEDGES
TOP LIMB 10" X 0.070
BTM LIMB 8" X 0.070
- FULL TAPER

.030 GLASS ⎤ BACK
.084 CARBON ⎦ BACK
.050 GLASS - BELLY

NOTE - REDUCED CORE 0.020 TO
COMPENSATE FOR CARBON
- LMT 2ND TOOK SET. REDUCED
WEDGE LENGTH/TAPER TO
REDUCE STRESS IN LIMB
AND INCREASED LIMB TAPER TO .006

BOTTOM   TOP
115   √120
115   √120 ⎤ CORE
115   √120 ⎦
149

RISER: 19" X 1 3/4"   1" X 3/4 DIA LAM PLUGS (18R)
BOW: 32'/34" (E TO STRIKE NOCK + 1/8" TO TIP
5/8" WIDE @ STRING NOCK
1 1/8" WIDE @ FADE

NOTES:
- CUT TO LINES, CAME IN @ 63# 6 1/2 BRACE H TOOMUCH TILLER
- CRONO 570 GRN (104 SPP) @ 178 FPS
- CRONO 630 GRN (11.5 GPP) @ 176 FPS (1-31-2015)
- FINAL TILLER 3/16 ⊕ ¢ SS# @ 26"

LIMB MEASUREMENTS   (X 3)

POSITION	TOP	BOTTOM	TOP	BOTTOM
0	120	115	360	345
12	76	71	288	273
24	72	67	216	102
36	48	43	144	521

NOTES: - PUT TIP WEDGES AGAINST BELLY GLASS
* CAST NOTCHES IN SLAM WOOD, SANDED AND GLUED
IN RISER. TOO MUCH OFFSET/WOOD DUST, MADE BONDED HARD.
- USED 302 PLASTIC CUPS. USED BIT MORE THAN 2:1 RATIO
OF HARDNER, JUST ENOUGH GLUE.

NEXT BOW - INCREASE TIP WEDGES TO 0.080"
- MAKE RISER BLANK 1.75" WIDE SO IT CAN BE
CUT SQUARED TO 1.5" WIDE

Sample notebook page

Back to business.

Making the Limb Template

The next step is to make a template of your desired limb profile, which will be used to mark the position of the limbs on the form and guide the router bit as it cuts the form surface to your desired profile. I usually use something like melamine board to make the template.

I shy away from plywood and other materials that tend to warp with temperature and humidity changes. While melamine is not very strong, it is stable.

Once you have your materials at hand, the challenge is to determine your limb profile and get it drawn onto your template.

At this point I will share with you what I have done to determine the best limb profile for an ASL, and what the results were. Hopefully this will save you some time and effort as you choose your limb profile.

I have made bows with straight limbs with parallel cores.

I have made bows with "ears" that extended one foot down the limb and provided 1 inch of backset. These bows had core tapers running from 0.002 - 0.005 inch per inch.

I have made bows with circular limb profiles that provided from 1 to 3 inches of backset.

I have made bows of these three configurations with limbs of even length, and with limbs where the upper limb was 2 inches longer than the lower limb.

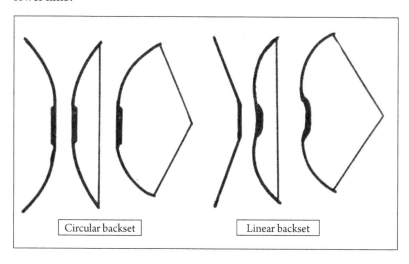

Circular backset   Linear backset

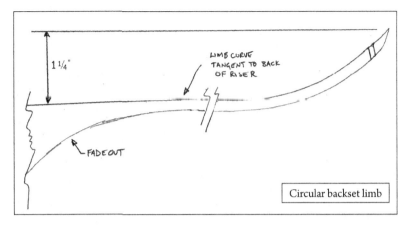

1 1/4"

LIMB CURVE
TANGENT TO BACK
OF RISER

FADE OUT

Circular backset limb

In the cases where the upper limb was longer than the lower limb, I
have made bows with circular limb profiles where the backset on the upper limb was greater than the backset on the lower limb to compensate for
the difference in limb length.

And finally, in the same cases where the upper limb was longer than
the lower limb, I have made bows with circular limb profiles where the
thickness of the upper limb is 0.015 inch greater than the lower limb to
compensate for the difference in limb length.

What I have found is that the bow that provides the greatest cast and
least hand shock and which is the most forgiving and easy to string is a
bow with a circular limb profile made on a form with 2 inches of backset.
By the time the bow is cut back to a length of 66 inches nock to nock, the
backset settles in around 1 1/4 inches. This bow will have an upper limb
which is 2 inches longer than the lower limb. The upper limb will run
0.015 inches thicker than the lower limb. Read Chapter 12 before accepting all the conclusions made in this paragraph.

That said, one profile I have not experimented with, but which I hope
to, is the simple linear backset limb. This limb is not tangent to the riser
where they meet, but heads off immediately at an angle to the riser in a
straight line. If you graph this profile over the simple circular curve, you
will immediately notice that it provides more backset to the limb than
does the circular profile. This is intriguing to me, but you will also notice that in this design, all the pre-stress glued into the laminations occurs
at this initial bend. I think this design would have merit for a flight bow,
which is expected to live fast and die young. But for a hunting bow, which
needs to be reliable, consistent, and long-lived, the more distributed pre-

stress of a circular profile is more dependable. As I said, I have not built this bow, so these conclusions are pure conjecture.

I will show how to make a form where the limb curve is tangent to the riser at its root and ends with 2 inches of backset for each limb. As mentioned before, 2 inches of backset in the form usually results in about 1 1/4 inches of backset in the bow. This method can be used to make a form of any design.

Determining the shape of your limb simply requires that you specify its end conditions. The limb has a root that ends at the riser fade outs, and it has a tip that, to no one's surprise, ends at the tip.

The limb curve should be tangent to the back of the riser at its root. What this means is that if you graphed the bow profile on a sheet of paper, the slope of the curve representing the riser should match the slope of the curve of the limb at the point they meet. For example, if the riser is horizontal on your graph paper, then its slope is zero. As the limb curve meets the riser, it should also have a slope of zero.

To define the limb tip requires determining only the amount of backset. Theoretically, you could build some string follow into the bow as well.

I happen to have some old CAD software that lets me graph a line easily, print out the curve, and glue it to my template material. It is then a simple matter of cutting the template out close to the line and sanding the remaining material down to the line. Another option is to use a few nails and a piece of flexible homogenous material to create a curve that you can follow with a pencil to trace onto the form. The temptation is to use a thin piece of wood for this simple method. I would caution against using wood as it is not a homogenous

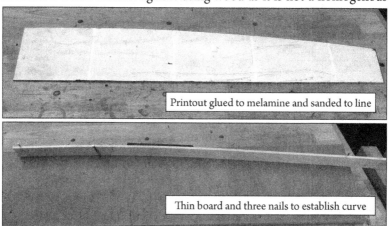

Printout glued to melamine and sanded to line

Thin board and three nails to establish curve

material, and it is thus prone to not bending in a perfect arc. A piece of plastic trim available from a home improvement store will work. To make this option work, you will need to place nails along the riser line for at least a foot to secure the flexible strip tangent to it. Then simply measure down 2 inches at the end of the form and place a nail. Insert the strip between the nails, and trace with a pencil.

Forms are traditionally 6 feet long and about 1 foot tall. As discussed earlier, for longbows they are 1 1/2 inches thick. I stick with this tradition.

With this in mind, our template should be 3 feet 6 inches long. It will include most of the riser and one limb. When the time comes, after having been used to trace out one side of the bow, it will be flipped over the centerline of the form to mark the other limb and remaining riser.

Once you have your profile traced onto your template material, it is time to cut it out. Use a bandsaw, saber saw, hacksaw, or whatever you have access to. Cut the template out wide of the line, leaving some material to gently sand away to the line.

To take the template to the line, use a belt sander or a sanding block. Either method is fine.

Once we have committed ourselves to the profile of our bow and produced a suitable template, it is now time to make ready the form blank.

<u>Making the Form Blank</u>

As discussed earlier, I have settled on simply using two pieces of one by twelve board, 6 feet long. The important thing is to carefully inspect

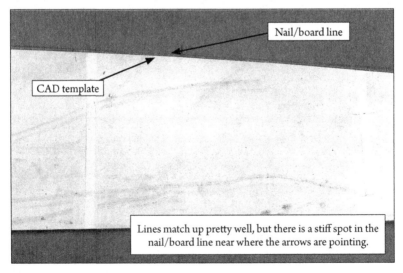

Nail/board line

CAD template

Lines match up pretty well, but there is a stiff spot in the nail/board line near where the arrows are pointing.

the wood before buying it. You will want to get two pieces that are as straight as possible. Try to minimize knots, but knots are acceptable.

After you get the boards home, look them over again with the understanding that these boards will be glued together. You need to determine which sides will be glued and which will be your faces. Here are some considerations:

- End grain - if possible, have the end grain opposed. This will provide the greatest protection against warping and cupping.
- Knots - if possible, put the big end of the knot to the glue side.
- Straight - if the boards do have any bow along their length, glue the boards together so that the bow is opposed. If possible, make the ends of the boards touch with the gap in the middle so they can be pulled together.

Once you have determined which faces will be glued together and how the boards will be oriented with respect to each other, it is a good idea to make marks to ensure you do, in the end, glue the boards together correctly.

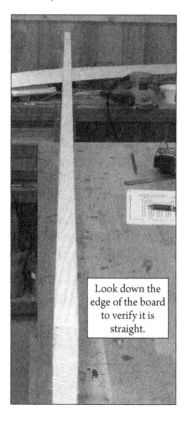

Look down the edge of the board to verify it is straight.

Opposing end grain

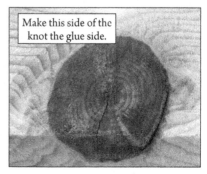

Make this side of the knot the glue side.

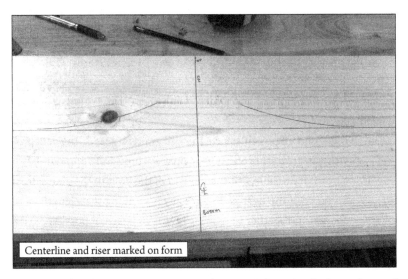

Centerline and riser marked on form

The next step is to lay your template onto the outside face of one of your boards. It is now time to determine where your form will be cut later on, after the boards are glued and screwed together.

Step one is to find the midpoint of the length of your board and mark a centerline. Measure your board. It is likely longer than 6 feet by half an inch or more. Make note of this. Mark the center point of your board. Now make a centerline across the face of your board and label it.

Now mark the ends of your form by placing a line 3 feet on each side of the centerline. We will cut this line later.

It is important at this point to consider the forces that will be applied to the form when the hose is pressurized to compress the laminations as the glue cures. As mentioned earlier, the form will see a total force of almost 6500 pounds when the hose is pressurized to 60 psi.

It is also important to remember that the riser has not been considered yet in the layout of our form. The space for the riser will be cut into what becomes the top of the form. We do not want the form to become too thin at this point. Because this is the thinnest part of the form, it is the weakest.

With the need to accommodate the riser in mind, lay your template onto the form so that it lines up with the center line. Move the template down toward the bottom of the form so that the tip side is about 2 1/2 inches from the bottom edge.

Draw the limb curve onto the form.

Repeat the process for the other limb.

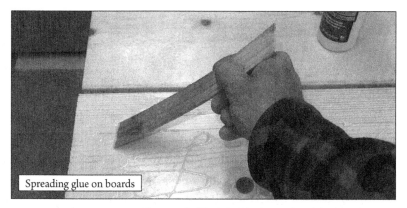

Spreading glue on boards

Draw the riser onto the top half of the form. It should lie right onto the curve drawn with the limb template.

Now we are beginning to see things take shape. The next step is to glue and screw the two pieces of wood together, but before we do that we need to mark the screw locations on the board.

To ensure adequate screw pressure, while avoiding interference between the screws and the bolt holes that will be drilled later, I space my screw pattern as follows: 1 inch in from each end, then, starting from the center, 6 inches apart going toward the ends. The last gap will be 5 inches, since the last row of screws is 1 inch in from the ends. My vertical spacing is dictated by the location of the limb line. I put two screws above and below the line, evenly spaced.

To glue the boards together, I use Titebond III as it is a good glue,

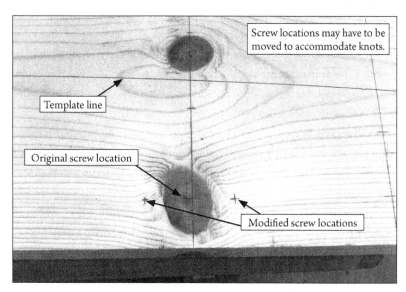

Screw locations may have to be moved to accommodate knots.

Template line

Original screw location

Modified screw locations

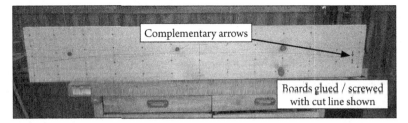

Complementary arrows

Boards glued / screwed
with cut line shown

inexpensive, and readily available. Wet the surface of both boards with
the glue. Spread it evenly and thinly. Put the two glued sides together
and screw them together. Start in the middle and move toward the ends.
As the boards are screwed together, excess glue will run out of the joint.
Clean up as required and leave the form blank to cure for at least a day.

At this point, I draw some complementary arrows on the right corner
so that I always orient the form halves together as they were cut. It's not
necessary as the screws can be used for orientation; I just prefer using a
mark to using the screws.

Shaping the Form

I like to square up the form. I cut the ends off at the lines made earlier
and then run the form lengthwise through the table saw to even up the
top and bottom edges. Now the form should be a nice squared-up piece
to work with.

The next step is to separate the top from the bottom along the limb
lines. You can use a bandsaw or a jigsaw to do this. It is important to leave
about 1/8 inch past the line.

The following step is the most critical step to get right so that your
form is true and produces bows with straight limbs. You may want to
practice this step on some scrap wood to make sure your setup is reliable.

Clamp your template to one side of the form so that it follows the
line. Make sure the clamps will not interfere with the path of the router
you will use to bring the form to the line. Now set the top and bottom
form pieces on a flat surface, oriented as they will go together with about
a 2-inch gap between them. Having the form pieces lined up this way will
give support to the router so that it will maintain a perpendicular cut.

Using the router, cut the form to the line. If your router bit is not long
enough to cut the entire 1 1/2-inch thickness of the form, lower the bit
and use the cut surface as your new guide to finish cutting the form face.

The final step to shaping the form is to cut out the riser section from

Template is clamped to form and ready for routing.

the top of the form.

Occasionally, the router will get away from you and gouge your form. For example, the bit can become loose and walk out of the chuck. If this happens, it is easy to fix. Simply fill the gouge with wood putty, wood epoxy, or wood filler. Sand by hand to bring to shape.

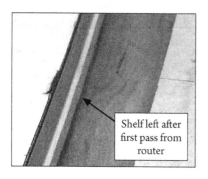

Shelf left after first pass from router

Router bit lowered down to remove shelf

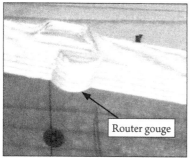

Router gouge

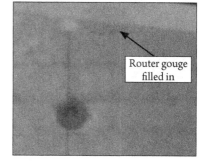

Router gouge filled in

Assembling the Form

Using spray contact cement, attach a Formica strip or fiberglass lamination to the face of the form. This serves to even out any odd spots on the face of the form and to provide a hard surface for the bow laminations to set upon.

The contact cement should allow you to affix the strip to the form without clamping. It is still a good idea to allow the strip to cure for several hours before handling it much.

Once the strip glue joint has cured sufficiently, it is time to sand and round off all corners of the top and bottom of the form. Be careful as you sand along the edge of the strip so you don't catch a splinter of fiberglass or Formica in your hand.

At this point, it's time to make the standoffs that will be used in conjunction with the metal brackets that affix the top and bottom halves together. Regarding the metal brackets, the bow press kit available from Bingham Projects is probably the best and easiest product to use for completing the form, as it comes with the metal brackets, hose, and other necessary components. It's also good to remember that these same components can be used on all future forms. It is easy to move the hardware from one form to another.

The standoffs serve to give space for the hose to extend past the edge of the form. This allows the hose to apply even pressure to the bow lami-

Formica strip

nations all the way to the edges.

The length of the standoffs will be determined by the curve of your limbs and the width of the form. The standoffs should be kept at least 1/8 inch below the face strip, and should be no more than 1/2 inch longer than the bracket.

The width should be about 1 1/2 inches.

The thickness is determined by the material you make the standoffs from. I use half-inch plywood to make

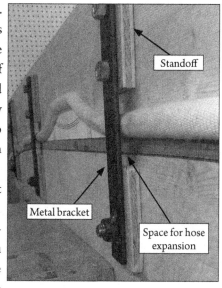

them. You will need a total of eight for the top half and eight for the bottom half of the form.

To determine the length of the standoffs, place your form pieces so that they lay about 1 1/4 inches apart. Lay your hardware on top of the form. The important thing in determining the spacing is to evenly distribute the force created by the pressure hose between the metal brackets. I space my brackets on center: 9 inches, 27 inches, 45 inches and 63 inches from one end. Now it is an easy matter to determine the length of each pair of standoffs.

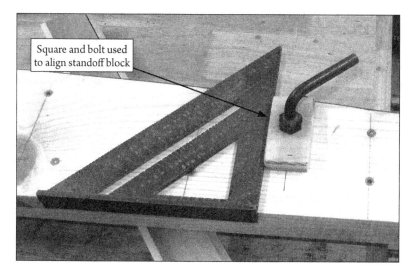

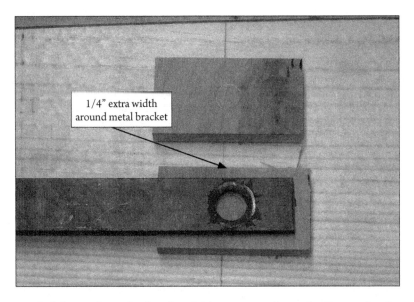

1/4" extra width around metal bracket

While you have the brackets laid out correctly on the form, take the time to mark the location of the bolt through holes in both the top and bottom halves by tracing the bolt holes in the brackets onto the form.

Now use the brackets to mark the location of the through holes on the standoffs.

Drill said holes. I use a 7/16-inch drill for the two holes in the top half of the form and a 9/16-inch drill bit for the single hole in the bottom half of the form.

Sand smooth the edges and surfaces of the standoff blocks. It is now time to affix them to the form. I affix the standoffs to the form using a staple gun. I orient the standoffs using the through bolts and a square.

At this point the form is complete. It is a good idea to coat your new form with furniture polish to help the form shed dirt and keep any epoxy that may come in contact with it from bonding.

Pressure Hose

Now consider the hose. As supplied, the hose has a pneumatic stem like those found on bicycle or car tires. The idea is to fill the hose with air to the correct pressure, then place the form into the bow oven so that the bow you are making can cure.

This method has worked for many thousands of bows. But I don't like the idea that I can't see what is happening to the pressure in the hose. Is there a leak? Did the bow cure under low pressure? There is no way to

NPT quick disconnect fitting installed in hose end fitting

know.

I want to ensure constant pressure on the hose, and thus on the bow, through the curing process. To do this, I replace the pneumatic stem with a 1/4-inch NPT quick disconnect fitting so I can connect it to my compressor.

To do this, you will need to remove the pneumatic stem from the hose end fitting. It has been installed using thread locking compound. Heating the stem with a propane torch will soften the compound and allow the stem to be removed.

The threaded hole in the hose end fitting must be retapped for a 1/4-inch NPT thread fitting. The appropriate drill bit and tap can be obtained from a hardware store to do the job.

Once installed, you will be able to keep your form pressurized while it is in the hot box. I stay with the recommended form pressure of 60 PSI as specified by Bingham Projects.

Building a Hotbox

Aside from your form, the only other piece of dedicated equipment you will need to build bows is a hotbox. A hotbox is simply an insulated box with a heat source into which you place your form, loaded with the bow blank, in order to cure the epoxy adhesive.

There is no need to go into detail describing its construction, as those details are not complicated and have been addressed by others including Bingham Projects in their instructional videos.

I deviated from their construction instructions in the following ways:

- Made my hot box shorter. The outside dimensions of my hot box are 7 feet long by 13 inches wide by 22 3/4 inches tall;
- Added caster wheels to the bottom to facilitate moving it around my shop as needed;
- Added a hole at one end to feed the compressor hose through so that it could be connected to the air hose in the form;
- Moved the light bulbs to the bottom of the hot box so that the heat would rise and keep the temperature more uniform;
- Added a meat probe thermometer to the hot box;
- Added handles to the ends to facilitate lifting the entire box;
- Added a timer for convenience.

Eventually, I did away with the light bulbs altogether. In the end, they are more trouble than they are worth. They eventually burn out, which can result in a low-temperature cure. They are a spot source of heat, which results in burns on the form and hot box. And eventually they will not be available as LEDs take over the lighting market.

I ended up using a 1000-watt base board heater and a digital temperature controller.

The cost of the baseboard heater was less than the cost of the light fixtures and junction boxes. The effort to install it was less, and it is a more reliable and efficient source of heat than light bulbs.

Another advantage to the baseboard heater is that it brought the hot-box to temperature in less than 10 minutes, as opposed to the 2 hours

Hot box sitting in corner, ready to use.

Meat thermometer

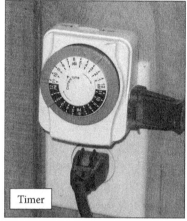

Timer

Hole for compressor hose

Standoff to keep form off light bulbs

Melt-out in foam under lights

required by the light bulbs.

The digital controller was surprisingly inexpensive and easy to install and use. I went with the Inkbird ITC-306T controller.

Chapter 5
Building a Riser

Before we can build a bow, we need to build a riser. The riser is the crossroads of the bow. It is the place where everything comes together: limbs, archer, and arrow. And it is also the place where the character of the bow is, for the most part, determined.

While the design of the limbs determines the cast of the bow, and to some extent the character of the bow, nothing matters as much as the riser. All our efforts to make a forgiving, efficient, and quiet bow can be lost if we neglect to make a good riser.

The riser must be durable. If the riser is not made to withstand the demands of repeated shooting, we will end up with scrap.

The riser must be ergonomic. If the riser does not communicate the forces applied to it by the archer in a repeatable and comfortable fashion, the bow will never shoot in a consistent and forgiving manner.

The riser should be attractive. What makes an attractive riser may be unique to each archer. There are some commonly held qualities of beauty that include simple flowing lines, rounded edges, smooth surfaces, and a sense of economy.

The qualities of a good riser include some of the trends we have seen as we build our understanding of what makes an ASL so appealing to the thoughtful, traditional bowhunter. A simple device, the ASL cannot be accused of promising great things while coming up short in the delivery.

When we look at a modern compound bow, we see lots of interesting shapes, mechanisms, devices, and materials that promise to give us a shooting experience beyond our wildest dreams. In fact, every year brings new and improved models that make the same promise. Some of us chase these promises and possibilities and buy that new bow. Usually, these new features leave us disappointed and serve mostly to separate us from our money, and from the simple joy of shooting.

As traditional archers, we have left mechanization behind. But even as we try to keep it simple, we are tempted to add just a little something or other to improve the performance or look of the riser. Of this crime, I am just as guilty as the next person. In fact, even with the knowledge that simple is better, I continue to find ways to complicate things. There is a fine line between innovation and claptrap.

So I will keep my discussion of what I have found to make a good riser as simple and to the point as I can. From there, you can explore all the possibilities.

The design of the riser goes hand in hand with the design of the bow, for where the riser ends, the limbs begin. This affects the layout of the form as well. Thankfully, there is a level of flexibility to the length and width of the riser with respect to the form, so experimentation with riser dimensions does not mean a new form is needed.

Once the overall dimensions of the riser are determined, the construction of the riser must be considered. We will take these discussions in order.

Riser Dimensions

A riser is made up of just three major features. Those features include the fadeouts, the grip, and the arrow shelf. Combining these features with the overall length of the riser completely defines the riser for us.

The fadeout length derives from the overall riser length minus the grip length. This number is then divided in two to give the fadeout lengths. The number is largely irrelevant. The grip dimensions and the overall length of the riser are the driving factors that determine the character of the riser. The important aspects of the fadeout design are that the slope is gentle enough to allow a smooth transition to the limb and that it promotes reliable construction.

The grip length has been a constant for me. I set my grip length at 4 inches and leave it there. I wear extra large gloves and tabs, so I expect that in most cases 4 inches should suffice. If you have larger hands, you may need to adjust. For smaller hands, I would still stay with a 4 inch length. A little extra grip is not a bad thing.

The depth of the grip, as well as its shape, are important to consider at this point. I have found that a riser blank made to a 1 3\4 inch thickness works well for me. If you have smaller hands, a grip of 1 1/2 inches may suit you better. It is important to keep the grip from being too shallow as this tends to encourage a tight grip, which in turn tends to push our arrow right and left of the bullseye.

The shape of the grip can be left until later to determine.

The arrow shelf depth and shape is a matter of personal choice and in my experience has very little effect on the shootability of the bow. It does not get cut into the riser until after the bow blank has been mostly shaped into a bow. I usually cut my arrow shelves in a little less than a half inch. Arrow shelves will be discussed in greater detail in Chapter 8 which outlines the construction of the bow.

The overall length of the riser will affect several things. Most obviously, it affects the length of the limbs. When considering the construction of a self bow, it is important to maximize the length of working limb. The longer the working limb is, the less work any one part of the limb has to do, and thus the longer the limb will last. When making bows using fiberglass back and bellies, the wood core is relieved from the duty of providing cast. Thus, the stress in the wood is significantly reduced and the need to maximize limb length is no longer the driving force.

With the need to maximize limb length set aside, we can consider making a longer riser. The longer riser will help to reduce the recoil shock, increase the cast, and improve the forgiveness of the bow. But we must be careful so that we don't go to extremes.

Before we consider longer risers, let's consider a shorter riser. A riser length of less than 14 inches results in fadeouts that, in my opinion, are too steep for the beginning bowyer. They can work, but they require excessive bow press force and perfectly shaped and thinned ends. If not executed perfectly, I think they detract from the slim elegance of an ASL too. They become the fat curves that draw the eye.

As mentioned above, longer risers have the potential to improve the performance of the bow, but there are limits. If they become too long, they no longer look proportional to the bow. An ASL with long slim lines that last just long enough to fade into the next curve will begin to look clunky with an overly large riser that overstays its welcome in the eye of the archer.

Aside from the aesthetic limitations of an overly large riser, it can begin to inhibit the action of an ASL. Where a reflex-deflex hybrid bow or a recurved bow can be constructed almost entirely of riser with just an afterthought of limbs attached at each end, the ASL depends upon its limbs' length for its drawing and shooting action. I have found that an ASL can benefit from shorter limbs, but only to a point.

So with all that said, for a beginning bowyer, making a bow of at least 66 inches nock to nock length, I would settle on a riser that is 17 inches long. I have run lengths from 14 to 18 inches, but I find 17 inches to be a happy medium. By comparison, on my 64-inch deflex-reflex bows, I had a riser length of 22 inches.

As you progress in your bowyer skills, exploring shorter and shorter risers with the accompanying need for better and better tillering is where the adventure lies.

Riser Construction

There are a number of ways to put a riser together. The methods I have adopted are the result of choosing to use local woods. As I have mentioned before, if you choose to use tropical woods with their heavy nature, superior strength, and ecological baggage, you need but to cut your riser from a single piece of wood and go on your way.

Use of North American wood, on the other hand, requires more understanding of the forces that your riser will be exposed to. But the knowledge that your future bow will not contribute to the continuing degradation of the planet should lighten the ethical load on your psyche and make the work all that more enjoyable.

Some North American woods, like sugar maple (otherwise known as hardrock maple), ash, hickory, osage, and dogwood, are very close in strength and even weight to tropical woods. I still like to laminate them back to belly to ensure that any unseen flaw in that particular piece of wood is prohibited from extending through the entire riser. Besides, it gives just a bit more style to the bow to make it from a couple contrasting woods. I will usually try to pair a piece of light maple with a piece of dark walnut or cherry to produce a nice contrast. I will use the stronger, more durable maple toward the back of the bow so that most of the fade out,

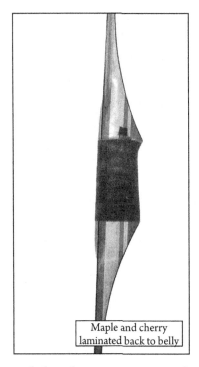

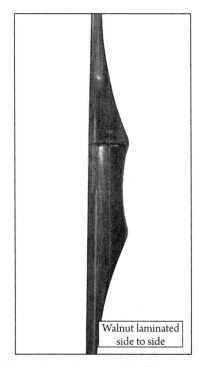

| Maple and cherry laminated back to belly | Walnut laminated side to side |

including the important paper-thin edge at the end, are made of this superior wood. The walnut will be used at the belly side, where its beautiful grain can be fully appreciated in the grip.

Sometimes I like to make just a simple riser from a single species of wood. I have made many bows using only walnut or cherry in the riser. In this case, I like to make the riser block from laminations that run side to side.

I have used this design for bows up to 55 pounds in draw weight. If I were to make a bow of greater draw weight, I would likely not use just walnut or cherry. I would add a sturdier wood like maple on the thin side of the fadeout.

When I first started making risers from laminations, I would glue the laminations together and then clamp the block to ensure good bonding. This worked, but it was a source of frustration. Anyone who has tried to clamp two flat pieces of wood that have been smeared with glue will appreciate how difficult it is to keep them together and straight. No matter how many clamps you use, or how diligent you are at getting the clamps straight, the wood slips and slides around like a little kid learning to ice skate.

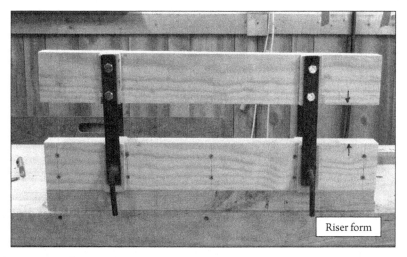

Riser form

Once the riser block has been cured, it must be cut square on all sides. Using the clamping method requires the use of wider and longer wood in order to guarantee that a square block can be cut out of it in the end.

So I made a form to glue up my riser blocks. This form is made in exactly the same way as the bow form is made, so I will not go into the details of its construction. The dimensions of the form are 2 feet long by 6 inches wide (top and bottom), with a gap of 2 3/4 inches.

You can use the same air hose and clamps that you use for your bow form. If you make enough bows, you may consider getting additional metal hardware and the short air hose that Bingham Projects sells for making take-down recurve limbs.

For purposes of illustration, I will show how to make a riser block that has seven laminations of 1/4-inch thickness laid together so that the glue seams run back to belly. This block will then be cut side to side and laminated again using accent strips. This will result in a riser block that has four glue lines parallel to the back of the bow and six glue lines parallel to the side of the bow.

If you were to make the riser using maple and walnut, you could skip the first lamination step and proceed with the second back-to-belly lamination step.

The dimensions of the riser block needed to make an ASL are as follows: width - 1 3/4 inches; length - 19 inches; thickness - 1 3/4 inches.

Once laminated together, this block will be cut down to the following dimensions: width - 1 1/2 inches; length - 17 inches; thickness - 1 3/4 inches. (After adding the accent strips, the thickness will be close to 2 inches, and then cut back to 1 3/4 inches.)

The wood you choose to make your riser should be free from knots or other defects. I like to cut my riser laminations from boards that have been cut flat grain. This means that you can see the grain patterns in the wide side of the board.

Cut a piece of wood from your stock board 1 3/4 inches wide. Then slice this piece of wood into laminations that are 1/4 inch thick. You will need to have access to a belt sander or drum sander to flatten the sides of your laminations to ensure a good bond and attractive finish. Divots, scratches, and blade burns will all affect the glue joints and the durability and appearance of the riser blank. You may want to cut your laminations a little thick so that you can sand them down to 1/4 inch.

You will need seven laminations to make your riser block.

Once your laminations are prepared, you will need to glue them together. I have made many risers using Unibond 800, which is a formaldehyde based glue. The advantage of using this glue to make risers is that it is cheaper than the Smooth-On epoxy I use for gluing the bow together. The disadvantage to using Unibond 800 is that it has a shelf life and will tend to harden after a year or so. I have had a few cans harden in a month. It will bond wood well, but it will not bond fiberglass or other plastics, so its use is limited. Keep it in the fridge to extend its life if you choose to use

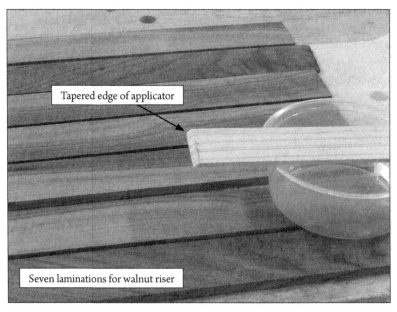

Tapered edge of applicator

Seven laminations for walnut riser

it. I am on the fence about using it as I have thrown a lot of it away, and thus it may not be more economical in the end.

I recently discovered Dap Weldwood Plastic Resin Glue. It is essentially the same glue as Unibond 800 but in powder form, which needs to be mixed with water to use, The dry powder will store forever in the fridge.

Apply glue to both surfaces that are to be glued together and ensure complete wetting of the surfaces. I use a thin piece of scrap wood as an applicator. No need for fancy brushes or rollers. I sand a 45-degree edge onto one end of the scrap wood, and then, using 400-grit paper, or finer, smooth the feathered edge. This works well to spread a thin, even layer of glue onto the laminations.

Once the laminations have been glued together, it is time to put them into the riser form. If you choose to simply clamp them together, make sure to use a generous number of clamps to ensure uniform pressure. Keep an eye on the clamped block for a while to make sure the laminations don't move out of position.

If you are using a form, simply put your riser block into the form, taking the precaution of putting a layer of plastic wrap onto the bottom of the form before laying your riser block into it. This will protect the form from the glue that squeezes out of the joints as pressure is applied to the form. Once the riser block has been placed on the form, add another layer of plastic wrap over it. Place a wood block on top of the riser block to help evenly distribute the pressure load. Then install the pressure hose and upper half of the form.

Place spacer blocks between the riser block and the metal brackets to keep the riser block laminations straight. Once this is done, you can bolt the metal brackets down tight.

Give the whole assembly a final look over to make sure that everything is lined up correctly and that there is no path for glue to migrate onto the form or hardware. Once you are satisfied that everything looks good, inflate the pressure hose to 60 PSI. Sixty PSI is the pressure Bingham Projects specifies in their form kits, and it has always worked for me.

At this point, I am usually done with bow making and head off to address the other chores of the day. I don't like to work too long at bow making, as it requires my complete attention. I limit my time so that I don't make any mistakes along the way.

Riser block in form

Assembling a bow by gluing a series of laminations together results in a fine weapon, but the process depends upon the bowyer's ability to work without mistakes. When a mistake is glued into a bow, it is hard to erase. Therefore I find it a good policy to work in shorter sessions than my enthusiasm might dictate. This helps me avoid those avoidable mistakes.

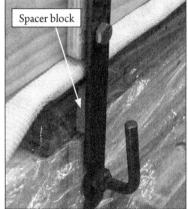

Spacer block

Even so, many mistakes that seem to throw up a barrier to completing the bow can be worked around. The process of correcting these mistakes is always improved if I take a break and come back later. I would encourage you to take this approach as well. Work a little, think a lot.

When you do return to bow making, you will have the pleasure of removing your first work from its form. This is always fun, like finding presents under the Christmas tree. And just as you have to be careful when collecting your presents to avoid knocking that delicate blown glass ornament to the floor where it shatters with that all-too-familiar sound all mothers know, you must be careful when removing your riser blank.

Bleed the pressure off the air hose first!

Once the pressure has been removed from the air hose, it is time to open the form and remove the riser blank. You will notice the sometimes sharp glue that has extruded from the edges of the laminations and is now

Glue waste on riser block

Riser block cleaned up

cured. It is time to remove it and square up the riser block.

I do this in steps. Sometimes I remove big pieces with a knife or a sander until the block will sit somewhat square upon the table saw. Then I run the block through the table saw, removing just enough material to get a somewhat straight edge. I work back and forth between the sides of the block a couple times until I have worked the block down so that it is relatively square. No need to get to final dimensions yet, as the sides will be cut again after contrast laminations have been added.

Be sure to keep straight what is side-to-side (side of laminations is side of bow), and what is back-to-belly (edge of laminations is back and belly). This is an opportune time to end up cutting your block to the wrong dimensions, so beware.

Once you are satisfied that the block is sufficiently cleaned up, you are ready to proceed with cutting the block side-to-side and gluing the contrast laminations in place. There are no technical limitations to the thickness or number of laminations. What I show here is for example only.

Since both the back and belly side of the riser block will be of walnut,

I like to have three contrast laminations - an inside lamination of walnut (0.150 inch thick) with the outside laminations of a lighter wood like maple (0.075 inch thick). I will then use this same theme on the limb nock overlays and the riser overlays to give a pleasing appearance to the entire bow.

Knowing how thick my contrast laminations will be, and anticipating where I want them to sit in the finished bow, inform where the riser block will be cut. There is some latitude to this cut, as the back and belly side of the block will be cut later to bring the block to final dimension. In this case I will cut the block 1/2 inch from what I have marked as the back of the block.

The contrast laminations and riser block are now ready to be glued and placed in the form to cure as done before.

The job of cleaning up the riser block and then gluing in the contrast laminations usually goes fairly quickly. It is now that the new bowyer realizes that a fair amount of the time spent making a bow is spent waiting for glue to cure.

Living on a subsistence farm as I do, there are always chores to take care of. I usually plan my bow work early in the day so that when I reach the stage of waiting for glue to cure, I can get on with the rest of my day. This is as close to multi-tasking as I am capable of getting.

In this case, however, before you stop bow work for the day, you may

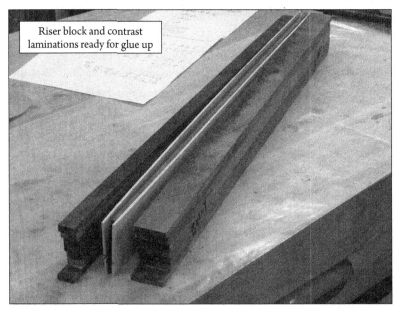

Riser block and contrast laminations ready for glue up

want to make sure you have your riser template ready to go. When the riser block comes out of the form this time, it will be ready to shape into its final form.

One of the great things about American Semi-Longbows is that they lend themselves to simple methods of construction. No need for fancy jigs or tools. There are no complex curves in an ASL, and thankfully no curves that need to match up between form and bow.

When building a hybrid bow, for example, the deflexed riser must mate perfectly to the form to ensure reliable construction. The curve that the back of the riser block must take is not simply the same curve as the form, which would be bad enough; it must take the curve that results after the back glass and core laminations have been laid onto the form. Bows of different draw weights have different core thicknesses, and thus have riser blocks with different curves on their backs.

All this is avoided with the ASL. The back of an ASL, from fadeout to fadeout, is straight. No curves to frustrate the bowyer and add hours sanding out high spots and low spots to perfection. Rip it on the table saw, touch it to the belt sander, and you are ready to go.

Shaping the Riser Block

While the back of the riser block is straight, there are the fadeout curves to contend with. But these curves do not need to mate up to anything on the form, so as long as they are smooth they will suffice.

As I mentioned before, I have an old CAD program, which allows me

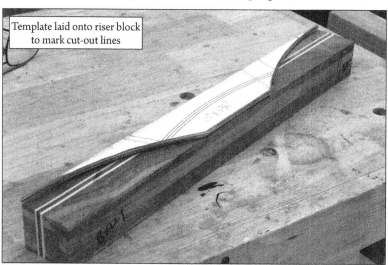

Template laid onto riser block to mark cut-out lines

to generate drawings that I can then glue onto a board to make a template. These curves can be made freehand, or with the use of a French curve, or in any other way you wish. Both fadeouts should have the same shape.

I make my risers 17 inches long by 1 3/4 inches thick, back to belly. I find this thickness fits my hand well. If you have a smaller hand, a thickness of 1 1/2 inches may suit you better.

The grip length is 4 inches centered on the centerline of the riser block. The fadeouts curve down from the ends of the grip and end tangential to the back of the bow at the thinnest point.

After I remove the riser block from the form for the last time, I run it through the table saw as required to obtain my final dimensions: 1 3/4 inches back-to-belly, 1 1/2 inches side-to-side. At this point, I am ready to cut the ends of the block to obtain the 17-inch length.

Look the block over for the best place to take the 17 inches out. I make my blanks 19 inches long so that I have 2 inches to play with. Sometimes one end or the other will not look good. Find where you will cut the ends. Cut one end, measure 17 inches, and then cut the other end.

Now lay your template upon the block and draw your fadeouts. I cut the fadeouts with a bandsaw. They can just as easily be cut with a jigsaw or a handsaw. The important thing is to stay at least 1/16 inch off the line so that there is no danger of cutting off the ends of the fadeouts.

I don't finish sanding the fadeouts until I am ready to laminate the bow together. I have found that if I take the fadeout ends to their paper-thin final dimensions and then leave the block to sit for a night, or a day or two, they can get broken through inadvertent accident, or warped by changing humidity. Finishing the fadeouts is the last thing I do before

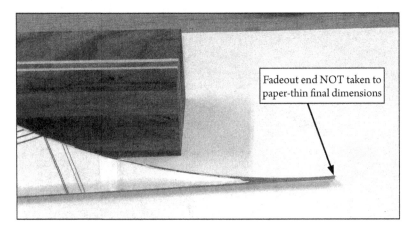

Fadeout end NOT taken to paper-thin final dimensions

mixing epoxy to laminate the bow.

To add weight to my risers, I add lead in the grip. I drill a pattern of four 3/4-inch holes 1 inch deep into the handle section using a forstner bit. These bits will allow the most accurate hole to be drilled.

I then have to make the lead weights to install into the riser. I have done this by simply pouring molten lead into the holes. This works and is easy. I've never had a problem with a bow I made this way. But recently I have precast the lead and then glued it into the riser. The advantage of this second method is that the lead is glued to the riser and may provide additional strength.

To form the precast lead, I drill out a block of scrap wood with the same forstner bit to a depth of 1 inch. I then line each hole with a piece

Weight holes marked and ready for drilling

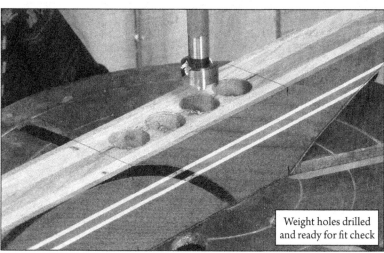

Weight holes drilled and ready for fit check

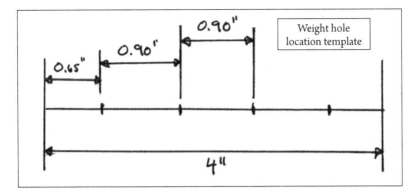

0.90"

0.90'

0.65"

Weight hole location template

4"

of paper. This paper will ensure that the lead weights, once removed from the form, will fit into the riser block.

Weight with air channel

After the lead weights have been re-moved from the wood block, I remove the paper and cut a channel in the side of the weight. This serves to let the air pass as the weight, covered with glue, is pushed into the hole in the riser.

Once the lead weights have been made and fit checked in the riser, the riser can be set aside to await final lay-up of the bow.

Final Thoughts on the Riser

I shared my hesitation about including any discussion of increasing the mass weight of the riser by building lead into it. I included the idea in

Tools and materials needed to cast weights

Chapter 2, and the instructions for doing it in this chapter, so that the option would be available to you.

My bows benefited from adding lead to the riser for a long time. This may have held me back in my efforts at improving my design by hiding the bow's true nature. Or it may have helped keep me going by giving me good shooting bows when my talents wouldn't otherwise merit it.

Maybe, by having the advantage of my experience, you can avoid this step and move on to good bows, made of good wood, without the need for extra mass.

Chapter 6
Catch It, Kill It, Grow It

Everything we do is informed by everything else we do.

As I ponder why I am drawn to spending so much time in the pursuit of food, I can't help but wonder why I am willing to spend so much time and effort to produce my own can of green beans. And likewise, my own American Semi-Longbow. Does one inform the other?

Committing this time to growing green beans, when I could more easily buy four cans of deluxe French-cut green beans packed in spring water for a dollar, doesn't mean I am eager to waste my time.

Our family has spent the last decade (and then some) trying to improve our gardening methods specifically so that we don't spend any more time, or money, growing our beans than we have to.

When we started our garden, shortly before we had kids, we did it in the time-tested way. We rented a roto-tiller from the local equipment company, tore up perfectly good grass, and commenced planting seeds. The package of seeds showed a perfect green bean and promised a bountiful harvest.

Yeah.

As I mentioned before, it's been many years since that first planting, and we have learned a lot. Some things we learned from books and articles; most things we learned from the school of hard knocks and back aches.

That first garden came up fast and looked beautiful for the first few weeks. Then the weeds grew and the bugs hatched out of their winter nests. By the time the beans were ready to harvest, I am not sure who looked more haggard, the bean plants or us.

And yet we kept at it. That first year, with only my wife and me to feed, we had plenty of extra produce. I brought it to work and left it in the snack room for my fellow employees to take. When the cucumbers, tomatoes, beans, and squash plants finally gave out is when I finally heard from folks. "When are you bringing in some more stuff?"

"Maybe next year" was my reply. But in my head I was trying to figure out how to preserve these things for the winter so we could eat more and give away less.

In that first garden was planted not only seeds in the ground, but a seed in my head. The seed of a question: "Could I feed my family from my garden and my hunting?"

At the time I was much younger and had more energy than sense. At the time it seemed like an interesting challenge. But looking back on it, I think of it as the beginnings of an awakening. I was beginning to awaken to the fact that I had been moving away from my connections to nature.

Going to college, and then working as an engineer, meant that I would live in a more urban environment. Study and project deadlines meant that I would have little time for outdoor adventure. Some form of this experience has been lived by every generation born since the Industrial Revolution.

Starting a family involves a lot of nature. For me, starting a family also served as a wakeup call. Did I want my kids to grow up without a connection to the land? Did I want to keep on living that way myself? Did I want

Kids watering terrace garden

Typical summertime picking

to build my children's bodies from partially hydrogenated soybean oil, or from deer?

Part of answering these questions involved deciding what, in my life, was important. Was it important to eat good food that I grew myself? Or was it important to spend as little money as possible on food?

As a society, we seem driven to value lowest cost above all else. The food industry has thrived off this tendency and spent much time and effort to foster it. The nutritional value of the food we eat is an afterthought to the cost, in dollars, of the things we consume.

And the story is the same for most everything we endeavor to do, including hunting. There is a gizmo, gadget, or widget that promises to make it easier - nay, almost guarantees - for us to kill that monster buck.

Gadgets serve to isolate us from our hunting in the same way that processed food delivered in vacuum-packed plastic film isolates us from real food.

"If we don't catch it, kill it, or grow it, we don't eat it" is how I have explained in concise terms the way our family lives. But the truth is that if you open our fridge, you will find plenty of things vacuum-packed in plastic film.

Condiments and the like are hard to catch, kill, or grow. And there are plenty of other things too. Living without ice cream seems to be a bridge too far.

Even though I have found it impossible to feed my family completely by my own hand, the effort has yielded fruit other than that grown on the vine. For one, it has shown me yet again that I must be ever vigilant against the all-too-easy-to-fall-into trap of relying on others to do my thinking for me.

I cannot write about food and our relationship to it without sharing some of the words of one of the most important writers on the topic of food. Michael Pollan has written many good and thoughtful books on the subject that have had a positive effect on the cultural conversation. The cultural conversation about food is remarkably similar to the conversation about bowhunting. Take these words for example from *In Defense of Food*:

> *The sheer novelty and glamour of the Western diet, with its seventeen thousand new food products every year and the marketing power - thirty-two billion dollars a year - used to sell us those products, has overwhelmed the force of tradition and left us where we now find ourselves: relying on science and journalism and government and marketing to help us decide what to eat.*

And compare Pollan's words with the words of Aldo Leopold as he decries gadgets in hunting in *A Sand County Almanac*:

> *Civilization has so cluttered this elemental man-earth relationship with gadgets and middlemen that awareness of it is growing dim. We fancy that industry supports us, forgetting what supports industry.*

The mistake of allowing other people to make our food for us is that it goes hand in hand with the mistake of allowing other people to do our thinking for us. It seldom works out in our favor.

The opportunity to make this mistake abounds in almost every as-

Maddie with basket of carrots

pect of living. Industry offers to make our lives easier for a price, if only we let them. But what is the true cost?

Our American Semi-Longbow goes hand in hand with our gardening. All things that serve to feed us directly seem to work together that way. What better example of this is there than killing a rabbit out of our lettuce patch and dropping him in a pot with some potatoes? Everything grown in the garden together ends up in the pot together. It is a symmetry that tells me that I am on the right track.

Could the same thing not be accomplished with a shotgun? Superficially yes, but let's consider it a little further. If I shoot the rabbit with the shotgun, I leave lead pellets in the garden, to be taken up by next year's crops and deposited in my soup. The sound of the shot disturbs not only the rabbit sitting somewhere down-range of the barrel, but all those critters not in danger of being shot. When the rabbit is killed with the longbow, the sound disturbs none of the local residents, and all that is left in the garden are his entrails, ready to enrich next year's lettuce.

One of the things I love best about my bow is simply holding it. In the winter and early spring months, long after hunting seasons are past, I walk with my bow through the woods. As I hold the bow, I occasionally look at

One of the few times it all worked out.

its structure. The way the riser fades into the limbs, and the way the string is connected, by simple notch, to the limbs.

The simple elegant nature of the bow serves to remind me of the simple elegant nature of nature, and of how all the elements in nature work together to produce a robust system that tolerates abuse.

If we take our compound bow on a long hard journey over mountain, valley, and river, we are likely to worry about its ability to function correctly, should the opportunity arise. We treat it as carefully as possible and must spend more time going over its various elements to assure ourselves they have survived the abuse, than we ever spend shooting it.

Contrast that experience with the experience of making the same journey with a longbow. A quick look for damage, a short tug on the string, and all is proven well.

It is a struggle these days to keep things simple. We are constantly barraged by messages that encourage us to buy gadgets to make our lives easier, make things happen faster, and "connect" us to the world. Ironically, most of these things tend to do the opposite.

Walking through the woods with my simple bow reminds me that these things are not necessary to live the good life. What is necessary are the skills to use the tools of the simple life. In hunting, we call these skills woodsmanship.

Woodsmanship is often seen as a badge of accomplishment worn by a few better-than-average hunters, an unobtainable goal. Most of us admire it, but we are resigned to the fact that we will not be able to obtain it. To me, it serves as a metaphor for living the good life.

The gadget industry has turned our reluctance to develop good woodsmanship into a niche. The commercialism we are exposed to praises the merits of good woodsmanship while at the same time promising us shortcuts to the end result without the trouble of developing the skill.

Why "hunt the wind" when we can don a suit made to eliminate our scent? Why look for buck trails when we can make a "mock scrape?" These things promise to increase our odds of killing a big deer, without the effort and uncertainty of hunting in the traditional manner.

If you are reading this book, then you have already answered one of these gadget questions: "Why hunt with a longbow when you can shoot a super efficient, fast, quiet, accurate compound bow equipped with sights and a release guaranteed to ensure that you hit your mark?"

You have learned that your pride and satisfaction in achieving your goal is proportional to the effort you expended in reaching it. Overcoming uncertainty, facing adversity, and perfecting skill are what fuel your satisfaction.

Everything we do is informed by everything else we do. There is a lesson in this simple choice we make to decline the advantages of a modern compound bow and instead pick up the longbow.

Hopefully, through this choice you discovered that shooting a longbow isn't really as hard as it was made out to be. Woodsmanship is the same. It requires you to be observant, and to be honest with yourself. But it isn't rocket science. While we may not all become the greatest outdoorsmen who ever lived, we can all become proficient at hunting with a longbow in the traditional way. By this effort we can all experience the satisfaction of killing a deer, without the mental noise that gadgets bring to the experience.

Everything about the simple American Semi-Longbow speaks to the truth that joy is found in keeping it simple. There are no unfulfilled promises in its straight limbs, only that promise that if I do what I am supposed to do (pick a spot, good form, etc.), it will do its job.

This simple lesson that joy is found in accomplishment, and accomplishment is found in overcoming adversity, is a lesson we should keep in mind as we mull over the rest of our lives.

I have found this lesson to be the most basic building block of a good life. Every purchase we make, every action we take, should be measured against this lesson.

I have also found that the repercussions of this lesson extend beyond my own experience. And this is where I begin to feel resistance to my choices.

Our economy is based on growth. Everything in our society seems to be held to that measure. When we hear about the status of the economy, it is described only in terms of its rate of growth. A positive rate is the only measure of a good economy.

It makes me wonder. The earth is a sphere of set proportion. It does not grow. If the earth does not grow, if its resources are finite, how can the economy continue to grow forever? How can we continue to think that all we have to do is "grow our way" out of our economic problems?

The intent of this book is not to answer these thorny questions, but simply to relay what my longbow has taught me about living in this world. I have found that if I resist the urge to look for happiness in the empty promises of the latest gadgets, whether they be for hunting or anything else, I am happier for it.

This happiness comes not only from the effort of doing things myself, but I am sure, subconsciously at least, I am happier because doing things this way allows me to live more gently on the earth.

It seems to me that the foundations of living the good life are based on living as simply as we can, and eating as well as we can. These things are hard to do in our fast-paced society. In the past, families spent hours

Canning applesauce

a day preparing meals and eating them together. Now the average family prepares few meals at home and spends little time eating them together.

This change may have been unavoidable. But again, I wonder. I wonder if this change is not so much the result of conscious choice as it is the result of the industrialization of our society.

Before the Industrial Revolution, there were many more beer pubs than there were coffee houses. Now coffee shops outnumber pubs. When we drink beer in pubs, it is to socialize with our friends and to enjoy life. Can the same be said of coffee houses? Aren't coffee shops there to help us get through our day?

As I walk through the woods with my longbow, I know these things cannot be walked back. All the same, I renew my commitment to live as simply as I can.

Another benefit to spending so much time in the pursuit, cultivation, and preparation of our food is that we spend that time with our family. Time spent together, working together for our shared benefit, helps us to stitch our family more tightly together. It helps us to see that the land is part of our family too.

Defining our food in purely economic terms endangers not only our bodies, but our families. Cheap food, easily acquired, may seem like a boon to our free time and family, but in truth it just borrows our time and money from the future.

What is the future cost to us when we opt for cheap margarine instead of real butter? Should we really be willing to mortgage our long-term cardiovascular health for a cheap biscuit today?

By canning our own tomatoes and apple sauce, and by involving our children in the process, we can instill in them the knowledge that the joy of living, the satisfaction of a job well done, are found not in ease but in effort.

Part of the lesson is to learn that the can of green beans bought in the store is not the same as the jar of green beans we put up ourselves. To this lesson, the physical contents are irrelevant.

What the homemade jar of beans contains, and what cannot be measured by nutritional scientists, is the family story of what it took to make that jar of beans. The preparation of the garden bed in early spring, the planting of the seeds in May, the watching of the plants as they sprout and grow, weeding, the picking of the beans in the heat of summer, the snap-

Liam with spring cabbage

ping of the beans on the front porch while the bobwhite proclaims the beauty of the day from a nearby fencepost, the hot and sweaty effort of canning the beans, and finally the good meal happily shared by the family. Think of all the conversations, and arguments too, that helped build that jar of beans.

It's the same stuff good hunting stories are made of. And what better time to share these stories than over a nice venison roast? If you have killed a deer, prepared it, and eaten it with your family, you surely know of what I speak.

When I discovered that I could make my own bow and extend my hunting story even further, I learned, yet again, that all things are connected. Everything we do informs everything else we do.

Which brings me to the point of this chapter. The founding fathers acknowledged that the pursuit of happiness is fundamental to living a good life. None of us needs to hunt, or garden, to survive. But I believe that most of us, if we could slow down enough to become aware of it, would be happier by the effort. It has been my experience that if I think of hunting, gardening, family, and meals not as separate things, but as parts of a whole, then I am indeed engaged in the pursuit of happiness.

If I see my American Semi-Longbow in this light, in the light of feeding my family, of building my family story, it gives this simple weapon deeper purpose.

I started out making my own bows because I thought I could maybe make a better bow more cheaply. Over time I have realized that a cheaper, better bow isn't the point.

The point is to craft a good bow, by my own hand, and to use it to feed my family. Not just to feed them good food so that my children can be made of strong and healthy deer and live strong and healthy lives, but to help stitch the family together.

What bow could better meet this challenge than the simple, honest American Semi-Longbow? If you should choose to make one of these bows, don't fret overly much about the effort or time spent. Share the experience with your family and friends. Build the effort into the fabric of your family. Just as the outcome of the hunt is not its sole or even primary purpose, the important results of your bow making are measured in things incalculable with scale and ruler.

There is an old Chinese Proverb that tells us: "Life begins the day you start a garden." I think whoever had this thought had in mind more than just planting seeds and waiting for them to grow.

If we allow ourselves to be part of the garden, and not apart from it, we can begin to see what makes the garden grow.

Chapter 7
Making or Collecting
Limb Laminations

Up to this point I have discussed the construction of the support equipment needed (forms) and the main chunk of wood in the bow (riser). I have not yet touched on what the limbs are made from, or the thickness of the limbs.

This feels like the most boring chapter in the book. A primary goal in writing this book was to lay out all the information and steps required to make a good American Semi-Longbow, leaving no important detail out. While I am sure it is impossible to achieve this goal totally, I am equally sure that some of the detail, like that contained in this chapter, borders on pedantic. For this I apologize.

In defense of this chapter I will point out that the spirit of the bow is contained in its limbs. A bow with thick, uneven limbs will be clubby, slow, and unresponsive. A bow made with smooth, even tapers, well designed and executed, will have the potential for speed, smoothness, durability, and responsiveness. If it is then shaped and tillered so that the stresses are uniform and within the working limits of the materials, it will have the potential to feel like an extension of your arms. It will point as naturally as a finger.

In this chapter, I will explain how I make the wood laminations for my bows. If you are just beginning your adventure as a bowyer, I would suggest you purchase your laminations from a supply house. Purchasing laminations will be more expensive than making your own in the long run, but it will save you the cost in equipment and setup required to make your own laminations.

For those who will wisely purchase their limb laminations instead of making them, you will find value in the first half of this chapter. For those who have been this way before and are ready to attempt making their own laminations, the entire chapter should be helpful.

Rather than present the topics in this chapter in chronological order, I present them in what I think is the most helpful order. As a result, you will have to read through the chapter and decide for yourself how you will use this information.

As mentioned previously, I have made bows that were straight (usually ending up with some string follow) and bows that had backset (usually ending up with about 1 1/4 inches of backset). On the whole, I prefer bows with some backset. They shoot faster, can have less hand shock (contrary to popular opinion), and are just as easy to point and shoot as any other bow. (Read Chapter 12 for a contrary point of view.)

I believe the reason they have less hand shock is due to the fact that the limbs have less mass (owing to the greater pre-stress) to reach a desired draw force. All other things being equal, the bow with the lightest limbs will have the least hand shock.

Before I get into how to make wood laminations, I will list, in tabular form, some lamination options for the lay-up of a bow. The collection of laminations (wood, fiberglass, and carbon) together is referred to as the stack. This table can be used to ballpark your target weight for a 66-inch bow.

There are a few rules you can use to predict draw weight for bows that have thicknesses or lengths other than those specified in the table. They are:

- For every 0.003 inch of core thickness added or removed, the draw weight will increase or decrease, respectively, by approximately 1 pound.
- For every 0.001 inch of fiberglass thickness added or removed, the draw weight will increase or decrease, respectively, by approximately one pound.
- For every 0.001 inch of carbon substituted for fiberglass (as listed in the table below), the draw weight will increase or decrease, respectively, by approximately 2 pounds.
- For every 2 inches in bow length added or removed (going from

a 66- to a 68- inch bow), draw weight will increase or decrease, respectively, by approximately 5 pounds.

Stack Thickness for 66-inch Backset Bow* (Limb Taper 0.006 inch / inch)						
Draw Weight	Upper Limb Cores			Belly Glass	Back Glass	Back Carbon
	1	2	3			
45 lbs.	105	105	110	50	30	20
	125	125	120	50	50	0
50 lbs.	110	110	120	50	30	20
	130	130	130	50	50	0
55 lbs.	120	120	130	50	30	20
	135	135	140	50	50	0
60 lbs.	130	130	140	50	30	20
	150	150	150	50	50	0

*Note:
1. All dimensions given in thousandths of an inch.
2. To make an ASL with the upper limb 2 inches longer than the lower limb, the lower limb needs to be 0.020 inch thinner than the upper limb.
3. Lower limb cores have not been specified in this table.
4. Back carbon must be placed under the back glass.
5. Bows made with these stack thicknesses will be about 5 pounds over weight when cut to lines. Extra draw force will be lost in tillering and final sanding.

In reviewing this table, you will notice that I have included stack dimensions for bows that include a carbon strip on the back, and for bows that don't. The debate as to whether carbon adds appreciably to the performance of a bow is ongoing and contentious.

There is no doubt that carbon is lighter, stronger, and more resilient than fiberglass. There is also no doubt that it is more prone to breakage. As a result, most bowyers put the carbon under a layer of fiberglass. This serves to protect the carbon, but it also keeps the carbon from yielding its maximum performance.

In my experience, adding carbon to a bow adds a few feet per second in speed and reduces hand vibration slightly, owing to the thinner and lighter limbs. Whether this justifies the additional cost of the carbon and effort to include it in the stack are not clear to me. The best justification I can make for using carbon is that it provides another opportunity to experiment and to have fun making bows.

You will also notice that for bows that do not include carbon, the fiberglass specified is 0.050 inch back and belly. I have tried other combinations (thinner on back than belly) and thicknesses (both back and belly) and have come to conclude that there is not much to gain by it. Keeping both back and belly at 0.050 inch allows me to minimize the fiberglass I have to buy and keeps it simple. Fifty thousandths glass is also very strong and makes a reliable bow.

That said, if you are going to make a lighter bow of less than 45 pounds, your bow may benefit from using less glass. In designing the perfect bow, the bowyer should attempt to bring all materials to their maximum stress, while not stepping over the threshold of failure. I leave it to you to adjust your designs accordingly.

Finally, you will notice that the preceding table specifies three core laminations (each with a taper of 0.002 inch/inch each). There are benefits to using fewer laminations, and maybe even more laminations. I like to make bows with one lamination of bamboo, but would not do that with cedar as the internal stresses might get too high. Fewer laminations allow for less work, while more laminations allow for more pre-stress to be built into the limbs. You will have to decide for yourself what is more important. In the end, I find very little difference in performance between single-lamination bows and three-lamination bows.

If you choose to make bows as a hobby (it may not be a choice, it may be a compulsion), you will eventually decide that it is worth making the core laminations yourself. By making the laminations yourself, you can reduce the monetary cost of your bows substantially. The only remaining items you cannot easily make are the fiberglass and the epoxy.

Making core laminations will require an investment in equipment and fixtures. The chief investment is in a drum sander, which will be used to taper the core laminations. The laminations will first need to be cut from your stock, which can be done with a table saw or a bandsaw. This may constitute an additional investment.

If you have a bandsaw, you will need to get a good blade for cutting the lamination blanks. I have had good luck with the Wood Slicer resaw blades available from Highland Woodworking.

There are many drum sanders available on the market. I have tried none of them, save for the 12-inch Grizzly drum sander that I own. I can say with confidence that the Grizzly sander is the most economical sander

I have found, but I have yet to grind the perfect lamination with it.

I can also say with confidence that I have not perfected my understanding of, or method for, making tapered laminations. The method I have arrived at will result in a good lamination that is very accurate. However, it is time-consuming, and I expect that there are better methods and equipment to be discovered.

That said, If you wisely choose to purchase laminations for your first few bows, check them carefully. I have found that most laminations vary quite a bit from the specified dimensions. Some of what follows may be helpful to you in correcting the imperfections found in purchased laminations.

Taking the time to make your laminations as accurate as possible to start with will reduce the effort you must expend in tillering the bow later. The better matched the limbs are through their thickness, the more efficient and thus fast-shooting they will be.

This point I cannot emphasize strongly enough. The design of your bow is dependent on a consistent limb thickness taper. The more your limb thickness varies from the design target, the more material you will need to remove from the sides and corners of your limbs to get them to match up and work together.

The thickness of the limb has a much greater effect on the performance of the bow than does the width. In fact, the character of the bow is determined by the limb thickness, not its width.

This characteristic of a bow limb will be discussed in more detail in Chapter 12, but it is so important it is worth mentioning here too. The thickness of a limb affects draw force by a factor of ten times as much as limb width. What this means is that while the draw force will increase 1 pound for every 0.003 inch of thickness increase, it will take 0.030 inch of additional width to achieve the same result. Add to this the fact that the natural frequency of the limb is determined solely by its thickness and length (the natural frequency of the limb determines the speed of the bow), and you can begin to understand that controlling the thickness accurately is crucial to realizing the full potential of your bow design.

To get a mental visualization of why width really has little effect on bow performance, imagine two identical bows locked in a vice next to each other. If you pull back on the limb of one bow and then let go, you will see a certain rate at which the limb returns to rest. Do the same thing to the other bow. You will see the same rate of return. Now tape the two limbs together in your mind. You have effectively doubled the width of the bow limb. But when you pull back on this new double limb and let go would you expect it to perform any differently than the individual limbs did? The answer is no.

Each bow by itself would shoot a 10 grains-per-pound arrow at the same velocity. By taping the bows together and shooting an arrow that is twice as heavy (thus resulting in 10 grains-per-pound), you will get the same speed as the individual bows.

Now consider the situation where the thickness varies instead of the width. If you have a bow that shoots, say, 20 pounds, and another that shoots, say, 40 pounds, the thickness of the 40-pound bow will be greater by some 0.060 inch than the 20-pound bow. A far cry from the exactly doubled mass of the two bows sitting side by side to achieve the doubling in draw force. Add to this much lighter mass the fact that the stiffer limb has an inherently faster rate of recovery (natural frequency), and you can see that the thickness of the limb, for a given length, is indeed the controlling dimension that determines bow performance.

Thus, it is very important to spend as much time as necessary to ensure that your core laminations meet your design specifications.

Now that we have an understanding of why the limb thickness is so important, we can feel confident that the time required to make the cores exact is not wasted.

<u>Choosing the Core Material</u>

There are many core materials available from which to make a bow. The American Semi-Longbow, having only a slight backset to its limbs and a simple, gentle curve when strung, can handle a greater variety of materials than can bows of other designs. This means the bowyer who chooses to make an American Semi-Longbow has a lot to choose from.

Those choices can be based on availability, economics, durability, performance, or aesthetics.

Availability and economics go hand in hand. I have found hardwoods to be the most available and economical materials to build bows from. Woods like maple, black walnut, and hickory make excellent bow limbs.

Bows made from maple, black walnut, and hickory will likely last a lifetime. But for sheer durability, I believe that maple or bamboo are probably the best choices.

Performance should be an objective measure of how fast the bow shoots per grain of arrow weight, but I think it ends up also including subjective measures like hand shock and noise. I have made bows from all the materials mentioned above except hickory. Additionally, I have made many bows from eastern red cedar. Eastern red cedar is my favorite wood to make bow limbs from because it yields bows with very little hand shock that seem to shoot 4 or 5 feet per second faster than bows made of other materials. I think it makes a nice looking limb, too.

The problem with eastern red cedar is that it is full of knots. Finding clean pieces of wood from which to cut laminations can be a challenge. I have made my own "action cedar" which helps to overcome this problem, but which also involves a great deal more work.

Bamboo, in particular "action boo" made from laminated strips of bamboo, is a very popular limb core material. It is very durable and makes a good bow, but it is very heavy compared to other core wood choices. Contrary to popular opinion, I have found that it makes a bow with a bit more hand shock than the other available materials. It is also more expensive to acquire than some good walnut, maple, or eastern red cedar. To balance all these limitations out, it is a very consistent material that is very easy to work with. Another big factor in its favor is that a single core lamination for the entire limb thickness can be made from action

Dad and I cutting cedar logs on his Woodmizer

boo, which significantly reduces the labor and materials required to make a bow. I have found that bows made from single core action boo are very good bows.

Making Action Cedar

Because I am such a fan of eastern red cedar, I will explain how I make action cedar here so that if you have some cedar that isn't free of knots, you will still be able to try this wonderful wood.

Before proceeding further, though, I need to point out that eastern red cedar is not western cedar or any other cedar. Eastern red cedar is actually a member of the juniper family. It has specific properties, which have been recognized by bowyers since ancient times, that make it a good bow wood. In fact, it can make a good self bow if tillered perfectly. Western cedar, or white cedar, or cyprus, while close in appearance to eastern red cedar, will fail fast and furiously if forced to be made into a bow. Do not try it!

The first thing to do is to collect some boards of eastern red cedar, hereafter referred to as cedar. I am lucky in that my dad has a saw mill and I can cut my own boards. I have had luck, too, in getting wood from local saw mills and our local hardwood store. The trick is to check often and buy when available. What you want in the end are boards at least 1 1/2 inches thick by 4 feet long.

Once you have a supply of cedar boards, you can cut them into strips. When I first made action cedar, I cut the strips all 1/4 inch wide. The bows I made from this were durable. But then I realized that if I varied the width and ended up with a non-symmetric action wood, I could ensure that the glue joints in the laminations of action cedar would not line up in the limb of the bow. Now I cut a few strips less than a quarter inch, and a few more than a quarter inch. The point is to end up with a stack of strips 1 1/2 inches tall.

Chances are you will have some strips that are clear (meaning no knots) and some that have many knots. The clear strips can be set aside for later use as lamination

Knotty cedar board, good for action cedar

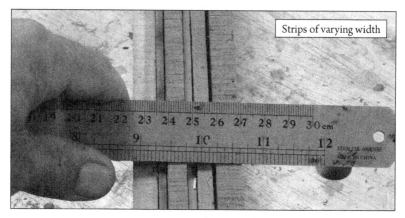

Strips of varying width

blanks. The strips that have knots will have to be cut to remove the knots. You will end up with a bunch of short pieces. I try to keep my short pieces at least 1 foot long. Anything less than that adds to the work.

Now the puzzling begins. Sort through the short pieces, matching them up so that you end up with a number of mated sets a few inches over 3 feet long. The small pieces will need to be butt glued together to form the strips for our action cedar.

Gluing butt joints never results in a strong union. With this in mind, it really doesn't matter what glue we use. The point is simply to keep the wood together so that we can glue the strips together into our action cedar blank. Thus, I use Titebond III. Cheap, easy, and available.

The overlapping nature of the strips protects the end joints and provides the durability that action woods are known for.

Once the 3-foot strips have been glued together, it's time to sand them flat so that when they are sistered together, the joints will be uniform and strong. Here again I use my trusty drum sander. I have a 5-foot sled for sanding laminations that I use for making walking sticks. This sled serves double duty as it works fine for sanding these action cedar strips too. I will get into how to make a sled (a tool used to guide the laminations

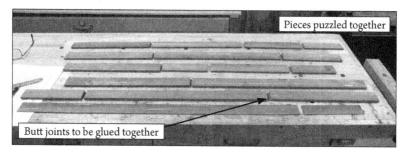

Pieces puzzled together

Butt joints to be glued together

through the drum sander) farther on in this chapter when we look at making one for the tapered laminations for the bow.

End joint glued using angle aluminum to ensure a straight joint

When sanding the strips flat, remove as little material as possible. The point is simply to flatten out the butted glue joints and any other irregularities so that a durable glue bond can be made when the slats are glued together into a stack.

Once the strips have been sanded, it's time to arrange the strips so that no butt joints, strip to strip, line up.

And now it's time to glue and press our strips together to form our action cedar. I have used both epoxy and unibond glues for this process. I tend to use unibond as it is easier to spread, and cheaper.

I have not used Titebond III, although its material specifications suggest that it is fully capable of serving as a good glue. The manufacturer does warn not to use the glue for structural applications. This warning has been enough to keep me from using it, although it makes me wonder if their warning is based on the limits of their product, or the limits of their lawyer's imagination.

I use the same press to make both walking sticks and action cedar. I pressurize the hose to 60 psi and wait 24 hours before removing the

Strips sanded flat and arranged for gluing and then curing in press

Action cedar blank in press

Action cedar block squared up and
ready for cutting into lamination blanks

action cedar blank from the press. At this point it is simply a matter of
cutting the blank to a length of 3 feet, squaring up one side, and cutting
lamination blanks from it.

If I make an action cedar block that is 1 1/2 inches wide by 2 inches thick, I can cut enough laminations blanks from it to make one bow,
sometimes two.

Measuring and Correcting Lamination Thickness

Whether you purchase core laminations or make your own, the method for testing and maximizing their dimensional accuracy is the same.

Before I make the laminations, I set up a table in my notebook that specifies the core thickness at the root (thick end) of the lamination and at a minimum of six more stations, 6 inches apart down the length of the lamination. Laminations are generally made 3 feet long. This allows for easy handling and, when two are butted together, provides the 6-foot length to match the fiberglass.

If you are using multiple laminations, and they are not all the same thickness (which can happen when you divide your total desired core thickness by the number of desired core laminations), you will need a table for each lamination of different thickness.

While I now measure the thickness at 6-inch intervals, I started measuring at 12-inch intervals. I did this for several years but ended up deciding that more measurements gave me better laminations. Measuring every 12 inches is easier and is sufficient to yield a good bow. Measuring every 6 inches takes more time but yields better results. The following table shows an example of how I define a lamination before beginning work.

Lam thickness for 0.006 in/in Taper				
Station	Lam 1	Lam 2	Lam 3	Total
Root	120	120	130	370
6 inch	108	108	118	334
12 inch	96	96	106	298
18 inch	84	84	94	262
24 inch	72	72	82	226
30 inch	60	60	70	190
36 inch	48	48	58	154
Note: All dimensions given in thousandths of an inch.				

This table describes the three laminations required to produce a core thickness of 0.370 inch with a total taper of 0.006 inch-per-inch (0.002 inch/inch taper per lamination).

You will notice that the thinnest end of the tapers are around 0.050 inch. I don't like to get much thinner than this, as it can be hard to control the sanding process and accidents happen. The thinner the lamination gets, the harder it is to work with.

If you purchase your laminations, you will find that most suppliers provide tapers down to 0.020 inch at the thin end. They can do this because they have equipment far superior to mine, and probably yours. If you buy your laminations, you are home free.

If you make your laminations, and you find that they are tapering to much less than 0.050 inch at the thin end, you may want to consider reducing the number of laminations in your core, which will allow you to use thicker ones.

Once you have defined the dimensions of your laminations and acquired them (by purchase or otherwise) it is time to measure and adjust them to final dimension.

I begin this process by aligning all laminations of the same thickness and taper, root to tip. Stand them on their edges, packed closely together, and mark the edges every 6 inches their entire length. Then write the desired thickness right on the taper at each measuring station.

Double check. Double check again.

Now begins the process of correcting any discrepancy down the length of the lamination. Measure the lamination at every measuring station. Take note of any trends in being too thick or too thin.

At this point, we also need to recognize the relationships between the individual laminations. I call laminations that lie next to each other "sister laminations." I call laminations that get glued together at the root ends "mated laminations." I will refer to these terms when discussing the relative position of a lamination within the stack.

If the lamination is too thick, it is a simple matter of bringing it to the desired dimension.

If the lamination in too thin at a point, the task is more complicated. You will need to measure its sister lamination, or laminations, and make arrangements to leave those laminations thicker than specified so that when you sister the entire stack together, the total design thickness and taper are achieved.

If you make a bow which has a core of just one lamination, you will need to be extra careful to ensure that the single core meets your design requirements. If it comes in thin somewhere, you must scrap it and start

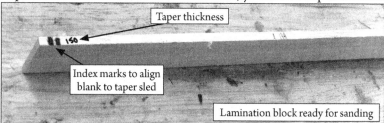

Taper thickness

Index marks to align
blank to taper sled

Lamination block ready for sanding

again. An error of just 0.005 inch can result in a weak spot in the limb, which can be tillered out by adjusting limb width later but will result in a slower bow. Don't give in to the temptation to use a bad lam. The work you invest now to make perfect laminations will pay dividends later.

The following method I share with you is what I have come to find works best for me. Doubtless many skilled bowyers (if they choose to read this book) will chuckle at my foolish toiling. Be that as it may, I humbly offer my method to you.

Place the lamination upon a non-slip surface. If you have elected to make your own, then you have a sanding sled already made. I find the sanding sled makes an excellent non-slip surface upon which to do any corrective sanding by hand. It also elevates the lamination off my work bench so that my sanding block can move freely.

I use a 30- or 40-grit 24-inch by 3-inch sanding belt stretched over a 12-inch by 3/4-inch-long wood block. This makes an excellent sanding block that takes material off quickly while maintaining flatness and uniform thickness across the lamination.

I usually take six to ten stokes off both sides of the lamination, working the area over the measuring station and halfway to the next one in each direction, while keeping in mind the thickness trend in each direction. Is it correct in one direction? Then go lightly that way. Is it thick in the other direction? Then go heavy that way.

Work your way down the entire lamination, taking the six to ten strokes, and measure again. Repeat until the entire lamination is within 0.001- or 0.002-inch of the target thickness as measured with a caliper.

I keep an air compressor handy to blow off the saw dust between

Taper on sled ready for sanding

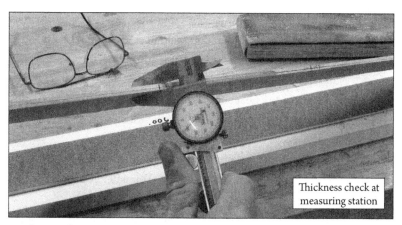

Thickness check at measuring station

sanding and measuring.

Once you have brought all the laminations to the specified tapers, it is time to stack up the sister laminations and take a stack reading. Refer to the last column in the previous table for the required dimensions. Take readings not just along the laminations, but across them.

Is one side thin? Is one side thick? Flipping sister laminations might help.

Is one stack (upper or lower limb) running thick while the other runs thin? Trading mated laminations might help.

You may need to go back and touch up a station or two to achieve the desired stack thickness.

I have found that this method will result in a lamination stack that is within 0.001 inch, plus or minus, of the desired total thickness without too much aggravation.

Some bowyers refer to this process of achieving the correct taper and thickness as "internal tiller." It sounds mysterious and impressive. In truth, it is a simple, though time-consuming, process that is most important. Making sure your laminations meet your design dimensions is a crucial step in ensuring that the resulting bow will be the best it can be.

Making Your Own Taper Sled and Laminations

If you spend enough time making bows, you will eventually begin to make your own core laminations. Making every part of the bow adds to the sense of accomplishment when a good bow shoots a good arrow.

Once you define your laminations, you will know what taper you need, per lamination, to achieve a total of 0.006 inch/inch. While bowyers are free to choose whatever limb taper they desire, I will illustrate this process assuming a taper of 0.006 inch/inch is used, as I have found this to be the best taper to achieve the best overall performance from a 66-inch American Semi-Longbow with backset.

This brings us to the next shop aid we will need to make: a sled upon which we can place our lamination blanks as we run them through the drum sander to achieve our desired taper.

Making a taper sled is a fairly straightforward effort that will take 30 minutes, once materials have been collected. You will need the following items:

- 4" x 1" x 3-foot piece of MDA board (available from Building Supply)
- Maple lamination of the correct taper (available from Bingham Projects and others)
- Rubber drawer liner
- 100-grit sheets of sandpaper
- Spray contact cement
- Blue painter's tape

I recommend that you buy a 2-inch-wide lamination of the correct taper, as it is the easiest way to get where you want to go. When you order the tapered lamination, you will receive two tapers (one for each limb). Choose the one that most closely matches your design taper for your sled. Once you choose the best lamination of the pair, inspect it and adjust it

Cutting sand paper using lamination as guide

until it matches the design taper perfectly.

Cut strips from the 100-grit sandpaper that match the width and run the full length of the taper. Using the contact cement, affix the sandpaper to the lamination.

Now lay the lamination on your sled base and mark the sides. Remove the lamination and apply painter's tape to the sled to protect it from adhesive overspray. Using the contact cement, affix the lamination to the sled.

Cut a piece of the rubber drawer liner to fit the bottom of the sled. Using the contact cement, affix the drawer liner to the bottom of the sled.

Having run the sled through the sander the wrong way more than once and thus ruining a lamination, I now mark the sleds not only with the taper that the sled will produce, but with the correct end to feed into the sander.

Your taper sled is now complete.

It is time to produce taper blanks.

I cut taper blanks with my bandsaw. If you use a table saw, you will not need to go through the following process of setting the bandsaw up to cut lamination blanks. There are advantages to the use of either tool. The table saw is fast and accurate, but wastes wood. The bandsaw is slow and accurate, but requires extra effort to set up. It has the smallest kerf and thus does not waste wood like the table saw. To each his own!

I have one bandsaw which I use for many purposes. This requires

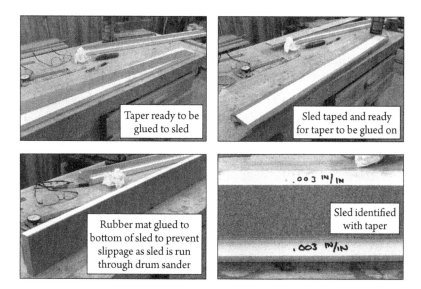

Taper ready to be glued to sled

Sled taped and ready for taper to be glued on

Rubber mat glued to bottom of sled to prevent slippage as sled is run through drum sander

.003 IN/IN

Sled identified with taper

.003 IN/IN

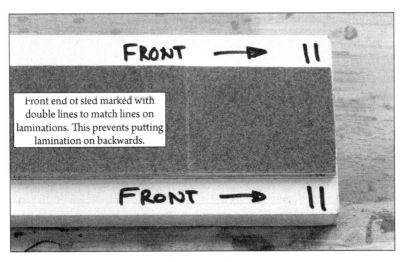

Front end of sled marked with double lines to match lines on laminations. This prevents putting lamination on backwards.

me to set the bandsaw up every time I cut tapers. Every time a blade is changed, the tune changes and the guide angle changes. So the first steps in cutting taper blanks are to set the guide distance from the blade, and to set the guide angle that will allow the blade to cut straight.

I cut my taper blanks about 0.020 inch thicker than my calculated lamination root thickness. To set the saw for this thickness, I take a scrap of wood, usually an old two-by-four, and mark it with a line at the desired thickness.

Put the guide on the bandsaw and loosen whatever mechanism is used to adjust the guide angle. Now begin to cut your scrap wood until you are confident you have found the correct angle. Stop the saw.

While holding the scrap wood in place, press the guide up to it, being careful not to move the scrap wood. Tighten the guide to the rail, and then tighten whatever mechanism keeps the angle. Now you have set the correct angle and depth with one step.

To test your setup, finish cutting your scrap block and measure the resulting lamination. Is it the correct thickness? If not, adjust the position of the guide and try again. Is it even across the lamination? If not, maybe the table is not set perpendicular to the blade.

Cut another strip from your test block and make sure you can duplicate acceptable results.

It is now time to cut your lamination blanks. Cut all you need to make the bow you have in mind. Leave the saw set up like it is in case you need to come back and cut more. It is not uncommon to overgrind a blank and

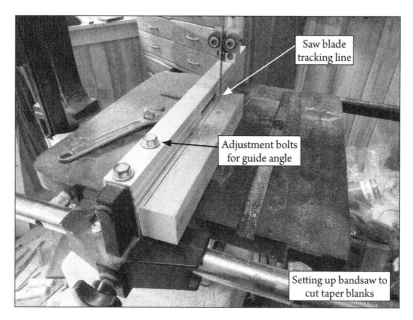

Saw blade tracking line

Adjustment bolts for guide angle

Setting up bandsaw to cut taper blanks

thus render it unusable. Having the saw already set up speeds the recovery time and gets you another blank ready to go.

You have your lamination blanks in hand. You have your taper sled ready to go. You are committed. At this point you must also have your drum sander ready to go. As I pointed out earlier, the quality of your tapered laminations in large part defines the quality of the bow they will produce. You have no doubt explored the myriad options available for drum sanders, both homemade and for sale. I will say nothing more about drum sanders except to point out that the quality of your taper laminations is directly proportional to the quality of the tools you use to produce them.

Step one is to mark your measuring stations on the side of your lamination blanks. I usually make a double mark at the end that matches up with the double marks on my sled. This helps me to keep the lamination correctly oriented on the sled each time I remove it for measuring.

The process of drum sanding laminations is still a mystery to me. Things happen that I cannot possibly explain to my own satisfaction. The best piece of advice I can give you is to follow the directions provided with your sander and take your time.

There are two anomalies I have encountered while sanding tapers. The first anomaly I noticed right away actually has a name. It is called snipe. Snipe is the effect that causes the last half inch or so of each side of

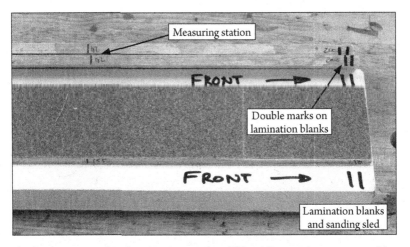

the lamination to be thinner than it should be. This can be minimized by not being too aggressive with the sanding pressure. Take a little bit off at a time.

The second, and most annoying, anomaly is that the lamination does not come to dimension along the entire lamination. This is important to monitor. If you just measure the root, or the tip, and sand until that station is correct, chances are your lamination will have other thin or thick spots. Sometimes the middle sands faster than the ends, sometimes the ends sand faster than the middle.

As a result of the above-referenced anomaly, it is important to measure several stations along your lamination. When you find a station that meets your design thickness, turn the drum sander off and finish the lamination by hand.

The only other suggestion I have regarding drum sanders is to use the coarsest grit paper you can find. This will speed the process and give a good glue surface.

Time to grind a lamination.

When I start a lamination, I inspect both sides first. I start to sand on the side with the most imperfections or scrapes. If both sides look equally good, I look to see if the lamination has a bow to it. If so, I place the lamination on the sled such that the middle is bowed up and the lamination touches the sled at the ends. Get this first side ground down till the sanding drum runs its entire length. Then flip the lamination over and repeat. Once the drum sander runs the entire length of the second side, begin taking measurements at several of the measurement stations marked on

Running taper through drum sander

the lamination. When you find a station that meets (or is close to) the design thickness, stop.

Now measure the lamination at each station and get a feel for how it runs. I usually find that there are a few stations where the thickness runs high.

Using the information presented in the previous section entitled "Measuring and Correcting Lamination Thickness," bring the taper to its design thickness. The goal should be to get the thickness within 0.002 inch of the design thickness.

If you have designed your ASL to have an upper limb that is 2 inches longer than the lower limb, then your lower limb laminations should be about 0.020 inch thinner than your upper limb laminations. I recommend that after you have sanded your lamination to its correct thickness and you are satisfied with it, you mark the thin end (limb tip end) of your lamination with the word "top" or "bottom," as appropriate. This will help you avoid confusion and mistakes during the layup of your bow.

I will stop to contradict myself here again. When you read Chapter 12, you will see that I eventually started making bows with asymmetrical risers that are offset on the form toward the lower limb by 1 inch. By doing this, a thickness differential between limbs is built in by the fact that the lamination joint is offset 1 inch toward the upper limb. This builds in a lower limb that is already thinner by twice the taper ratio. For example, if the taper ratio is 0.004 inch/inch, then the delta between limbs is 0.008

inch.

I would encourage the new bowyer to start out with bows that have symmetrical risers and laminations centered in the handle. I found these easier to learn from. If, however, you understand the previous paragraph, proceed as you see fit.

Mating Laminations Together

Once you have the individual laminations made, you will need to join them together at their root ends to produce the 6-foot-long laminations required to make a bow.

Being a hobbyist, I am strapped with the tools of a hobbyist. I cannot justify the expense, and don't have the room, for professional equipment.

Square line marked

Marking tapers to square up on sander

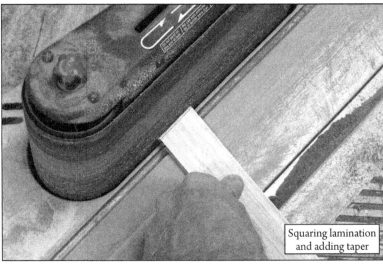

Squaring lamination and adding taper

Laminations butt clamped on angle

Butt joint before sanding

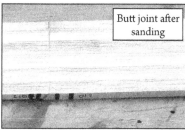

Butt joint after sanding

I have tried various mechanical ways to cut the root ends square to get a good mate. Suffice it to say that the best way I have found, with my limited tooling that must be used to keep the farm running and to fix the house and that cannot be adjusted "just so" and left that way, is simply to use a square to draw a line. Then I freehand that line on my vertical sander. I like to add a bit of a taper to the line as well.

I then lay the laminations upon my aluminum angle (to ensure straightness), glue, and clamp. This works well enough.

When the glue joint has dried, I remove the lamination from the aluminum angle and lightly sand the joint until it is flat. The lamination has now been prepared for use.

Limb Tip Wedges

Limb tip wedges are short laminations that are placed at the limb tips in order to thicken and thus stiffen the limb tips. I have tried a variety of configurations and lengths of these wedges to achieve a smooth, circular limb profile at full draw.

What I have found to work best, and is counterintuitive to me, is to

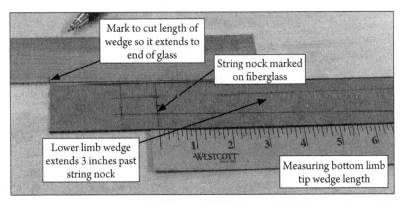

Mark to cut length of wedge so it extends to end of glass

String nock marked on fiberglass

Lower limb wedge extends 3 inches past string nock

Measuring bottom limb tip wedge length

have the lower limb tip wedge longer than the upper limb tip wedge. After seeing that this worked to produce a circular tiller, I had the confidence to hypothesize why it might be so: Since the lower limb is stiffer than the upper limb (because it is shorter), it requires more stiffness in the tip to bend it around into the desired arc. The longer wedge provides that extra tip stiffness.

I have also tried a variety of thicknesses and tapers for these wedges. I have settled on fairly short wedges with a thickness of around 0.050 inch that taper for 1 1/2 inches.

I make the upper limb tip wedge extend 2 inches in front of the string nock. I make the lower limb wedge extend 3 inches in front of the string nock. I make the tapers freehand on my vertical belt sander.

These tapers are placed in the limbs so that they are even with the end of the lamination stack. For a 66-inch bow, the end of the lamination stack does not match up to where the end of the limb will eventually be. Therefore, it is necessary to make the limb tip wedges longer than they will end up being in the finished limb. To do this, simply make a lamination that is 0.050 inch thick and long enough to extend from the end of the lamination stack to the desired distance in front of the string nock (2 inches for

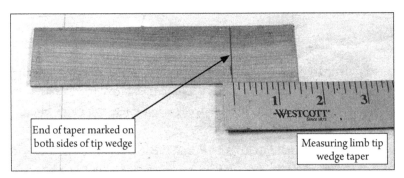

End of taper marked on both sides of tip wedge

Measuring limb tip wedge taper

the upper limb, 3 inches for the lower limb).

As we complete the laminations and wedges, we arrive at a milestone. Together with the riser we made earlier, we have made all the parts of the bow. This is a good time to contemplate the fact that all the work done to this point determines the character of the bow. It is a good time to check and recheck dimensions.

Chapter 8
Performing the Lay-Up

I like to think of the process of gluing up the bow as the moment when the bow is born.

Everything that has happened up to this point has been either theoretical, or building jigs in support of this process, or making the parts and pieces that will make up our new bow. At every stage, if we made mistakes those mistakes were not detrimental to the final outcome. The faulty part could be tossed, a new one made in its place.

From this point on, everything done, every successful step or unintentional mistake, will affect how the bow performs and how it acts in the hand. Not unlike the process of raising a child.

Just like the process of raising a child, things can be done to fix most of our mistakes. And just like a child, the bow will almost always come out OK, despite what we do. In the end, we must accept the bow for what it is. If we do that, we will be successful.

When we design our bows, we do it with a desired performance in mind. We expect our bows to have a certain draw force, and we expect them to be forgiving of our foibles and send the arrow to the target reliably.

We must keep in mind that once the bow is born, it will have its own personality. It will have its own aptitude for casting the arrow and its own way of reacting to the shooter. If we recognize these things and bring the bow to its best self without trying to force our preconceptions of what the bow should be upon it, we will end up with a good bow.

If the bow comes out too light, surely there is someone who would like to give it a good home. If the bow comes out too heavy, the same must be true.

Bows are like children, too, in that I tend to learn more from my bows than they learn from me. Each bow teaches me something. So no matter how it turns out, the effort is not wasted.

If I keep these things in mind, then my worry about the final outcome fades away and I can enjoy the process of laying up the bow.

There are, however, a few things that can ruin an otherwise good bow. These things are easily avoided:

Dirtiness. Make sure that your work area is clean. Brush off all your laminations and riser to remove dust and dirt. Make sure your form is clean and that the area you will use to glue up your bow is dust-free. Inclusions between laminations can weaken the bond and, if you use clear glass, mar the look of whatever wood lays beneath.

Solvents. Resist the temptation to use acetone or other harsh solvents to clean your bow parts. These solvents can bring additional oils to the surface of the wood, which can ruin the glue bond. Once these oils have been raised, they are almost impossible to remove. I use Smooth-On epoxy to glue my bows together. Smooth-On is easily removed from your hands and bow surfaces with simple isopropyl alcohol (rubbing alcohol). I find this is the only cleaning agent I need.

Unprotected table. I use wax paper on my lay-up table. It is cheap, biodegradable, and easy to use. The wax will come off the paper when scraped, so again, resist the temptation to scrape epoxy off the paper and apply it to your laminations. Let it go.

Paper cups. Just as the wax on wax paper easily contaminates epoxy, so does the wax on paper cups. Use plastic cups to measure your epoxy to avoid this problem.

Old epoxy. The hardening agent in Smooth-On ages. As it ages, it takes on a strong smell. The stronger the smell, the more likely the hardener has gone bad. I have no empirical method to guard against hardener that has gone too far. But if the odor gets too bad, I just use that batch of epoxy for tip overlays, or broken things around the farm. It has never let me down in this regard.

Poor fit to form. When using a form for the first time, or when making changes to the bow design, it is always a good policy to do a dry run.

Place your bow laminations and riser in your form and bring the hose to pressure. Make sure that everything lies as expected and that there are no gaps, particularly around the fades.

Missing items. Make sure you have all the fiberglass laminations, core laminations, wedges, riser, etc. that you will need before starting. Remembering a missing part after the others have been coated with glue can be stressful, to say the least.

Incomplete glue spread. Make sure that as you apply glue to your laminations, you leave no dry spots. First-time bowyers tend to use too much glue, which squeezes out the sides when pressure is applied to the bow form. This extra glue can cause mischief if it collects around the mounting hardware on the form, or gets under the edge of the strip glued down on the form. It can make removing the bow blank from the form a challenge. Learn to spread the glue evenly and thinly, while at the same time ensuring that there are no dry spots.

Time. Give yourself several hours for your first glue-up. Gluing up the bow in a rush is not good for your nerves, or for the bow.

Preparing the Work

As I mentioned earlier, it is important to have everything clean and ready to glue up. Keeping dust off laminations and working surfaces can be a challenge in a shop. Do the best you can.

It is important to have a work surface a little longer than your lamina-

All components laid out on workbench ready for lay-up

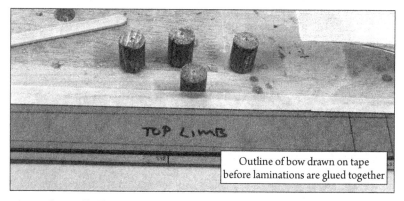

TOP LIMB

Outline of bow drawn on tape
before laminations are glued together

tions. This will allow you to apply glue without having to shift the laminations back and forth. The glue gets everywhere and on everything. To help minimize this problem, it is a good policy to have a workspace and work plan that will allow you to apply glue to the laminations with as little movement as possible.

Since my workbench is not 6 feet long, I have made a simple plywood lamination table that I lay on my workbench and secure with the vice. When not in use, it gets stored in the curing oven. I stage this table on one side of my workbench. My form gets staged on the other side.

After cleaning the fiberglass that will make the back and belly of the bow, I apply blue painter's tape to the smooth side.

Here, my process diverges from most other folks'.

At this point, most folks proceed with the lay-up. I take the time, while the fiberglass that will become the back of the bow is still flat and easily handled, to draw the outline of the bow on it. This makes sense to me for several reasons:

First, drawing the outline is much easier and more accurately done before the bow blank is put together taking on curves and thickness that make it harder to work with.

Second, by drawing the outline now, the edges of the bow blank don't need to be cleaned up much before the bow is cut to the outline. Grinding the glue off to make way for rulers, straight edges, pencils and fingers is a lot of work I like to avoid.

Third, since the bow has a longer top limb, everything is predetermined. There is no option to pick limbs later. By drawing the outline now, I can also write "Top Limb" on the top limb. This helps avoid mistakes later.

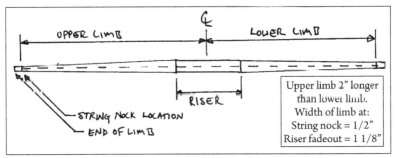

UPPER LIMB   ¢   LOWER LIMB

RISER

— STRING NOCK LOCATION
— END OF LIMB

Upper limb 2" longer
than lower limb.
Width of limb at:
String nock = 1/2"
Riser fadeout = 1 1/8"

Finally, if I pull the bow blank out of the form and something has slipped sideways (lamination or riser) so that the bow can't be cut out on its original center, I haven't lost much. I just sand the edges down, peel the tape off, apply new tape, and redraw the outline. So far, I have never had to do this.

Cut the belly glass at this time. Since one limb of the bow is longer by 2 inches than the other limb, I usually mark the centerline 1 inch off center. I then cut about 3 inches out of the middle using a hacksaw. Mark the top limb glass at this point with the words "top limb." The belly glass should be long enough so that when it is laid in the stack, it extends no more than 1/4 inch above the fades, and no more than 1/4 inch over the end of the stack at the tip of the limb. Extending too far above the fades can cut the pressure hose, or cause the glass to rise off the fades when pressure is applied. The danger in having the glass not extend above the fades is that as pressure is applied to the form, the glass will slide down the fadeouts. This is mostly a cosmetic problem.

With practice, it is possible to position the belly glass maybe 1/8 inch

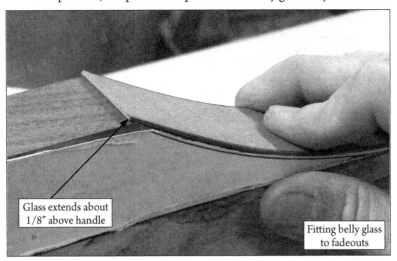

Glass extends about
1/8" above handle

Fitting belly glass
to fadeouts

above the fadeouts and have it stay there. This is about the ideal overhang. Keeping all the laminations even on the tip end will facilitate good positioning of the tip wedges. Taking time to get the belly laminations cut to the correct length will make a better bow blank, and thus a better bow. Take the time to get this right.

After my lamination table is covered with wax paper, I stage the bow laminations on it in the correct order. I make sure that the back glass is on the top, and the belly glass is on the bottom.

I cover the form with plastic wrap to protect it from glue.

Then I prepare the wooden glue spreader as discussed in the riser chapter. I use the same stick for a long time. It will usually need the end taper cleaned up. Some fine grit sandpaper does the job nicely. You want to have a smooth edge and sides for the spreader so that the glue flows evenly off of it. This will speed the process of spreading glue and help it wet the glass and wood more evenly.

The last thing I do before mixing my glue is to shape the fadeouts on the riser. I wait until this moment so that the fadeouts are not subject to breakage, and so that they don't warp, wrinkle, or crack from humidity changes.

The fadeouts must be sanded to the point of being paper thin, or thinner. You should be able to see light through the end of the fadeout when you are finished.

As you sand the fadeouts, hold a flat block of wood behind them to support the fadeouts as you work. Work slowly and carefully so that you don't ruin the riser block at this point.

The reason I don't mix the glue before finishing the fadeouts is so that if I do mess them up, at least I haven't wasted the glue. So far, knock on the proverbial wood, I haven't ruined a riser at this stage. I am sure it will happen one day...

If you are making a bow for the first time, using a new form, or making changes to the form or riser block, it is always a good policy to do a dry run. Put all parts of your bow blank into the form dry. Add the pressure strips and the pressure hose and secure the form. Apply pressure and carefully inspect the bow blank for any gaps between the laminations and riser block. Look the whole thing over for any discrepancies. Take your time.

Once you are satisfied that everything is in order, mix the glue according to instructions and take a breath. If you need a bathroom break, take it now. You don't want to stop if you don't need to. The pot life of AE-40 is at least six hours, so you have plenty of time. That said, removing gloves and cleaning up is extra work and wastes materials that could be saved with a little forethought.

Gluing the Bow Blank

As I glue the bow blank together, I utilize two stacks of laminations. I start out with all the laminations stacked together dry, with the back lamination on top of the stack. When I am done gluing the stack together, the back lamination is now on the bottom.

Lift the back fiberglass off the dry stack and lay it on the wax paper tape side down. Make sure no dust has collected on the lamination and then proceed to apply a thin layer of glue to it. Then apply a thin layer of glue to the next lamination while it sits on the dry stack. When complete, move the first core lamination to the wet stack, glue surface to glue surface.

Repeat the process through the entire stack.

When the entire stack is glued together, lift it and set it on the form. Align the center line of the stack with the center line on your form.

Now apply a generous amount of glue to the bonding surfaces of your riser. If you have elected to use lead weights in your riser, and once all bonding surfaces have been coated, coat the insides of the weight wells and lead weights with epoxy. Drop them in and make sure there is plenty of glue across the tops of the weights to fill any gaps.

Applying glue to laminations

The riser is the one piece that doesn't have an orientation. It is symmetric, so give it a look over and decide which end you want on the top limb. Is there some pretty grain you don't want to lose if it were to be cut away for the arrow shelf? Is there a chip out, or bad area you might want to get rid of? Once you decide, lay it on the form, centerline to centerline.

Finally, apply glue to the

Fiber-reinforced tape applied over end of laminations to keep wedges in place

bonding surface of the belly glass pieces and lay them on the rest of the stack already placed on the form.

At this point, things may seem unwieldy. Things are sliding around, nothing is following the curves of your form. No problem.

Now that all the parts of the bow blank have been mated together, we can start to secure them so that they stay that way. The first thing to do is secure the limb tip wedges. The tip wedges have been known to squirt out the ends as pressure is applied to the form. This will not do. So I use some of the fiber-reinforced tape to cover the ends of the limbs by running a couple pieces of tape, back to belly, along both edges of the blank. If the belly glass extends too far past the end of the limbs, it can prevent the tape from holding the tip wedges in place.

It helps to have an assistant at this point, but it is not necessary. The next steps involve taping the laminations to the form so that when the form is assembled, together with the pressure hose, everything stays in position.

I like to get the riser secured before worrying too much about the limbs. To do this, I cover the riser section with some plastic wrap extending just past the fades.

Press the riser down onto the form, holding the centerlines aligned. Then wrap tape around the riser and form to hold it in position. I tightly wrap tape about an inch on both sides of the centerline. Try not to cover the centerline, so that you can use it to gauge any movement and make corrections.

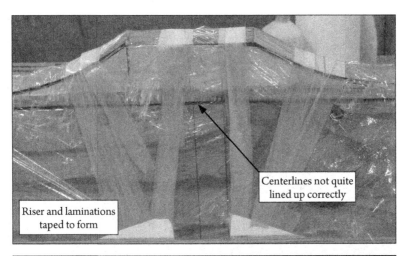

Centerlines not quite lined up correctly

Riser and laminations taped to form

Spacer block to take stress off edge of belly glass and pressure strip

Pressure strips taped to form

Once the center of the riser is taped down, I tape the glass down to the fadeouts. This tape runs perpendicular to the center of the fadeouts and around the base of the form. Notches can be cut in the base of the form to better wrap the tape and keep it from slipping.

Pay attention to this step. The side forces applied by the tape to the riser at this point tend to push it off center. Taping one fadeout will push the riser one way; hopefully taping the other fadeout will move it back to center. You will have to do the final adjustment to ensure that the riser and laminations stay centered.

Make sure the belly glass does not extend more than 1/4 inch above what will be the grip of the bow. If the glass extends too far up the fade, it can cut the pressure hose. Additionally, the pressure hose will deform the glass while it tries to push it down. This can result in a poor bond to the fadeout, which can make the bow blank unusable.

Now cover the entire bow blank with another piece of plastic wrap. Lay the pressure strips (thin steel sheet metal) onto the bow blank. Tape it down along the fades and at least once along the limbs.

Take another breath. Give things a good look over to make sure everything is in order. Ask yourself one more time, are all the laminations oriented so that the limbs will come out correctly?

Now lay the pressure hose onto the stack and place the top of the form onto the stack. Bolt together.

At this point, I usually move the form to my workbench clamp. This keeps it stable while the final work is done to the form.

I have a collection of small blocks of wood of varying thickness I have acquired over the years as I have fit various bow blanks to the form. You would think that every bow would be the same, as all the wood is cut to 1 1/2 inches wide. For the most part this is true, but sometimes a thinner block or two is needed.

Take these blocks and place them between the bow blank and the metal form brackets. These blocks will help keep the limb alignment correct. Make sure the blocks are about the same size as the stack and won't interfere with the pressure hose.

For the next step, I have seen a variety of methods. As you progress through your bow building adventure, I am sure you will find or invent other (better) ways of doing it. In the meantime, I humbly offer my method, such as it is.

The purpose of the next step is to keep the riser from slipping around as the air hose is brought to full pressure.

I use four wood screws and four 1/8-inch diameter by 1 1/2-inch

Spacer block

Using spacer block to control limb alignment

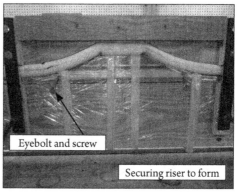

Eyebolt and screw

Securing riser to form

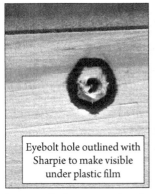

Eyebolt hole outlined with Sharpie to make visible under plastic film

Eyebolt and screw

Securing limb tips to form

long eyebolts screwed to the side of the form and extending past the limb laminations onto the riser block for this job.

Outlining the existing holes with a Sharpie allows me to find them through the plastic film. Hold the eyebolts vertical and gently screw them in place.

So now the riser and limbs are secured to the form and will likely not move as pressure is applied to the hose. The only things left to secure are the limb tips.

How the limb tips respond to pressure can be unpredictable. I used to clamp them in from side to side using a couple blocks and a small clamp.

A better option is to employ the same sort of mechanism used to retain the riser block to retain the limb ends. This is simpler than using the clamps/block method mentioned in the previous paragraph.

At this point, for my first few bows, I applied pressure to the hose and inspected my bow blanks for any misalignment or other problems. I then left the form alone for 24 hours to cure. I then disconnected the form from the compressor so I could move it to the oven. I stuck the bow in the bow oven, repressurized it, and cured it again at 180 degrees Fahrenheit, per manufacturer's instructions.

The makers of Smooth-On glue used to specify that the strongest bond would be achieved by curing the epoxy at room temperature for 24 hours, followed by 6 hours of curing at high temperature.

As I was in no rush, I followed these instructions.

Since that time, the manufacturer has modified its instructions to state that the glue can just be cured with 6 hours of high temperature heat followed by 6 hours of cool-down in the form.

I have done it both ways without any problem.

The second, shorter, cure does present a potential problem though.

I don't like to apply pressure to the form more than once while the glue is wet. If pressure is applied and the glue squeezes out of the laminations, and then pressure is relieved, I think there is ample opportunity for air to leak back in as the glass relaxes away from the fadeouts. This is not good.

When pressure is again applied to the bow blank within the form, there may not be enough glue to displace all the air. This results in air bubbles under the glass and between laminations. These bubbles may or may not affect the integrity of the bow. They surely will ruin the appearance of a bow constructed with clear glass.

Using the shorter method requires a little faith in your preparations. Where before I would apply pressure to the form and then inspect the bow blank to ensure everything was aligned correctly and there were no gaps, I now have to assume, based on the dry run and adequate clamps and taping, that the bow blank will not move when pressure is applied to the hose. Once the form is put into the bow oven and pressure is applied, it is not possible to see what happens to the blank.

If you choose to use the pressure hose as it was originally designed to be used (pressurized through a temporary connection to the tire valve before placing in the oven), then you will not face the question of whether or not your bow blank behaved upon pressurization. But I believe the advantages of constant pressure on the hose outweigh the disadvantages. Your choice.

To avoid disappointment with the outcome, take your time. Inspect the form and blank to ensure you have done everything to secure it. Then inspect it again.

Curing the Bow Blank

The time has come. You have done all you can do. Place the form into the bow oven. Connect your compressor to the pressure hose. Bring the pressure up to 60 to 70 PSI.

I like to let the form sit in this state for a couple hours before applying heat to it. I cannot give you a concrete proven reason why I do this. I can tell you that Smooth-On is a very viscous glue. I like to give it plenty of time to move as much as it wants to so that it can completely wet the wood and fill every void and pore. I think giving a couple hours at room

Analog timer

Digital temperature
control

Temperature and
time controls

temperature for this to happen allows trapped air time to migrate out of
the bow and is good insurance that the bow blank will turn out as good
as it can be.

After a couple hours at room temperature, turn the heat on. If you use
light bulbs as your heat source, it can take several hours to reach curing
temperature. If you use a baseboard heater or some other heat source, the
oven can reach curing temperature faster.

Just as your grandmother will caution you that the holiday turkey
takes a lot longer than the oven to get hot inside, the bow blank, nestled
inside the form, takes much longer to reach curing temperature. I like to
give the bow blank at least 2 hours (after the oven has reached temperature) to come to temperature before beginning the 6-hour clock.

For the first several bows I made, I checked the oven periodically to
determine when the milestones were reached. Now I simply use a cheap
timer. My oven, equipped with a baseboard heater, comes to temperature
in about 10 minutes with the form in it. So I set the timer to turn on about
2 hours after I put the form in the oven. Then I set the timer to turn off
about 8 hours later.

Finally, according to Smooth-On instructions, I leave the bow blank in the form at room temperature and under pressure for 6 hours. This is easily accomplished as the bow blank usually goes into the oven in the afternoon. By the next morning it is ready to be removed from the form.

Roughing the Bow to Lines

Arguably the most exciting time in making a bow is the moment when you remove it from the oven. It is indeed like Christmas morning. All that planning, preparation, and work comes to a head. Did it cure correctly? Did anything slip? How will it work?

All this anticipation can lead to ruin. But ruin is not likely if you take your time. Enjoy the anticipation. Work slowly. Take joy in what you have done.

Making a bow is not nearly as important as raising a child. But, as I said before, it is similar in many ways. If you have raised a child you know the challenge of trying to provide all the necessities of life, while at the same time instilling what you believe are the core ingredients of a good life.

You spend 18 years (to start with) feeding, teaching, and helping your young one to become an adult. And then what? What kind of adult will he or she be? Will your child make you proud?

Part of being a good parent is to let go of these questions and concerns, which are mainly self-centered, and just focus on doing the best job you can do to raise your wee one. We must learn that the outcome, while dependent on what we do as parents, is really not up to us. It is up to our children. This is a hard truth to learn as a parent. Especially hard to learn if you, like me, believe that perfection can be achieved simply through hard work and grit. In truth, you can mold your child only so much. In the end, your child will be their own person, just as you are. And almost without exception they will be beautiful in wholly unexpected ways.

And so it is with your new bow. As I mentioned at the beginning of this chapter, I like to think of the curing process as the time when the bow is born. Up to this point, everything we did to prepare for the lay-up of the bow contributed, for better or worse, to the final quality of the bow. Once the bow has been glued together and cured, everything we did to establish the character of the bow, and those things we have no control over, such as the nature of the specific pieces of wood we used, are blended together.

Together, these qualities will determine the character of the bow.

From this point on, there is only so much we can do to change the nature of that character. We can shape the bow and tiller the bow to get close to the desired weight and draw force characteristics, but we must be careful to pay attention to what the bow is telling us. If we ignore what our bow tells us as we work with it, and we force the bow to meet our preconceived notion of the exact draw weight or limb length or tiller profile, we are in danger of destroying the character of the bow.

I will get a little ahead of myself here and describe the goals to strive for and the pitfalls to avoid as we bring our bow to its finished state. The final steps that will optimize the bow are collectively called tillering and are addressed in Chapter 10. When we rough the bow to the lines we drew on the back of the bow, we must keep these points in mind.

If we are hell-bent on achieving a certain draw weight and cut the limbs too short, we may indeed achieve that weight, but the bow will be tortured by excessive stresses and may stack on the draw as a result.

If we work the limbs down pursuing the perfect tiller, we may find we have weakened the limbs at the fades so much that the cast of the bow is diminished.

If we forget to exercise the bow between adjustments, we may find that we have overshot our goal and we have broken the spirit of the bow.

The lesson here is to proceed slowly and to keep in mind all the core qualities that make an American Semi-Longbow such a pleasure to shoot.

Minimizing the string angle at the limb tips will contribute to the gentle nature of the bow, making it smooth to draw. Maximizing the string angle at the fingers will minimize finger pinch and add to the forgiving nature of the bow. Maximum string angle is achieved by making sure the limb bends uniformly from the fades to the tips. The last few inches of the limb should, ideally, be stiff and not bend as much as the rest of the limb. Bending too much at the fades can

Harry floor tillering his bow

Using weighted string to test straightness

help maximize string angle, but it can rob cast from the bow.

Keeping the limbs bending evenly helps to add cast to the bow and minimize hand shock.

By being attentive to all these things, we can take note if something seems amiss. It is easier to leave the limbs a little wide or a little long in order to bring the bow closer to our specifications.

After I remove the bow blank from the form and remove all the plastic film that clings to it, I look the blank over for any obvious problems.

Did the fade outs get glued together without any issues? No sliding? No gaps?

Did the laminations behave along the limbs? No bubbles, bumps, gaps, or twists?

Did the laminations behave at the tips?

If things look pretty good, I cut the ends off the limbs to square them up along the line I drew on the back of the bow. I use a carbide-tipped band saw blade for this step. A hacksaw would work too.

Once this is done I gently floor tiller the bow. Cracking and popping is normal at this point as the glue that built up on the sides cracks. No worries. Be gentle; don't push the bow too far. The goal is to feel if the bow seems like it will meet your desired draw force. This is something that comes with practice. A bow blank bends differently than a bow cut to lines. When you first do this, you will not be able to make any judgments. After a few bows, this test will start to have value.

If the blank seems a bit light, you can make mental note of it and plan on making a shorter bow. If it seems heavy, you may consider making a slimmer bow.

The next step is to ensure that the bow blank is straight, with no twisting in the limbs.

Set the blank on a couple blocks to raise it off your work bench. Lay a weighted string across the length of the bow, lined up with the centerline marks you made when drawing the profile of the bow. Lean over the bow and verify that the string lines up with all the centerline marks.

Most of the time, the string lines up perfectly. If it doesn't, there can be a couple causes.

The most likely cause is that your form is not perfectly straight or square. This can happen when the form is made, or it can happen if the form warps from repeated exposure to heat or humidity.

It can also happen if the core woods warp or the laminations slip during the curing process.

There is not much advice I can give you to help deal with warped bow blanks, except to be honest about the cause. If warping is due to a faulty form, fix it or get rid of it. Making a form takes a lot of time and effort, so it is hard to part with a bad one. But scrapping a warped form is often the best choice.

If the blank is warped for some reason other than a faulty form, there is still not much advice I can give you, since each blank is unique. The one piece of encouragement I can offer is to be patient. Leave the blank alone for a few days and see what happens. As it rests and stabilizes after being heated in the oven, it may come back to straight on its own, given enough time.

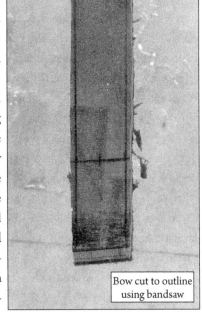

Now that the bow has been verified to be straight, it is time to cut the blank to the layout drawn on the back of the bow.

Using my carbide-tipped bandsaw, I cut the bow out, staying at least a heavy 1/16 inch outside the lines. It is a personal choice how much material you want to remove with the sander. People who make bows for a living, and committed hobbyists, usually have a vertical sander long enough to sand the entire limb at once. These folks often skip the bandsaw step and go di-

Bow cut to outline using bandsaw

rectly to the sander.

One day I hope to have such a vertical sander. But for now, my vertical sander is not big enough, or powerful enough, to handle such a chore. So I remove most of the extra material with my bandsaw and clean up the remaining material with the sander.

If you use a bandsaw as I do, be careful to not remove too much material. Bandsaws have a habit of getting out of control when you least expect it, which can leave a dimple in your limb or riser. Sanding more and cutting less is a good policy. With practice, you will find the right balance.

If I think the bow may come out with a low draw force based on floor tillering the blank, I may leave a little extra material outside the lines. If I think it is going to have a heavier draw than I'd like, I come closer to the lines.

Cutting String Nocks and Stringing the Bow

Once I get somewhere in the ballpark, it is time to cut in the string nocks and check the weight and tiller.

So far the making of the bow has not been so much an iterative process as it has been a serial process. Up to this point, parts and pieces have been made. Once the part was made, that step was complete and it was time for the next step.

From here on out, until the bow is ready for a coat of finish, the process changes to a circular one, which seems particularly appropriate since we are chasing a basically circular tiller. This is again a reference to Chapter 10.

This circular process includes: shaping the limbs, bringing them to the lines, adjusting the string nock depth as required, checking bow draw force, adjusting string length to maintain brace height, and checking tiller.

It is important to take your time as you juggle these jobs. Forgetting to make the string nocks deeper after having sanded the sides down a bit could result in the string popping out and your bow jumping across your shop in a very undignified manner!

Back to the string nocks. I use a 5/32 chainsaw file. These are cheap and readily available.

I draw a line 45 degrees from the back of the bow on both sides of the limb. I aim to make this line the front edge of the string groove. I cut the groove so that the file lays in the groove to about its centerline. Make sure

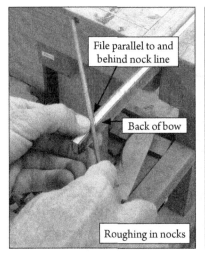
File parallel to and behind nock line

Back of bow

Roughing in nocks

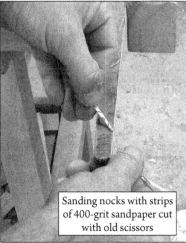
Sanding nocks with strips of 400-grit sandpaper cut with old scissors

that the grooves on each side of the limb are even on both the belly and the back of the bow.

The edges of the string grooves will be sharp enough to abrade the string. Before adding a string to the bow, I sand the string grooves with a narrow piece of 400-grit paper. Then I blow the grooves out so that the string won't pick up fiberglass dust, which will also abrade the string over time.

Before stringing the bow, I run some 150-grit sandpaper along the edges of the last 6 inches of each limb so that neither the string nor my hand pick up any fiberglass splinters. Again I blow the dust off, or wipe it away with a paper towel, before introducing the string.

We have arrived at yet another exciting moment in our bow building adventure: putting the string on the bow for the first time. Will it meet my draw force expectations? Will the limbs work together so the bow will tiller correctly? Will the bow stack when drawn? Will the bow be straight, or will it have a twist?

Again I must defer to Chapter 10 for the specifics on tillering. For the remainder of this chapter I will stick to the mechanics of making the bow. Reading this chapter and Chapter 10, and thinking of them together as you make your bow, will help you arrive at a finished bow that meets your draw force requirements, while at the same time is as forgiving and as efficient as it can be.

Now that the bow has been strung, the next step is to make sure the bow limbs are straight and that the string tracks down the centerline of

the bow.

To do this, simply lean one tip of the strung bow on the edge of a chair or your work bench and let it hang there as you gently hold the other tip. Look down the string with one eye and align the string with the center of the far limb. Then track down the bow with your eye. Does the string follow the centerline of the riser and opposing limb?

If something seems askew, flip the bow, adjust your orientation to it, use your other eye, move to a different location in the room, and repeat your observation. Sometimes things can look wrong from one perspective, and right from another. Make several observations to confirm any twists you may see.

String tracks down center of bow

If you see a twist in a limb, it is usually the result of uneven string nock depth. Even if the twist is not a result of uneven string nock depth, it can usually be resolved by adjusting the depth of one of the string nocks.

The weaker side of the limb will bend more than the stronger side of the limb. This results in the twist. To fix it, make the string nock slightly

Sanding station set up outside with appropriate safety gear

deeper on the weak side of the limb. Go slowly, a few strokes of the file at a time. Test, repeat.

If everything goes according to plan, which it usually does, my bow will come to the desired draw force, the string will track down the center of the bow, and the tiller will look pretty good. At this point, I will usually dress up the riser and limb tips with overlays, and cut out the arrow shelf before trying to achieve final tiller. Cutting out the arrow shelf slightly weakens the upper fade. This contributes to the tiller of the bow. It is important to cut out the arrow shelf before finishing the tillering process.

It seems I should describe how to cut out the arrow shelf at this point, but I prefer to cut it out after adding overlays. So I will describe how I cut out the arrow shelf in the next section.

Adding Overlays

The beauty in an American Semi-Longbow, the real beauty, can be found in its honesty. It is true, in form and function, to its purpose.

Adding anything unnecessary to an American Semi-Longbow seems almost garish to me, like an overly bejeweled courtesan. Overlays could fall into this category.

Adding anything unnecessary to the tip of a bow detracts from its performance, even if it is hardly measurable. I am torn about the merits of tip overlays, vacillating back and forth between the stark but truly functional no-overlay tip and the dressed-up, trimmed-out overlay tip. In truth, the overlay can be justified in that it protects the tips from the added shock they must endure from newer bowstring materials like Fast Flight.

But if we stay the course and are honest with ourselves, we must admit that the tip wedge that we use, if made from the right material, like linen phenolic, can do the job of stiffening the tip, as well as securing it against the hard use of non-stretch strings.

Adding overlays to the back of the riser, on the other hand, can be justified by function. Overlays on the back of the riser allow me to shape the riser more roundly on the back, and thus fit the hand better.

Making the overlays on the back match the overlays on the tips

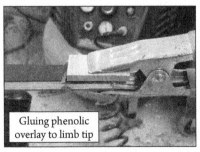

Gluing phenolic overlay to limb tip

gives a finished look. I never add one without the other.

As I have continued my association with the ASL, I have become accustomed to its clean form. Some may call it stark, but I believe there is deep beauty in utility. I can see that, over time, I will probably leave the overlays behind.

However, that is the future, and this is now.

I am tempted to continue my thoughts on what makes the American Semi-Longbow beautiful, and in doing so complain about how it is treated in advertising. Suffice it to say that when bows of any stripe are shown in ads, the risers get all the attention. Rarely are the limbs shown.

While I acknowledge that it is difficult to take a good picture of such a long, thin thing as a bow, I think more effort should be put into it. The limb is where the action is.

The character of an ASL is mostly determined by its limbs, not its riser. Looking at an advertisement for a bow that shows only the riser is like looking at an advertisement for a car that shows only the door handle.

Enough said.

When I add overlays to the riser and tips, I do so before I cut out the arrow shelf. This saves the time and effort of cleaning up the arrow shelf twice.

For the riser overlays, I generally use the same woods I have in the riser. I make two pieces around 0.040 inch thick that are a little wider than

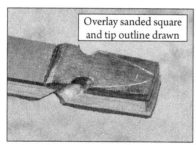
Overlay sanded square and tip outline drawn

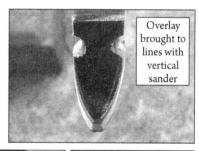
Overlay brought to lines with vertical sander

Belly of tip rounded with sander

Overlay sanded to rough shape with 150-grit paper

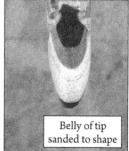
Belly of tip sanded to shape

the riser and about 8 inches long.

I roughen the riser using a hacksaw blade. This allows me to really prepare the surface for bonding. The riser bends more than you would think as the bow is drawn. If the overlays are not bonded well to it, they will eventually lift off.

Hold the hacksaw blade across the riser and tension it with a little bend. Then gently scrape the back of the bow until the entire surface is abraded.

I center my 8-inch overlays on the center of the handle. This allows the overlay to extend about 2 inches up the arrow shelf area, and about 2 inches below the handle grip area. It is pleasing to the eye.

I apply epoxy and clamp them, lighter color on the bottom, to the riser. The riser fadeouts pose a clamping challenge. There is more than one way to meet this challenge, and I expect there are better ways than I have found. But hopefully the following methods that work for me will be helpful to you.

One way is to use a single clamp and a slat to spread the force out to the ends of the overlays.

Another way, which is more secure but requires more preparation, is to make a jig that fits your riser area and provides the necessary flats for your clamps. I find this the best and easiest method.

Once the overlays have been glued onto the riser, I move to the tips. I use the same woods on the tips, with the addition of a layer of the afore-mentioned linen phenolic. A couple pieces of wood about 0.030 inch thick, and a standard 1/16-inch thick piece of phenolic make up the tip overlay.

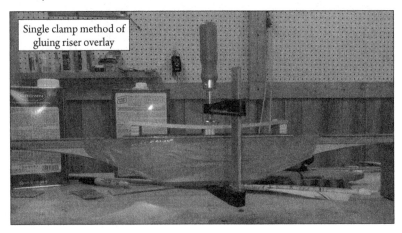
Single clamp method of gluing riser overlay

Using wood jig shaped like belly of bow to give flats for clamping

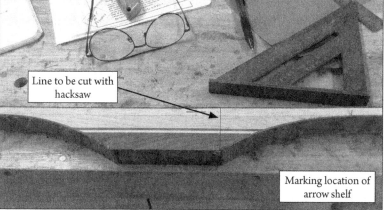

Line to be cut with hacksaw

Marking location of arrow shelf

Prepare the surfaces for bonding with coarse sandpaper (the hacksaw treatment is not necessary on the tips), glue the tip material on with the phenolic against the back of the bow, clamp, and wait.

Cutting the Arrow Shelf and Finishing Out the Grip

Once all the overlays have cured overnight, it is time to sand flat and cut out the arrow shelf.

Sand the overlays flat to the riser. Then mark the location of the arrow shelf. This is a simple but critical step. The best piece of advice I can give you for this is to make sure you mark the correct side of the correct limb. I have oopsed this more than once (and ended up with a left-handed bow).

Draw a line across the handle at the beginning of the fade. This marks where the arrow shelf will be. After confirming, and reconfirming, that I have the correct side of the correct limb, I cut this line with a hacksaw to almost the depth of the blade (about 7/16 inch).

Now rotate the bow so that you are looking at the back of the bow. I make the next mark 2 3/4 inches above the arrow shelf cut. I then draw a line connecting the inside of the arrow shelf with the outside of the riser. Cut this with your bandsaw or hacksaw.

The shelf is now cut out.

It is now time to start sanding and shaping the bow to bring it to its final form and tiller.

I usually wait until the bow has been brought to its final tiller and the limbs are ready for a final sanding before cutting out and shaping the grip. This allows me to set the bow securely on the tillering tree.

Finishing out the grip, tips, and limbs requires some rasping and a lot of sandpaper work. It is best to do some shaping, then do some shooting, then do some more shaping. You will arrive at the best final dimensions by this iterative process. It's fun, too.

I have come to favor the simple, narrow, dished grip. There is no absolute best grip, or best way of making it. But for your reference, here is how I do it.

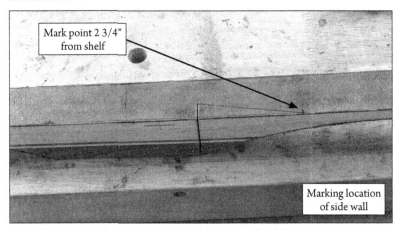

Mark point 2 3/4" from shelf

Marking location of side wall

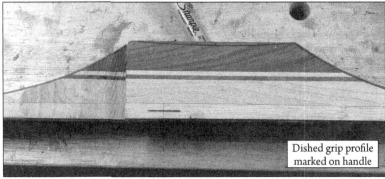

Dished grip profile marked on handle

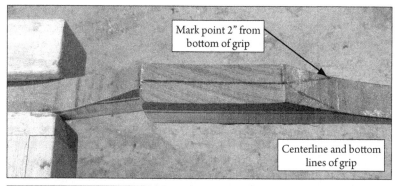

Mark point 2" from bottom of grip

Centerline and bottom lines of grip

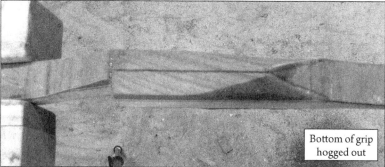

Bottom of grip hogged out

Lay the bow on its side and mark the profile of your desired grip. Cut this out.

Lay the bow on its back and find the centerline of the grip and mark it. Then mark 2 inches down the fades and mark each side. Next, draw a line connecting these points. Hog this material out. Fiberglass is very hard on tools. Don't commit an expensive wood rasp to this task, as it will soon be ruined. Use an old rasp, or sand it, or (if you are confident) cut it out with the band saw.

Finally, round the grip sides out so that it fits well in your hand. I like to add a little indention in the back of the bow for my index finger. It helps me locate the grip in my hand, and it feels comfortable.

One tool that helps make light work of shaping the grip and rounding the sides of the limbs is my pneumatic sander. It consists of a pressurized bag covered in a sandpaper cylinder that mounts to my drill press. Lightly passing the bow limbs and riser along this sander leaves a pleasing round-ness.

Once the grip has been brought to this roughed-in shape, the final work on the tips and limbs follows the same routine. Thin strips of in-creasingly finer sandpaper are used to smooth, round, and blend the vari-

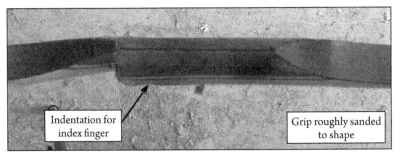

Indentation for index finger

Grip roughly sanded to shape

ous angles and sides of the bow.

If I were under the pressures of being a professional bowyer, I would have to find an efficient and fast way to bring the bow to its final condition. But since I am just a hobbyist, I can take my time and enjoy the adventure of bringing the bow to its final form. This usually takes me several weeks.

I usually add a little rug rest to the arrow shelf during this process of sanding and shooting and tillering. It can be easily removed when it comes time to apply finish to the bow. Having the rug rest in place allows me to more easily see how the bow is shooting. Shooting off a bare shelf is harder and can result in poor arrow flight. A little lift makes all the difference.

Chapter 9
More Than Just a Stick and String

Emergent properties. One of the most interesting concepts to me, and seemingly a property of almost every organic system, is the phenomenon of emergent properties.

Emergent properties are properties or characteristics of a system that could not be predicted from analyzing the individual properties or characteristics of the individual parts of that system. They are properties or characteristics that emerge, somehow, as a result of the interconnections and interactions within the system. In this age of computers, we might understand this notion of emergent properties as the result of networking.

In 1875, a philosopher named George Henry Lewes recognized this effect and discussed it in his work *Problems of Life and Mind*. In this book, he illustrates the idea by observing that all processes of life can be broken down into their constituent inorganic chemical reactions, and yet when taken together they become organic and lead to life.

Emergent properties include all things emergent. Life, thought, behavior, love, sex, and death. While we can easily recognize these things, these emergent properties, we have a hard time defining them. Our questions of what they are, and how they come to be, still provide humanity with our greatest intellectual mysteries.

Imagine the emergent property of reason trying to determine how it emerged. Is it possible?

The physicist Mark Bedau observed that:

Although strong emergence is logically possible, it is uncomfortably

like magic. How does an irreducible [property] arise, since by defini-
tion it cannot be due to the aggregation of the micro-level potenti-
alities? Such causal powers would be quite unlike anything within
our scientific ken.... Their mysteriousness will only heighten the tradi-
tional worry that emergence entails illogitimately getting something
from nothing.

Indeed, emergent properties can make us feel uncomfortable, especially true for those of us who are used to the idea of explaining our world
in rational terms. This discomfort has led some to the church. It has led
others to the woods.

Emergent properties are not unlike the notion of unintended consequences. While consequences may seem unintended to some, to others those very same consequences are no surprise. Still, there are consequences that simply cannot be predicted, and are thus unintended.

Unintended seems to imply unwanted. This unwanted connotation
has risen out of the perception that on balance, the majority of unintended consequences are bad. But strictly speaking, unintended just means
unplanned or unexpected.

Which brings me back to my American Semi-Longbow. I can see
now that my hunting adventure has been about more than simply stepping outside to see if I could kill a deer.

Over the years, I have hunted with gun, compound, and traditional
bow. As some do, I have gravitated toward the traditional bow as I have
aged. On the surface of it, it seems like the natural thing to do. As hunting
skill increases, the use of a more primitive weapon challenges the hunter's
skill. Obviously.

This was my feeling about it until I started shooting the ASL. As my
experience with the ASL grew, so did my awareness that what I did with
the bow would affect me, as well as the deer or squirrel I was aiming at.
Whether this correlation between my awareness and my ASL was causal
or simply coincidental, I cannot say.

But I do know that the more I became aware of where my meat came
from and how I killed the animals that provided it, the more I came to
value living what I call the good life.

To value something, you must know what it is. This requirement has
forced me to think about, and attempt to define, what a good life is.

What makes a good life?

I don't really know, but I think that it is not a thing in the sense that oxygen is a thing, and it is not a process like fire is a process. I think that the good life (whatever that may be) might just be yet another emergent property that we cannot easily define, but that we instantly recognize as something real.

Look again at an ASL. It is a simple thing consisting of just a bent stick and a string. Analyzing the properties of these two components, which together make the bow, will lead the rational observer to conclude that such a device might have many uses, from starting a fire to making music. Add a few more constraints and hints, like an empty stomach and an arrow, and the rational observer will again be led by the evidence to conclude that such a device could certainly be used as a weapon.

But how confounded would this rational observer be when he or she finds out that the simple act of shooting an arrow at a stump provides the archer with satisfaction and joy? What is the connection?

How confounded would this rational observer be to learn that the act of killing a deer for food becomes almost holy when performed with an ASL, where it was simply a challenge with a gun? What is the rationale?

I cannot answer these questions, but I can confirm the truth of the experience.

I can also confirm that for me the effect is greater when using an American Semi-Longbow than it was when using other traditional bow styles.

I expect that my experience of hunting and killing is enhanced with the ASL as compared to other traditional bows because there is less between me and the deer.

There is less technology, less weight, fewer curves, and less stress in the wood. This forces me to be more present in the moment, more focused, and more mindful.

If everything goes according to plan, the circle of life is rounded one more time.

So when the simple device that is the American Semi-Longbow is taken up by a person, that person now becomes an archer. When that archer takes aim at a deer or a squirrel, that archer now becomes a hunter.

There is a common belief that a person hunts with a traditional bow, or specifically an American Semi-Longbow, because it is more difficult than hunting with a rifle or compound bow. I don't believe this is entirely true.

In fact, I secretly wish that hunting with the longbow weren't so hard, and that I could kill as many deer with it as with my rifle. I spend so much time practicing not only to ensure that I will be ready when the moment comes, but also in the hope that shooting and hunting with the longbow will become easier through so much practice.

In the end I know that no matter how much I practice, hunting with the longbow will never be as efficient, and killing will never be as sure, as it is with my rifle. And yet I continue to do it, and I even prefer it to hunting with any other weapon.

The reason has to be wrapped up in the fact that the entire experience of a hunt with the longbow is somehow better. That it adds to the good life.

I sit in my stand or blind. I creep through the woods, standing still more than moving. I spend hours in the presence of squirrels and birds, watching the yellow, red, and golden leaves of autumn. Tired from their summer of gathering sunlight, they finally let go their stubborn hold upon the branches and fall crisply to earth.

Rarely, and always unexpectedly, I will glimpse the shape of a deer as it moves quietly through the underbrush in its relentless search for browse. Even more rarely, that same deer will wander within range of my trusty ASL and my not-so-trusty aim.

When this happens, and if the deer is big enough to make me want to kill it, my heart rate always quickens and I begin that often repeated, and always the same, conversation with myself:

"Stay calm! OK, breathe and stay calm. Is it broadside? Loosen up your grip and don't crab the string. It's OK to let her pass. Do I want to shoot her? Yes, I want to shoot her. Why? Do you want to look for her this late in the evening? Is it going to rain? Don't breathe so hard, she's going to smell your adrenaline. I can't believe it, she's still coming. Oh my gosh, she's only ten yards. I can make that shot."

"I'm going to shoot her now."

I immediately calm down. All shaking from cold or excitement stops. No more talk. Focus, pick a spot. Draw, settle, shoot.

Or not.

So much can happen at every step of the way that loosing the arrow may happen only one time in ten for such a scenario. Even when the arrow is loosed, branches can appear out of nowhere to deflect the arrow, the deer can supernaturally duck out of the way of the arrow, or I can just plain miss.

But when I don't, the payoff in meat and memories is incomparable.

When I look at the antlers that adorn the walls of my shop or home, I can remember with explicit detail almost everything about those final moments that resulted in my good fortune.

I remember where I was hunting and what the woods were like. How the air smelled. How I felt. I remember how the arrow flew, where it struck the deer, and how the deer reacted. I remember how I felt at that instant. Whether I had total confidence in the outcome, or I had doubt. How long it took me to track the mortally wounded deer, and the exact path I followed to find it.

If I was hunting with friends, I remember telling them the story as soon as I could. Sometimes this story is told in real time as the deer is being followed, sometimes the story is told after the fact around the campfire.

Those who hunt with a more efficient weapon will recognize some parts of this process, but I doubt they will recognize all of them. Many of the feelings, thoughts, and words associated with the doubt inherent to hunting with the longbow will be foreign to the rifle hunter and unfamiliar to a hunter who uses a compound bow.

It is these unfamiliar and maybe even foreign experiences and thoughts that contribute to the fullness of the experience of hunting with an American Semi-Longbow. These are the things that add substance to the experience and that make hunting with a longbow something more than just hunting.

When I hunt with a rifle, I see many more deer than I ever intend to shoot. In fact, even when the freezer is mostly empty I still find it hard to kill a deer with a gun. When I return from hunting on a crisp winter morning, my wife doubts my resolve to fill the freezer when she hears me tell her of the many deer I saw, while I stand there with nothing to show for it.

When I hunt with the longbow, I am much more intent on killing that deer. I seldom let a bona fide opportunity pass. What is the difference?

Why should I be so ambivalent about killing a deer with a gun and so enthusiastic to do it with a longbow?

I am sure that no small part of the reason is the state of my stomach. No man, who is very hungry, would experience such a dilemma. In fact, when we study what we did to hunt meat in the days of our Pleistocene ancestors, we see that no opportunity was lost. We would light entire for ests on fire to drive animals to their death. We would build walls designed to help herd herbivores over some convenient cliff to their death on the rocks below. When one is hungry, other concerns take a back seat.

Killing a deer with a gun adds very little to my life other than the quality meat it provides. When I kill a deer with a gun, it is usually not the result of careful premeditated planning. It doesn't require me to figure out how I can get close to the deer, and it doesn't result in the self-reflection often associated with a botched attempt.

When those that have come before me faced these questions and tried to figure out for themselves why it was that they chose to hunt with their longbows instead of their trusty guns, they would often settle on the increased challenge and perceived ethical superiority of voluntarily hunting with a more primitive weapon. In one word, sport.

This conclusion was concisely expressed by Saxton Pope in his book *Hunting with the Bow and Arrow*:

After all, it is not the killing that brings satisfaction; it is the contest of skill and cunning. The true hunter counts his achievement in proportion to the effort involved and the fairness of the sport.

While I believe this is part of it, I don't think it completely explains the compulsion some of us feel to hunt with a traditional bow. More specifically, I don't think it completely explains the compulsion to hunt with the American Semi-Longbow.

Some of us discover that it does indeed feel good to count the proportion of our achievement that is based in skill and measured in antler inches, and to stay there for most of our lives. Some others of us learn that who we are is more affected by what we do, and how we do it, than we might have thought.

Which brings me back to this idea of emergence. The act of hunting with a longbow is, no doubt, more sporting. I believe that enhanced sense of sport directly results from the free choice to hunt with a more challenging weapon. But what else comes from this free choice? The other enhancements to the experience of hunting with a longbow are not easily predicted because they are... emergent properties. These new things are not merely the feelings of satisfaction I derive from meeting the greater challenge of hunting with a longbow; they are changes to what it is that I call me.

These changes were not predicted, anticipated, or even considered as part of my decision to hunt with the American Semi-Longbow. Why did I start in the first place? I honestly cannot remember what it was that first sparked my interest in such a bow.

In fact, I clearly recall being unimpressed with the bow and even being somewhat repulsed by it. The first time I remember thinking about the bow for any length of time was many years ago in the mountains of Colorado.

A friend and I were hunting mule deer with our flintlocks and were camped at the end of a long firebreak. One evening, while we were enjoying our campfire and whiskey, we saw a light coming off the mountain. The light eventually made its way to our campfire and turned out to be attached to a man carrying an American Semi-Longbow.

His bow was unstrung and appeared thin and weak as he leaned on it, telling us of his day on the mountain. He had shot an elk a few days earlier and was now trying to kill a bear. He was hanging around the gut pile of his elk, waiting for a hungry ursine to show up.

After trading stories about the day and a few rounds of George Dickel Number Twelve, our longbow hunter thanked us for the guiding light of our fire and continued on his way. As he walked away, my friend and I talked about his bow and how crazy he was for hunting with it.

I was much younger then and had the benefit of complete confidence in my conclusions about the limited utility and plain ugliness of his weapon. It would be eight years before I would reconsider this verdict.

So while I can remember seeing the bow in different situations and rejecting it out of hand for its obvious shortcomings in power and style, I cannot remember the moment when I decided to pick the bow up and shoot it.

I wonder how many of the transformational moments of our lives we forget? I wonder if forgetting is part of the process?

I know that I had run the gamut from guns to tweaked-out compound bows to recurves and hybrid bows. And so maybe it was the simple desire for greater challenge that brought me to the American Semi-Longbow. I cannot say.

Once I began to shoot this new bow, things changed almost immediately. In straight narrow limbs that I once, and for most of my life, saw as weak and uninteresting, I now saw elegant strength. I saw a path toward perfection.

When I started to shoot this new bow, my shooting went to hell. It took me a while to understand why. It took me even longer to bring my shooting back. When I finally figured out why my shooting was suffering, I figured out why I associated shooting the American Semi-Longbow with the good life.

There are two fundamental ways of living. We can dominate our immediate environment to suit us, and in so doing likely destroy the integrity of the land, or we can learn to live within our means and by doing so add to the fertility and integrity of the land. I use the phrase "within our means" here alluding to the new understanding Leopold gave us that our economy includes more than just dollars and other humans. It includes the wealth of the land and all its member species.

We can dominate our environment by building river dams to hold reserves of water in a dry land, which we can then use to water unnatural grass and wash our cars and blissfully disregard the fish. Disregard the fish that have for eons travelled up this river to procreate and rightfully ensure the survival of their own species. Or we can learn to live within the limits of the environment, and in so doing ensure the survival of all species, including our own.

Compound bows, and to some extent recurves, are designed to accommodate us. In a sense, these bows are dams designed to provide a reservoir of features to facilitate our shooting. These bows appeal to the engineer in me. These bows don't require me to compromise or negotiate with myself to improve my form or mental focus. They are designed around my limitations.

By comparison, the American Semi-Longbow has few accommodations. I say few, because it does have some. Take the arrow shelf, for example. Not necessary, but very helpful. The arrow shelf is where my pragmatism parts with my idealism.

Shooting the American Semi-Longbow requires that I work with the bow, that I recognize that I have to do my part in order to achieve a good shot. Some people claim this makes the bow hard to shoot. I say it makes the bow honest.

If I do my part, the arrow will fly true, for the bow always does its part. Bows of more complex design hide the line between what is my part and what is the bow's part. Bows of more complex design move the line closer to the archer, requiring the archer to do less and the bow to do more.

It is a tricky proposition to design a thing to improve some outcome by any means other than simply moving the line. When we build a dam to hold back the waters, the benefits are recognized by those who live around the dam. But what of those who live downstream? What of those who live in the stream?

When I recognized that to shoot the American Semi-Longbow meant that I had to do my part, I began to see better results and feel less frustration.

The grip of an ASL is not designed to conform to the shape of the hand and cradle it like a sleeping baby in a crib, but to be held by the archer with commitment and relaxed confidence, sure in the knowledge that if she holds the bow on target and follows through on the shot, the arrow will hit the mark, or close to it.

The riser is not designed to swoop back toward the archer, giving a generous brace height to compensate for a poor release, instead it is straight or even slightly backset to deliver the most energy possible to the arrow.

The limbs are not designed with recurved tips to minimize string angle and smooth out the draw cycle. Instead, they are straight, deep, and narrow to ensure they move in a straight line with the most efficiency and dependability. While the recurved tips play to our need for speed, they do so at the expense of durability. Unlike the owners of a compound or a recurve bow, you will never hear the owner of an American Semi-Longbow complain that his limbs are twisted.

Designing bows is a game of sums and balances. Whenever we shift the balance toward a quality that we see as making the bow better and faster, we shift away from some other quality (known or unknown) which diminishes the bow.

I have come to realize that if I want a better experience shooting my bow, it is up to me to improve. Asking more of the bow rarely works out. I see this same lesson, learned more generally, adding to the good life.

When we build a dam to hold back water and make our lives better, we cheat ourselves and the land. Over time we have learned that dams are a temporary fix. But the damage they cause is permanent, at least within the time frame of a human life.

I think of these things as I hold my ASL in my hands, standing in the woods. I see the convergence of what I think of as the good life and the idea of simplifying. I see the same convergence with beauty.

Where once I saw an ugly stick, I now see a beautiful bow bent in a simple curve. I am beginning to see the power of durability.

Where once I saw simple relationships between squirrels and acorns, I am beginning to see that these two citizens of the land are connected not just to each other, but to every other living thing. I am beginning to see that I too am connected to all these things.

When I started shooting traditional bows, I expected that with enough practice and commitment I would become a proficient shot. And that would be it. Like sighting in a rifle scope.

You lay the rifle upon the rest, place the cross hairs on the bullseye, and fire. Based on the point of impact, adjust the elevation and windage as required, and shoot again. Repeat until the bullet strikes the bullseye. After this exercise is complete, there is no point in shooting again, until a deer walks by.

Yet again, I discovered that what I expected to be true was not true. Giving credit where credit is due, it is not true for any traditional bow. It is particularly not true with the American Semi-Longbow.

No matter how much I shoot my American Semi-Longbow, I never achieve the perfect shot, at least not twice in a row. I shoot well enough to kill a deer, but I never seem to shoot well enough to conclude that I can shoot no better.

I have learned that practicing with my bow is not for the purpose of achieving and maintaining the perfect shot, but rather a never-ending journey toward the ever-elusive perfect shot.

Once I realized this, the frustration I felt at not achieving the perfect shot diminished. It has not gone away, as I still have an ego that needs to be satisfied. My perceived relationship to the bow has changed from one of competition to one of cooperation.

Now I see my bow as a partner in my effort to become a better shot, not as a thing to be conquered. Yet again, this emergent relationship mirrors the relationship I must have with the land in order to try to live the good life.

If we see the land, nature, as something that must be conquered in order to be happy, we will never be happy. The more we conquer the land, the sicker it becomes and the poorer we are for it.

There is an old farming adage that tells us that liming the land makes the father rich and the son poor. What this refers to is the practice of liming the soil to make its nutrients immediately available to the planted crops. For a few years, the crops will be good and the farmer will profit from them. But eventually, the soil will be drained of its wealth and the crops will fail. Liming the soil allows us to withdraw from the soil bank without making any deposits. In the end, we are bankrupt.

If we can learn to live with the land, to live within its means and ability to support us, we can have the good life. If we give to the land as much as we take from it, the land can sustain us, and our children and their children. Living the good life in the end means more than simply sustaining ourselves, it means sustaining the land and the generations to come. How can we be happy knowing that we have diminished the land and, hence, our children's lives?

I am thick-headed. This is why I love the American Semi-Longbow and why it is so good for me. It patiently teaches me the same lessons over and over.

It teaches me that a good shot cannot be bargained for. A good shot cannot be designed and baked into my equipment so that I am relieved of any obligation.

It teaches me that a good shot is not the result of hitting the bullseye but is the result of everything that had to happen for the arrow to end up in the bullseye.

There is an old Japanese saying about archery that goes something like: "It is no business of yours where the arrow flies." It took me a long time to find meaning in this statement. But I now believe the author was trying to express the truth that a good shot is not defined by where the arrow goes, but by what the archer does before the arrow is loosed, and by the feeling we get when the arrow is finally released.

In the great cosmological scheme of things, what happens on this planet is irrelevant. But what it means to us is everything. When I make a perfect shot, I am satisfied. The day is good. I have done my part, and my ever-honest bow has done its part.

Making a good shot adds to my life. And by doing so, it adds, imperceptibly, to the lives of my family. Trying to live the good life, whatever that is, does the same thing not only for my family, but just as importantly for the land.

For me, living the good life means clearing the irrelevant clutter from my mind and living honestly on the land. If I am honest with the land, it will be honest with me. It can be no other way.

We can try to change this relationship by designing ways and means to get what we want, but in the end these efforts simply serve to move the line. There is only so much earth that we live on. When we come to grips with this truth, then we can begin to live the good life.

All these relationships that I have with my American Semi-Longbow have resulted in a new emergent quality in me. A new awareness of the land and the web of life. An awareness that I am not just on this earth, I am of it. If I care for myself, I must, by necessity, care for the earth as well.

What a lucky thing it is that I came around to shooting the American Semi-Longbow! I must reluctantly add that it has been lucky for the deer and squirrels too. For had I stayed with the rifle or compound, there would be far fewer deer in my woods to appreciate my beautiful bow.

The American Semi-Longbow is indeed more than just a stick and string. It has served as both map and compass to lead me to a better life, and hopefully, it has helped me live that better life more in harmony with the land.

If we leave this world a better place than we found it, is that not a clue that we have lived a good life?

Chapter 10
Tillering

Tillering was invented along with the self bow in the distant unwritten past of our Pleistocene ancestors. I don't know why we are constantly surprised by their ingenuity and intelligence, but we are. Tillering is yet another case where we get the opportunity to appreciate their thinking and take note of how little we have changed in the intervening years.

Unless you are one of those lucky few that can win a lottery, chances are that when you make a self bow you will see the same thing our ancestors did, a bow with one limb overly bent and the other limb almost straight. We intuitively know this is not right.

But what to do? The answer is obvious: scrape belly wood off the stronger limb until both limbs bend the same. In this observation is all the truth we need to make an efficient self bow. But as with most things, the truth is easier seen than achieved.

Our ancient ancestors set out to achieve this goal forthwith. They scraped the stronger limb until the bow appeared to bend evenly in both limbs, and then they set off to make meat with it. Hungry children have little patience. The end result was largely a measure of luck and artistry. The sweetness of the tiller was calibrated by the sensitivity of the bowyer's eye and the touch of his hand. Here the process was left.

It has been left there, for the most part, even to this day

I could keep this chapter short by simply outlining my method for tillering bows. It would indeed be short. But it might not be convincing or helpful. So I have taken pains to write out my thinking and the evolution of what I did so that you can not only know what I do, but hopefully learn from my mistakes. Since a bow is given life through its tiller, the importance of a good tillering job cannot be overstated. And so I think this topic warrants some indulgence.

The Way It Has Always Been

I have read all that I could find about tiller. What I have read about tillering self bows has informed my understanding about trying to get the bow to look good at full draw on a tillering tree, and to feel good when shooting. But it still left me in the dark. One of the most artistic writers on the topic of self bows is Dean Torges. It is unusual for a bowyer writer to devote an entire chapter to the process of tillering, but Torges does in his book *Hunting the Osage Bow*. As a builder of laminated bows, I had to pick and choose that which applied to my efforts. One particular paragraph has stuck in my mind:

> *The only meaningful criterion which should be applied to the tillered bow is what it does at full draw. Not what it measures at brace height, at the dips, nor anywhere else along its length. Not even what it looks like at brace height. Not what a caliper says. Neither what a graph, nor a grid nor a thickness gauge says or reads. The tillered bow always looks and feels tillered at full draw.*

I have used this as a guiding principal in my tillering efforts. One of the most interesting things I have learned is that I don't have a very good eye for what a tillered bow should look like. This may be because I tend more toward the literal end of the scale, farther away from the artistic end.

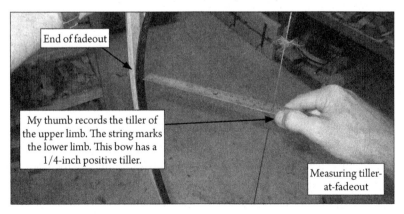

End of fadeout

My thumb records the tiller of the upper limb. The string marks the lower limb. This bow has a 1/4-inch positive tiller.

Measuring tiller-at-fadeout

168

Another guiding principle I have used is one that seems to come up in every discussion of tillering. It is the bedrock of all modern tillering conversations and is usually the only measurement discussed with, or specified by, bowyers and archers alike: tiller-at-fadeouts.

Tiller-at-fadeouts is the difference in length between the measurements taken from fadeout to string on each limb. Using a ruler, measure the distance from the belly of the bow at the end of the fadeout to the inside of the string on the upper limb. Do the same for the lower limb. If the distances are the same, the bow is said to have even tiller. If the distance measured at the top limb is greater than the distance measured at the lower limb, the bow is said to have positive tiller. The reverse being negative tiller.

Even tiller means the limbs are equally strong.

Positive tiller means the upper limb is weaker.

Negative tiller means the lower limb is weaker.

This entire discussion would be moot if we could shoot a bow with even limbs, having the arrow shelf at the center of the bow, in the center of the grip. And herein lies the problem. Unless we are willing to surgically alter our hand to build a hole for the arrow to pass through, we are left with the necessity to grip the bow below the arrow.

As soon as we move our hand down, we have destroyed the symmetry of forces that would nullify this discussion of tiller.

When we move our hand down, we increase the force we apply to the lower limb and decrease the force we apply to the upper limb. It is the classic see-saw shuffle. The smaller child must sit farther out on the end to balance the bigger child.

Modern discussions about what tiller-at-fadeout is best, are centered around a small range of numbers. Usually the range varies from even tiller to about 1/4-inch positive tiller. That's pretty much the whole discussion. For those who shoot three fingers under, even tiller is the answer. For those who shoot split finger, something positive (up to 1/4 inch) is the answer.

I have merged these two guiding principles into what has been my method of tillering: I shape and narrow the limbs to achieve draw weight and a slightly positive tiller. When I get close, I put the bow on the tillering tree and look to see that the limbs are bending in a pleasing way. I make smaller and smaller adjustments until the bow meets the draw weight and the tiller. Then I am done.

The mystery of what makes a bow shoot so well, and what makes it so pleasing to the eye, can be alluring to the budding bowyer. I find it irksome. I will rely, again, on Torges to put his finger on it for me:

> *...we will concentrate exclusively on refining the tiller of the drawn bow, relying primarily on our spring steel cabinet scraper or some similar scraping device. I can't tell you where to remove wood to make these adjustments. You must trust the critical eye which you developed for this purpose.*

So when I finish a bow, I reassure myself that I have tillered the bow to my shooting style (positive tiller for split fingers) and I have dutifully drawn the bow upon my tillering tree to make sure that the limbs appear to be bending equally and smoothly. I reassure myself that I have done all that I can do.

The Next Step

One of the joys of being human is the joy of sharing our knowledge with others. This joy is a defining characteristic of being human. It's also fun.

I have helped several folks make bows over the years. I expect it may be my collection of tools, and not my collection of knowledge, that attracts them to my shop. Be that as it may, I have provided some small guidance as they have built their bows. In one case at least, I also learned something.

Harry Angel gave me a kick in the pants when it comes to tillering a bow. Harry, like all of us aspiring bowyers, believes he can make a better bow. In his case it's a deflex/reflex, otherwise known as a hybrid, bow. We made a form to his specifications, and I have helped him make many bows.

During the construction of his first few bows, we did most all the work in my shop. But as Harry became more comfortable with the job of making a bow, he would take the bows home after they had been profiled to the lines and finish the work in his garage. At that stage of the game, power tools are no longer required. The only things needed are sandpaper and diligence.

After a while, Harry asked me what it was that I was looking for when I tillered a bow. I gave him the usual vague answers about putting the bow on the tillering tree and watching the limbs bend. He would nod his head at this without much comment.

Harry is a very good shot. He's one of those annoying people who seem to have better eye-hand coordination than the rest of us. He's able to pick up a sport and excel at it in short order. I won't bore you with the details of his skills in golf or his abilities with the shotgun. Suffice it to say that to some of us, it seems unnatural.

One of these annoying traits he brings to archery is the ability to feel in his bow hand any imbalance between the upper and lower limbs. He can tell when they are not working together perfectly. As he gained experience with making bows, he put this skill to work.

We have had a number of conversations about what exactly is happening when a bow is shot. I tried to impress him with my knowledge of statics, dynamics, kinematics, and energy. Largely without effect. Harry is a practical sort and has no use for complicated sophistry.

The physical characteristics of what is happening when a bow is shot are well understood. They fall neatly within the limits of a basic understanding of the aforementioned subjects. What makes them hard to translate from the theoretical to the practical is twofold: The time frame in which they happen is too short for human observation, and no two archers will shoot the same bow in the same way.

If we could watch the bow relax after the shot with the same level of detail that we can watch the bow being drawn, the mysteries would be removed. But we can't.

What about slow motion cameras, you ask? These would undoubtedly be helpful for the archer trying to perfect his shot. But as I observed earlier, since each archer is different, a camera would be most useful in a case-by-case study. As this is not a commonly available device, meaning I don't have one, I will leave that to others.

I could calculate the acceleration rate an arrow experiences when loosed from a bow that I make, but instead I will rely on C.W. Hickman, a doctor of engineering who spent more than a decade characterizing the performance of bows. He states that for his self bows that shoot about 150 feet per second, an arrow accelerates at a rate of 12,000 feet per second per second (*Archery, the Technical Side*, page 6). With this figure accepted, it is an easy thing to determine that an arrow stays on the bow for about 0.025 seconds (page 7). Within this very short time, the fate of the shot has been decided by the perfection of the archer's form, and aim.

We can measure the bow's brace height in the traditional way. We can draw the bow upon a tillering tree to watch the limbs bend, paying attention to whether the top limb is leading or lagging, and we can shoot the bow.

What else can we do?

This brings us back to Harry and his bow hand. When Harry discovered that he could feel in the bow grip the difference between the upper and lower limb forces, it got him to thinking and experimenting.

What he did next was to measure the tiller of the braced bow not just at the fadeouts, as is traditional, but at even increments of 3 inches down the entire length of the limb. What he found was that the tiller varied one way or the other, positive or negative, as he moved down the limb.

And so he set out to make the tiller the same. Using his sandpaper he worked to even the tiller all the way down the limbs. It should be mentioned at this point that Harry's bows are of even limb length.

What he found is that if he tillered his bows so that they had an even 3/16 inch to 1/4 inch of positive tiller (meaning the upper limb is weaker than the lower limb) every 3 inches down the entire length of the bow, his bows shot with more forgiveness, less noise, and faster speed.

The faster speed is an interesting clue. What Harry found is that as he changed from the traditional measured-only-at-the-fades tiller to his even-all-the-way-down-the-limb tiller, the bow would lose a couple pounds. And yet it would pick up several feet per second in speed.

How can this be? A weaker bow shooting faster than a stronger bow?

Here is where we must examine our assumptions. It is generally assumed, and I have said it myself in this book, that by making the limbs from several layers of materials (wood, fiberglass, carbon), the limbs become homogeneous and behave as though they were made of some uniform material like steel. This is mostly true. But what Harry discovered is that when it comes to achieving the best tiller for a bow, the organic nature of the limbs (laminated or not) still causes variations that can't be ignored.

By accepting that our assumption of homogenous limbs does not apply completely to tillering, we can go on to explain why a weaker bow shoots faster than it did when it was stronger: The bow has become more efficient.

Whether Harry himself realized it, he did that thing that Galileo Galilei calls out as the deepest truth of science and the scientific method:

In questions of science, the authority of a thousand is not worth the humble reasoning of a single individual.

Harry made an observation about his bow: The limbs are not pulling equally. He devised an experiment to see if he could correct the problem: He changed his tillering to include measuring the entire limb. And he tested the results of his experiment against the current known facts: Harry compared the speed of the old tillering method to the new tillering method and found that the new method had increased the arrow's speed.

Is this method Harry has devised unique? I am sure not. Archery has been discovered and rediscovered so many times through history that it is highly unlikely to be original, and impossible to prove one way or the other.

Is this the best method of tillering to employ? While I am sure there are even better ways to tiller a bow, so far it is the best method I have tried.

Will the results of tillering a bow this way always be better than the traditional methods of measuring tiller at the fades and observing limb action on a tillering tree? No. I am sure there are plenty of bowyers with an artist's eye and a finer hand that can tiller a bow in short order to perform as well as or better than any bow I can make.

The advantage of this method is that it allows a person of average skill to approach perfect tiller using a process that is well defined.

And therein lies its beauty, at least to me.

Application of Tillering Method to the ASL

So now the question arises, can we use this method to tiller our American Semi-Longbows? I believe the answer is a qualified yes. Qualified, because we must make allowances for the differences between Harry's hybrid bow and our ASL. There are two differences we must consider.

The first is limb length. Harry's hybrid has limbs of even length. Our ASL has an upper limb that is two inches longer than the lower limb. This will require additional thought.

The second difference is the profile of the bow. Harry's hybrid bow has a straighter limb profile than our ASL when strung, and it has a slight recurve at the end of the limb. Of course our ASL has a smooth curve from fadeout to string nock. This will work in our favor.

As Harry told me of his new tillering method and showed me the results, it got me thinking about how to apply this method to the ASL.

One of the dangers in designing and building a device is that we may operate under the false impression that there is only one way to skin the proverbial cat, and that if we pick the wrong way, we have failed. I have found that there are usually many ways to solve a problem, and that the most important step in solving it is to begin.

And so I will begin by thinking about the longer upper limb of the ASL and why I made it so.

I made the upper limb longer because many better bowyers before me did it that way, and they said it worked. So I did it and found that it did indeed make a better bow than a bow of equal-length limbs. The improvements are numerous, but they all hinge upon the fact that the center of balance of the bow has been moved from the center of the grip up toward the arrow shelf. The result of moving the center of balance toward the arrow shelf is to better balance the forces applied to the limbs. Uneven limb length means more even forces.

As the forces become more balanced, the requirement to positively tiller the upper limb is diminished. By this reasoning, it appears that if Harry's method does apply to the ASL, it will need to be modified in that the positive tiller should be reduced.

And now for the second difference: that of different limb profiles. If the limbs are of a deflex/reflex design, then when the bow is strung their shape can vary from a straight line fadeout to string nock; to a straight line from fadeout to a slight recurve at the string nock; to even a shape which appears to look like a true ASL. Which of these shapes will provide the best combination of performance and forgiveness? And how should these shapes compare, bottom limb to top limb? I really don't know. I am sure there are as many answers as there are people who prefer these bows.

When we ask the same questions about an ASL, the questions become somewhat simplified by the character of the bow. An ASL will have limbs that generally take the same curve from fadeout to string nock. They will appear to gently bend more and more as the eye moves from fadeout to string nock. But is the curve circular, elliptical, or a combination of the two? Should the last few inches of the limb actually be straight?

Again, I do not know absolutely, what is the best profile for the bow to take to ensure best performance and forgiveness. All I can do is approximate it to the best of my ability. In keeping with the spirit of simplicity that defines the ASL, and relying on those smarter and wiser than I am, I can come to only one obvious conclusion.

Occam's razor is a problem-solving principle devised by a Franciscan friar named William of Ockham in the 14th century. The principle states that among competing hypotheses that predict equally well, the one with the fewest assumptions should be selected. To put it in his own words:

Entities must not be multiplied beyond necessity.

I have found that if I live by this rule of thumb, I cannot go too far off track. Keep the limb profile simple, and the resulting bow will come very close to being as good as it can be. And so what simple shape should it take? Here again I turn to a person whose thoughts on the technical aspects of the bow have stood the test of time. Dr. C.N. Hickman wrote in the 1930s an article for the book *Archery, the Technical Side* in which he analyzed the profile of bows to determine what shape might work best. He observed:

If the curvature [of a bow] is constant for all parts, then [the bow] is bending in the arc of a circle. This fact does not seem to have been previously observed... in archery where it is desired to work all parts of a stressed member to equal values with a simple practical shape. (page 30)

Dr. Hickman's experimental proof and mathematical analysis proved to him that a bow made so that its limbs would bend in a circular arc would yield a bow with better cast, durability, and forgiveness than bows that bend in some other, non-circular, arc.

By following this path and tillering my bow so that all parts of the limb see equal stress, I know that no part shall be in danger of being stressed too much. And I will have the additional advantage of having a bow that will take a simple and pleasing shape.

So now I have the desired shape to which I will tiller the bow. And I have a method which I can use to allow me to shape the limbs to bring them to this desired shape of a circle. I know too that because the limbs are not of the same length, the radius of the arc each limb will take must be different.

Take a minute to mull over the previous paragraph. And then read the following description of how the tillering sketch was generated several times as needed.

Look at the following figure of a bow titled "Tillering sketch - even tiller lines." This is a figure I generated using my aforementioned modeling software. In this figure, you will see several collections of lines and dimensions.

You will see the shape of a braced American Semi-Longbow. This model is of a bow 66 inches nock-to-nock with an upper limb 2 inches longer than the lower limb. It has been braced to a height of 8 5/8 inches as measured from the back.

You will see two pie-slice-shaped sections. These sections help to define the limb by specifying limb length. The upper limb is 34 inches long as measured from the center of the bow. But the working part of the limb is only 25 1/2 inches as measured from the end of the fadeout. By the same reasoning, the lower limb is 23 1/2 inches. Using the dimensions shown, and the fact that the length of the arc is equal to the ratio of the contained angle divided by 360 times the radius, we can set the length of the limb as it bends through its arc.

The limb is tangent to the end of the riser.

The string is parallel to the riser.

The string is 8 5/8 inches from the riser.

The geometry of the bow is now fully defined.

Now let's look at the dotted lines contained within the arc of each limb.

The dimension groups A and D define the distances between the marks we will use to tiller a bow.

The dimensions in groups B and C represent the height, or tillering distance, we will measure when tillering our bow. Notice that the dimensions in groups B and C are all the same.

The approach I chose to make tillering the bow as easy as possible was to find where on the upper and lower limbs I could take my mea-

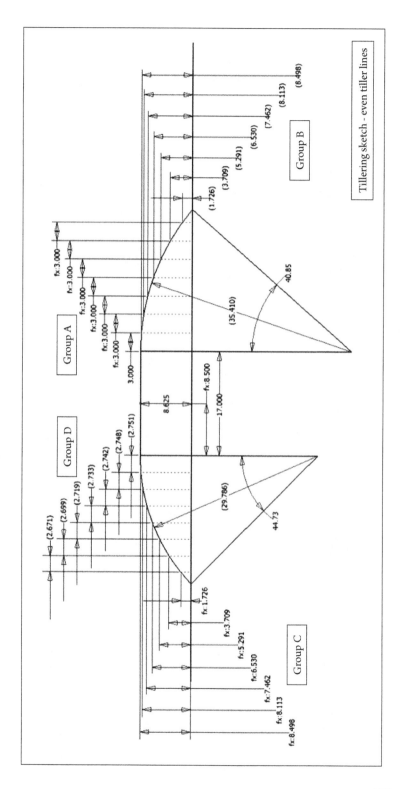

Tillering sketch - even tiller lines

177

surements such that both points would show the same brace height. Remember, the limbs are of different lengths, thus they bend with a different radius and will approach the string at different rates.

The ultimate purpose of this model was to allow me to specify the dimensions contained in group A, and to have the software provide me with the values of the dimensions in group D.

I specify values in group A. The model calculates the values in group B. I set the values in group C equal to the values in group B. And finally, the software calculates the values in group D.

By modifying the geometry of this model, it is possible to get measuring distances for bows of any length. I have included dimensions for bows from 62 to 70 inches in the table titled "Limb Tillering Marks" in the following section.

It must be mentioned that the brace height on which these models were based is not intended necessarily to be the brace height to which the actual bow is set for shooting.

It must also be mentioned that for purposes of tillering the bow, the brace height must be specified relative to the back of the bow, not the lowest point of the grip (as is common these days). Measure it from the glass, not from any overlay that may be on top of the grip area.

And finally it must be mentioned that the dimensions specified in groups A and D cannot be directly measured on the limb. The limb takes a curve, and the dimensions are in line only with the string. Therefore, to get an accurate measurement, the dimensions would have to be made on the string, and then transferred to the limb with the use of a square. To simplify this so that these steps can be avoided, the table includes dimensions that are the length of the hypotenuse formed by the vertical and horizonal legs of the triangle formed at each measuring station. This allows us to make our measurements directly on the limb.

Tillering an Actual Bow

Now that I have fully explained the method of tillering that I use to make my ASL bows shoot as best they can, we will look at the steps of tillering an actual bow.

As mentioned at the beginning of this chapter, by retillering bows that Harry had thought were tillered well, he gained speed and forgiveness in his bows. I saw the same thing in my bows. In fact, I have seen as much as 10 feet per second of speed gained by tillering the bow so that both limbs take a circular profile at even tiller. Retillering a bow is often more difficult than tillering a bow for the first time.

We will look at an example of tillering a new bow now.

After a bow has been removed from the hot box, cut to length, and brought roughly to the profile lines, I then cut the string nocks into the limb tips.

At this point, I will string the bow and check the weight. I will also observe the limbs to see if one is grossly overpowering the other. If all looks well, I don't worry about tiller at this point.

I continue to work the limb profile until I get within 5 pounds of the desired drawing force. Hopefully this will not involve much sanding.

Once the bow has been brought within 5 pounds of the desired drawing force and the handle section has been sanded down to a width of 1 1/8 inch, I cut the arrow shelf out.

These steps were explained in detail in Chapter 8. With the bow brought to this point, we have now come to the job of tillering.

The first step is to mark measuring points on the sides of the limb for each measuring station. These measuring station points are taken from the following table:

Limb Tillering Marks							
Bow	Station						
	1	2	3	4	5	6	7
62 inch (15 in riser)							
Top limb	3.00	3.03	3.08	3.16	3.28	3.46	3.70
Bottom limb	2.74	2.76	2.81	2.89	3.01	3.17	3.42
64 inch (15 in riser)							
Top limb	3.00	3.02	3.07	3.14	3.23	3.37	3.56
Bottom limb	2.76	2.78	2.82	2.88	2.98	3.11	3.30
66 Inch (17 in riser)							
Top limb	3.00	3.02	3.07	3.14	3.24	3.40	3.60
Bottom limb	2.75	2.77	2.82	2.89	2.99	3.13	3.33
68 inch (17 in riser)							
Top limb	3.00	3.02	3.06	3.12	3.20	3.31	3.46
Bottom limb	2.76	2.78	2.82	2.87	2.95	3.06	3.21
70 inch (17 in riser)							
Top limb	3.00	3.02	3.05	3.10	3.17	3.26	3.38
Bottom limb	2.78	2.79	2.82	2.87	2.93	3.02	3.14
--All dimensions are in inches--							

Tillering marks on
back and side of bow

Once these side marks are made, I transfer those marks to the back
of the bow so that when the side marks are removed by sanding, they can
be easily restored.

The next step is to make a table into which you will record your measurements. Don't rely on memory, as you will make these measurements
multiple times. By writing them down, you can preserve a record of your
progress as well as the outcome. Leave room in your table for many, many
measurements.

String the bow so that the brace height measured at the handle is 8
5/8 inches. Measure from the glass on the back of the bow.

Take note of how the limbs are bending as your measurements progress down the limbs. Often you will see some measurements that tend to
be positive, and some that tend to be negative. The actual measurement is
not important. What is important is the difference between the readings
at the matching station on each limb. The goal is to approach even tiller,
or just slightly positive tiller.

To adjust the tiller, do not remove material from the back or belly
face, but rather from the corners of the limbs. Take more from the back
corners of the bow than from the belly if you need to reduce the draw
force. Take more from the belly corners than from the back if you need to
change the shape of the limb. Take gentle strokes so that the shape of the
bow is not drastically changed, and so that you don't make narrow or wide

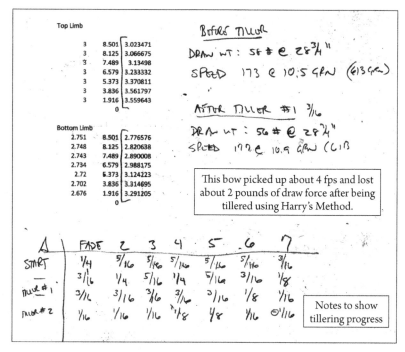

	FADE	2	3	4	5	6	7	
START	1/4	5/16	5/16	5/16	5/16	5/16	3/16	
TILLER #1	3/16	1/4	5/16	1/4	5/16	3/16	1/8	
TILLER #1	3/16	3/16	3/16	3/16	3/16	1/8	1/16	
TILLER #2	1/16	1/16	1/16	1/8	1/8	1/16	0 1/16	Notes to show tillering progress

places in the limb.

As you make adjustments, you will need to consider the effect on the entire limb. Make small changes, measure often. Draw the bow repeatedly so that the changes can register in the wood.

When you get close, stop.

Shoot the bow a lot. Don't worry about fine tuning arrows or doing anything about accuracy. The reason to shoot the bow at this point is to allow the limbs to settle in and take set. As they do, your tillering measurements will change.

Each adjustment you make will result in smaller and smaller changes in the bow until everything balances out.

I have found that the process of tillering, shooting, and tillering some more can take two weeks of dedicated effort. If you shoot only on the weekends, it could take a month or more.

Don't shortchange this process.

New bowyers, myself included, seem hell-bent on getting a coat of poly on the bow as soon as possible. Try to resist this temptation. A bow covered with glass on back and belly can be shot reliably without a finish forever, so long as it is kept out of the rain.

We have a bit of a chicken-and-egg conundrum at this point. Take note: It's hard to shoot a bow if the handle isn't at least mostly shaped. But once the handle is mostly shaped, it's hard to get a good reading on a tillering tree since the shelf on a tillering tree doesn't really mimic a human hand too well.

What I have found to answer this conundrum is that the value of observing the bow on the tillering tree is more of a confirmation of good tiller than a tool to achieve that tiller. So I pretty quickly shape the handle just enough to allow me to comfortably shoot the bow, while still allowing meaningful observation on the tillering tree.

Once the bow has been tillered at a brace height of about 8 5/8 inches, it seems to respond well through the rest of the draw.

After I have the bow tillered and shooting well, I like to put it on the tillering tree one more time. Draw the bow to 28 inches and take a picture.

I can then put this picture on my computer and overlay graphics on top of it. I can add circles to the limbs to verify they are bending smoothly, and I can add an arrow shaft to verify that the arrow will lay on the bow and be about perpendicular to a line connecting the string nocks in the limbs.

In this figure of the bow on the tillering tree, you can see that the bow is drawn from about where your middle finger would be under the arrow. The line that connects the string nocks intersects the arrow line at about 90 degrees. I am not sure that this is necessary, but it is pleasing to the eye. You can see that the limbs take a circular tiller until about the last 6 inches of the limb, at which point they become more straight.

It is interesting to note that when the bow is braced to 8 5/8 inches, the limbs bend in circles that have different diameters; but when drawn, they bend in circles that have the same diameter. The circles shown in the figure have the same diameter.

This can be explained by the fact that when braced, there are no external forces acting on the bow. Therefore the bow will bend in response to the internal forces created between the string and the bow. When drawn, there are external forces acting on the bow at the grip and at the string. When these forces are balanced out, the result is that the limbs of a well tillered bow will take the same arc.

It is also interesting to note that a line drawn from the intersection points of the two circles will intersect the handle at about the center of pressure of the grip.

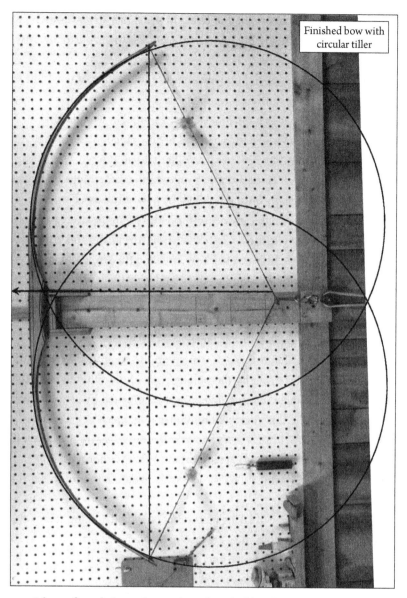

Finished bow with circular tiller

I have found that when a bow bends like this, it shows the most forgiveness, is quiet, and gives the best cast I have achieved. In short, it makes meat.

Further Study

Something that hinders us closet bowyers (we would probably be more accurately described as garage bowyers), is the lack of opportunity to compare notes and designs with others of our ilk. When reading good books on making bows, like the *Bowyers Bible*, I am always jealous of the good fortune those fellows had of living in proximity to each other and seeming to have so much time, effort, and materials to devote to their passion.

In an attempt to see and understand what others have done, I like to take pictures of bows others have made to see how their tillers worked out. What they felt was a good job. What they thought would work.

Another advantage of taking pictures of bows and looking at them on my computer is that I can zoom in on different parts to see what is happening up close. It gives me an opportunity to measure things I couldn't measure while biting my lip and holding the bow at full draw.

One of the things I can measure on the computer screen easily, safely, and accurately is the angle between the string and the bow limb. The smaller the angle between the bow limb and the string, the more efficiently the bow will pull, and the more smoothly the bow will draw. As we discussed in the first design chapter, the sense of stacking in the draw can be blamed one hundred percent on the angle between the bow limb and the string. We call this string angle.

Another thing that is easily measured on the computer screen is the angle formed in the string by the pulling rope of the tillering tree. This is effectively the angle that the fingers will be pinched by as the bow is drawn. Maximizing this angle will minimize finger pinch and reduce errors caused by the release. I don't like to call it the release; I prefer to call it the loose. What it is called isn't important. What is important is to realize that the less the string pinches the fingers together, the smoother the loose will be.

Another advantage of taking pictures of bows and looking at the tiller is to distill the truth from the advertising. I have heard many arguments and claims made about mysterious and secret tillering that supposedly makes the best and fastest bows. What I have found, though, is that when bows are drawn on a tillering tree and exposed to the lens of a camera, the fact is that they all bend in a circle. This is true regardless of their braced profiles. (I must qualify this statement with the fact that I have not studied every bow ever made.)

I have to make another confession too.

I have printed out the profile shown in the tillering sketch figure to full scale. I don't have to take the time to transfer tillering marks to my bow and then measure and record the values at each station. I simply have to lay the bow on top of the tillering sketch and see what's what.

This saves me much time, but the results are no different than what you will see by going through the tillering process as I described it.

As my tillering experience has increased, and my skills have improved, I rely more and more on the sketch upon which I lay the bow. I rely less and less on the tillering tree. That said, I always take a picture of the bow at full draw and superimpose circles upon it to verify that the limbs are indeed bending correctly at full draw. I have yet to find a full draw bow picture that contradicts the results of the bow laid upon the tillering sketch.

All of this adds up to give me a pretty high level of confidence that I understand what makes a well tillered bow, and how to achieve it. As I stated in the beginning of this chapter, I am sure there are many better bowyers who are more artistic and have a better natural feel for "what's right" than I do. This chapter was not meant for them.

That said, as we improve the design of our bows by nailing down the perfect taper, limb length, riser length, material, number of laminations, etc., etc., tillering will become easier. The bows will mostly come to tiller when they are cut and sanded to their outlines.

The process of tillering will become more a process of confirmation and less a process of change.

I have included some pictures of bows at full draw for your consideration at the end of this section. Some are made by other bowyers more experienced than myself. Some are made by me. The bows of my own manufacture I include to show the tiller from different limb profiles.

By studying these profiles, you will be able to draw your own conclusions about what is important.

I encourage you to take pictures of your bows as you tiller them and gain experience. I have taken as many as 10 pictures through the tillering process. It almost provides a "stop-action" perspective on tillering a bow.

Keep these pictures in a folder on your computer. Label them so you can keep them organized and maintain the connection to each bow.

It's not only informative to see how the tiller changes, it's fun to look back on what you have done and see how you have improved.

I won't go into too much detail about how I take the pictures or process them to get the circles superimposed on them, as the software will, no doubt, change over time. Suffice it to say that the software I use is what has come free on my computer. The camera I use is a point-and-shoot digital camera mounted on the same tripod I use with my chronograph.

I try to stage the camera exactly the same for every picture so that the scale will not vary too much picture to picture, bow to bow.

The trick is to hold the tillering rope while at the same time taking the picture. If I bite my tongue just right, it's not too hard. I use the timer, set to two seconds, to take the picture. This eliminates any movement due to my hand.

I include a text box in the pictures to record basic relevant data. A few of the acronyms used may need explaining:

- LLSA - lower limb string angle
- ULSA - upper limb string angle
- FA - finger angle
- NTN - nock to nock

And now to the pictures...

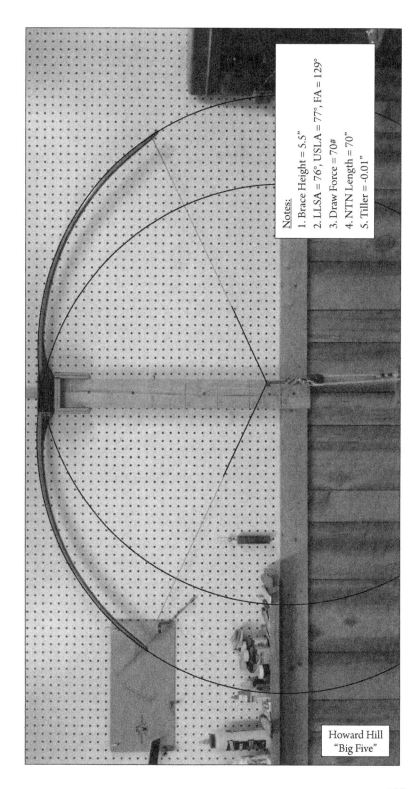

Notes:
1. Brace Height = 5.5"
2. LLSA = 76°, USLA = 77°, FA = 129°
3. Draw Force = 70#
4. NTN Length = 70"
5. Tiller = -0.01"

Howard Hill
"Big Five"

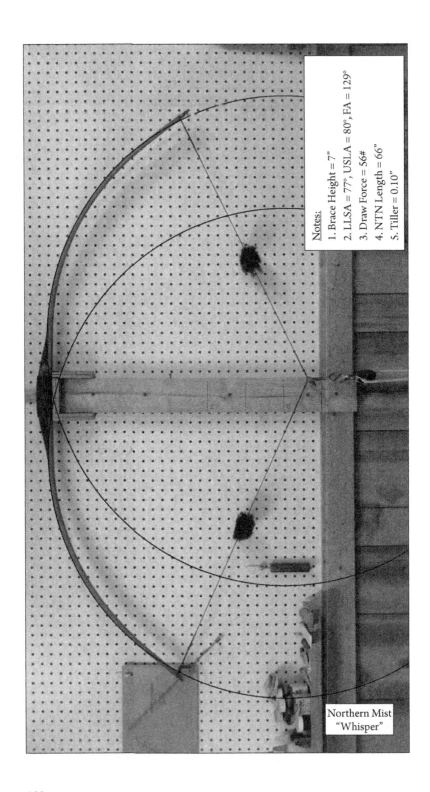

Notes:
1. Brace Height = 7"
2. LLSA = 77°, USLA = 80°, FA = 129°
3. Draw Force = 56#
4. NTN Length = 66"
5. Tiller = 0.10"

Northern Mist
"Whisper"

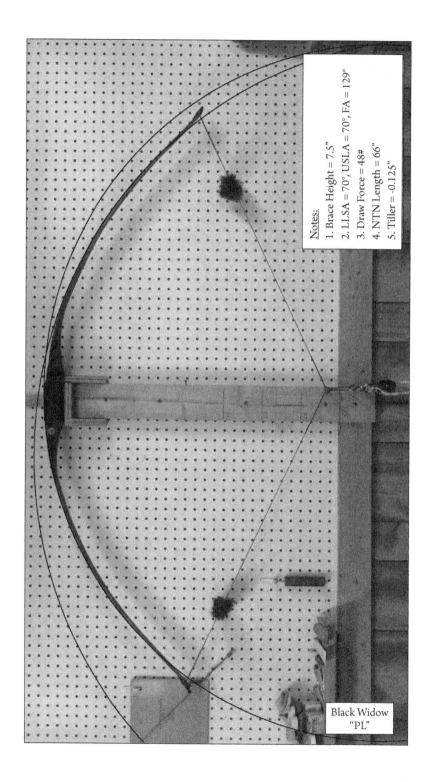

Notes:
1. Brace Height = 7.5"
2. LLSA = 70°, USLA = 70°, FA = 129°
3. Draw Force = 48#
4. NTN Length = 66"
5. Tiller = -0.125"

Black Widow
"PL"

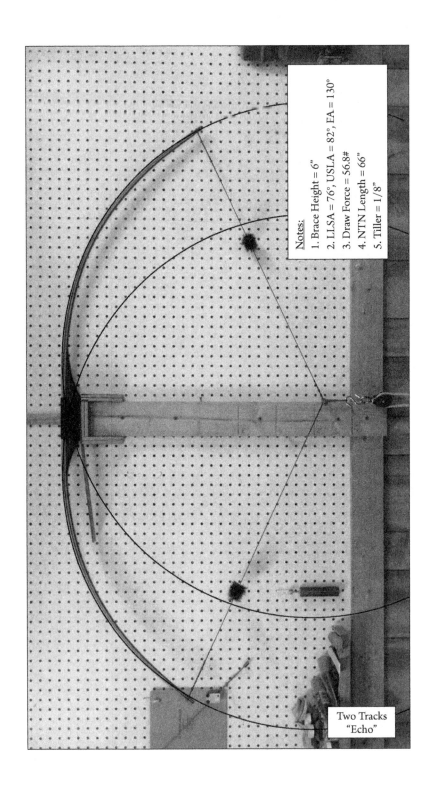

Notes:
1. Brace Height = 6"
2. LLSA = 76°, USLA = 82°, EA = 130°
3. Draw Force = 56.8#
4. NTN Length = 66"
5. Tiller = 1/8"

Two Tracks
"Echo"

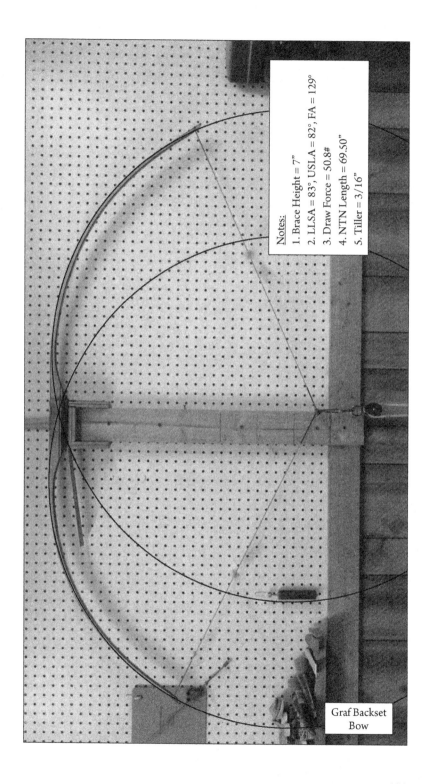

Notes:
1. Brace Height = 7"
2. LLSA = 83°, USLA = 82°, FA = 129°
3. Draw Force = 50.8#
4. NTN Length = 69.50"
5. Tiller = 3/16"

Graf Backset Bow

191

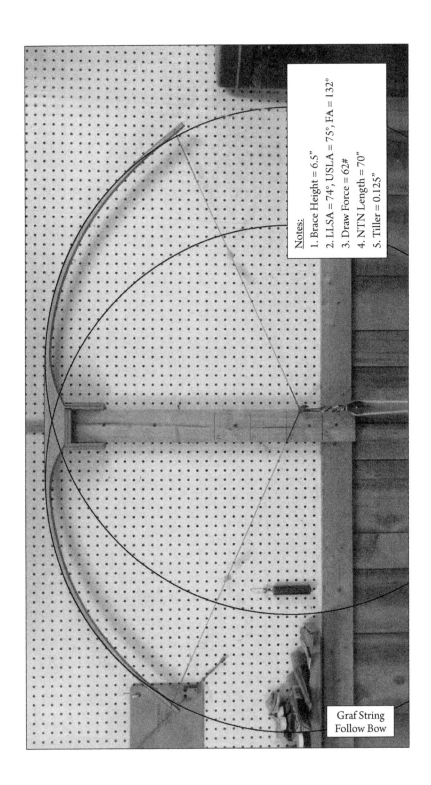

Notes:
1. Brace Height = 6.5"
2. LLSA = 74°, USLA = 75°, FA = 132°
3. Draw Force = 62#
4. NTN Length = 70"
5. Tiller = 0.125"

Graf String
Follow Bow

192

One More Tillering Tool

As I stated before, the character of the limb is determined by its length and its thickness. Width has almost nothing to do with it.

Once you have made the same bow ten, twenty, or a hundred times over, there will be very few surprises. That's in the domain of professional bowyers. For me, a strictly amateur hobbyist, I rarely make the same bow twice.

Since I am always treading where I haven't tread before, I sometimes have trouble not only getting the limbs to statically balance, but also have trouble getting both limbs of the bow to move at the same rate.

This brings up the notion of the difference between static balance and dynamic balance.

For a bow to be statically balanced, all that is required is that both limbs bend about the same amount when drawn.

For a bow to be dynamically balanced, both limbs must return to their braced position at essentially the same rate and must come to rest at the same moment in time.

If I were concerned about only static balance when I tillered a bow, I would simply cut the nocks in the bow, and then proceed to narrow the back of the stronger bow limb until the limbs come into balance.

If the limbs are pretty close to start with, this usually works fine.

If, for some reason, the limbs are not close to being in static balance (for example, if the tiller at fades is out by a half inch or more), it may be more prudent to shorten the weaker limb until the limbs come into balance.

I have found that when the tiller is out so dramatically, the limbs are often not in dynamic balance. This can be felt in the bow as extra shock when it is shot. It also serves to make the bow less forgiving, slower, and more jumpy.

I have found that shortening the weaker limb instead of narrowing the stronger limb serves to bring the limbs into static balance as well as bringing them into dynamic balance.

The first few times I shortened the weaker limb, I did it by simply filing in some new string nocks; making the limb 1/8 to 1/4 inch shorter. This works, but makes for more effort in finishing the bow. It also involves guesswork to get the position of the new string nocks correct.

I wish I had a technique that would allow me to find where the string nocks belong, exactly, without having to cut the nocks in until I know where they need to be. While this necessity has led to invention, the inventions have not panned out, thus far.

What I have done is sand the bow limbs down to the layout line (or close to it). I then cut the nocks in the upper limb according to my layout drawn on the back of the bow.

Then I affix my adjustable string nock tool to the bottom limb and position the nock about where I think it needs to be.

I then string the bow and see how it looks. Note the weight, draw the bow, and feel it. Check all my tillering marks, etc.

If I find I need to move the bottom nock to make the limb stronger or weaker, I do it by adjusting my nock tool in or out.

Once I find the correct position of the string nock, I mark it with a pencil, unstring the bow, and cut the nocks into the limb as usual.

The problem is the tool. What I have tried to do is make an adjustable nock that sits on the back of the bow and is anchored on the square end of the limb. This allows me to move the lower nock as required to achieve tiller. The problem is that I have not come up with a reliable tool that does not threaten to come off at every instant and cause calamity.

So far, this method has mostly been a failure. But I mention it here in the hopes that it will stir imagination and that someone who reads these words will be inspired to come up with something that works.

Final Thoughts

As I mentioned at the beginning of this chapter, the techniques I outline here are intended for the new bowyer. No matter how well you ride a bike now, you must have started out not knowing how to ride. You either used training wheels, or you had a trusted ally steady your seat as you picked up speed.

The profile dimensions I laid out in this chapter were for 15- and 17-inch risers. (I have found that longer risers make for more stable, easy-shooting bows more forgiving of a new bowyer's skill.) As my tillering skills have improved and I have been able to make the limbs work together well, I have been able to utilize shorter risers. Shorter risers mean longer limbs, which in turn mean smaller string angles and more forgiving and faster bows. As I made this transition, I was also making better laminations and thus better bow blanks. I found that I didn't need to rely so heavily on my tillering method as the bow blanks got better and as my eye improved. Since there is a lot of math and effort required to produce the tillering tables, and as I wasn't dependent on them, I didn't update them with shorter risers.

I understand now that training wheels have fallen out of fashion, and so I hesitate to compare this tillering method to them. That said, the method described here is intended as an aid to get you going. If you build bows, you will need a place to start. Where you go from there is part of the great adventure.

Chapter 11
Finishing the Bow

Right up front here I must say that I know very little about all of the different types of finishes that can be applied to a bow. I expect an entire book could be written just on finishing a bow, but because of my limited experience with it, this will be, not surprisingly, the shortest chapter in the book.

I have tried a variety of the rub-on oils and polyurethanes. I can say to stay away from acrylics and lacquers as they are not flexible enough or durable enough for bows. I have not tried the epoxy coatings as they require air brushes to apply.

I mostly just use spray-on polyurethane that I buy from the local hardware store. The only choice I need to make is the level of gloss desired.

The level of gloss is controlled by additives that serve to dull the finish. The more additives, the duller the finish. It is also true that the more additives in a finish, the less durable it is.

Therefore, a gloss finish provides the best protection to the bow. I like to apply four or five coats of gloss finish. I then apply a final coat of semi-gloss. This gives me the desired level of protection while keeping the shine down.

Preparing the Bow and Applying the Finish

Once your bow has been shot in and is ready to finish, it will need a final sanding. Usually by this time, I have gone over the entire bow with 150-grit sandpaper. What is needed now is to simply bring the surface

India ink and pen

Wood stabilizer

to its final smoothness and to remove from the grip the oils and dirt that have accumulated while shooting.

I do this with 350- to 400-grit sandpaper. Whatever is available.

I like to cover the entire exposed wood surface of the bow with Elmer's Rotted Wood Stabilizer before applying the polyurethane. I have tried a variety of grain fillers, but none seems to work as well. The Elmer's product fills the grain the best and produces a nice, deep finish. That said, liquid super glue works well too. I just prefer to work with the non-toxic stabilizer formula.

After the stabilizer has dried overnight, a final rub-down with fine steel wool is the next step. Most folks warn against the use of steel wool, as it can cause rust spots in the finish if small particles of steel are left on the bow. I avoid this by blowing the bow off with my compressor before applying the finish. It has never been a problem for me.

At this point, it is customary to mark the bow with its draw weight, maker, and name, if appropriate. I do this with a fine nib pen and India ink. I keep black and white ink on hand and use whichever is appropriate, based on the color of the belly glass. Allow the ink to dry for 20 minutes before proceed-

Bow ready for spray

ing to apply the finish.

I hang the bow in my tractor shed by a small wire wrapped around the nock of the lower limb, which is then looped over a chain affixed to the roof of the shed.

I then apply the finish to the bow and allow it to hang for two days before putting the bow into service. I leave it in the tractor shed for a couple hours before moving it into the shop.

Obviously my precautions are not nearly enough to keep dust out of the finish. If you want to have a perfect finish on your bow, you will need a better method than this. This method does produce a good finish that will protect the bow and look nice too. It's just not quite the finish you would expect when buying a bow.

Adding the Trim

Once the bow has been sealed and protected with a finish, all that is left to do is decide upon an arrow rest and strike plate combination, and what to do about the grip.

I find that a small piece of rug rest serves me just fine for an arrow rest. A small piece of leather works well too. I am not a good enough shot to judge whether lifting the arrow off the shelf contributes to a better arrow group, but I can say that having an arrow rest on the bow reduces the sound of the arrow being drawn. It also protects the bow finish.

The strike plate is another matter. What you do to the side of the arrow shelf affects how the arrow flies. It can also be used as a tuning aid.

If your arrows are showing weak, one option is to add material to the strike plate to move the arrow away from bow center. As you do this, a weak arrow will begin to fly better.

Rug rest and leather strike plate

Rug rest and no strike plate

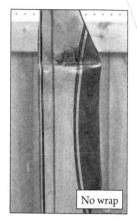

Sport wrap | Leather wrap | No wrap

Lately, I have found myself leaving the strike plate off the side of the arrow shelf. If I get my arrows tuned up for this configuration, then I get the arrow sitting as far into the shelf as possible. This is a reliable way to keep the arrow on the shelf. Moving the arrow out increases the chance that it will fall off the shelf at an inopportune moment.

Since the side of the arrow shelf is usually well rounded, I have not noticed that leaving it bare adds to the noise of the draw.

I don't care for the style of arrow rest that incorporates a single piece of leather that forms a strike plate and arrow rest and is then tucked into the handle wrap. Every arrow rest will eventually wear out. Replacing it is more work if it is tucked into the handle wrap.

Which brings us to the handle wrap.

I have tried a number of wraps on the handle, and I can say that, for the most part, it's hard to go wrong. Most anything will work. What I have found too, is that no wrap is needed.

Leather wraps look great when they are first applied, and they feel good in the hand. But if you shoot your bow a lot, they get pretty dirty pretty fast. A summer spent shooting and sweating makes for a grungy grip.

Sport wraps, available from any sporting goods store that sells tennis racquets, work well and are easy to put on and remove. They are cheap and easy and provide a good grip. They last a surprisingly long time and don't seem to get as dirty as leather.

Another option, especially if you do anything fancy to the handle section, is simply to skip the step of adding anything to the grip at all. I find a bare grip just as nice as a covered grip. So give that a try too.

Chapter 12
More Design Consideration

There is a fine line between tradition and dogma. Tradition being that body of knowledge and custom, handed down through the generations, that still adds to the good life. Dogma being that body of knowledge and custom, handed down through the generations, that doesn't. We humans are complex animals that seem to have a hard time walking these fine lines and making these distinctions.

The words tradition and dogma have almost the same definition and share synonyms. I think the difference lies not in the denotation, but in the connotation of the words. Traditions are knowledge and customs that still improve our lot in this "modern" life. Dogmas are knowledge and customs that, for whatever reason, no longer add anything positive to our lives, yet are still practiced.

In order to practice the good life as best we can, we must constantly be mindful of the things we do, and why we do them. Do they make us better people? Do they add to the fertility of the land? Are they respectful of others? If the answers are yes, then we can call this knowledge and these customs tradition. If not, maybe we shouldn't.

The American Semi-Longbow is, in part, attractive to me because it embodies the joy of casting arrows by the simplest of means. Which makes me wonder: "Why ask too many questions?" There are those that say the best American Semi-Longbow is the bow that most closely matches the bows built in the early 20th century by the greatest archer of all time, Howard Hill.

Some folks want to leave it there and resent it when anyone dares to change a thing. I come up against this attitude a lot.

If we look more closely, we will see that those lucky people who were taught by Hill, those great bowyers that came after him, all contributed something to the design, even if it was just to put a finer touch on the craftsmanship of the bow.

The characteristics of the bow that make it shoot so well, be so reliable, and look like it does seem well defined. But that shouldn't keep us from experimenting, from adding to the tradition.

The bow that Howard Hill designed worked well for him. I have to point out, though, that he was the only Howard Hill. There might be changes to the bow that would make it work better for someone else — in my case — me.

One obvious change that is hopefully acceptable and allowable is the draw force. We can't all shoot a 100-pound bow. If we were to stick absolutely to the bow that Hill designed, we would all have to shoot a high draw force bow.

If we can accept this change, can't we accept others too?

In the spirit of embracing the American Semi-Longbow for what it is, and not trying to make it into something it isn't, I offer these last few observations about bow design as tools that can be used to understand why the bow does what it does, and to help you make the best bow/archer/arrow machine you can make.

Limb Dimensions

I have mentioned several times in this book that the nature of the bow limb is determined by its length and its thickness. I will talk about it once again, as understanding this is so important to the bowyer who hopes to make an efficient bow.

To design an efficient bow, and by efficient I mean a bow that casts an arrow as fast as it can for its given draw force, the limbs must be stressed close to their maximum working limit. If they are stressed more, they would be in danger of breaking. If they are stressed less, they cannot reach their full potential.

Taking a bow close to its maximum working limit is what makes a winning flight bow. Flight bows live fast and die young by design. They are taken to the very edge of failure so that they can cast their arrows as far as possible. To do this, durability is sacrificed.

Because durability is paramount in a reliable hunting bow, a good hunting bow must not be taken to this limit. But to achieve the fastest arrow we can get, we must approach this limit.

How close you want to get is personal choice.

Regardless of how close you want to get, it is helpful to know what affects the stress in the bow, and how to optimize it.

Bowyers used to struggle with things like cross section. What is the best cross section? Flat back and round belly like the English Long Bow? Completely round? Oval?

Thankfully Paul Klopsteg, in his article "Physics of Bow and Arrows" in *Archery, The Technical Side*, makes a convincing argument that the rectangular cross section, with some trapping as desired, makes the best bow limb because it results in the most balanced stress, back to belly. Luckily for us, making laminated bows as I have discussed lends itself to using this efficient cross section.

Bowyers also used to struggle with what profile their bow should take when brought to full draw. Should it bend in an ellipse? Should it bend in a circle? Should it only bend out of the fades?

C. N. Hickman, in his article "Effects of Thickness and Width on Its Form of Bending" in *Archery, The Technical Side*, proved mathematically that a bow limb will store the most energy when every part of the limb is stressed equally. He went on to prove that the shape a bow limb will take, when equally stressed at all points, is a circle.

Strictly speaking, Hickman's work was based on a limb of either constant thickness and tapered width, or tapered thickness and constant width. Our modern glassed bows have both a tapered width and a tapered thickness. This means they do not truly meet the condition of constant stress. But the tapers are so slight that they come close, and the fiberglass can handle the extra stress.

If we accept what these engineers and scientists, who loved the bow as much as we do, discovered by their experimentation and analysis, we can conclude that there are only two dimensions left to consider: length and thickness.

These two properties of the limb work to affect not only the draw force a limb displays, but also its dynamic response to being loosed by the archer.

202

The longer a limb is for a given thickness, the weaker it is. We can understand this easily by our understanding of a lever. The dynamic property we may not be so familiar with is the fact that the longer a limb is, the more slowly it will return to its rest position after being let go.

Do not jump to conclusions and think that a longer-limbed bow is necessarily slower than a shorter-limbed bow. You will have forgotten that a longer limb does not have to move as far as a shorter limb during the draw cycle.

You must remember too that a longer limb experiences less stress than shorter limbs for a given draw length.

If you have your thinking cap on just now, you will realize that if the riser of the bow is long (resulting in an overall long bow) and the limbs are short (resulting in a faster natural frequency), you can make a fast and durable bow. This is true, but will it still be an ASL?

The thicker a limb is for a given length, the stronger it is. We can understand this easily too by our experience with a lever. The dynamic property we may not be so familiar with is the fact that a thicker limb will return more quickly to its rest position after being let go.

This is why you hear that a good American Semi-Longbow will always have a thick core. A thicker bow will shoot faster.

As always, there is a balancing act. With thickness comes stress. Too much stress will undo your bow and turn it into scrap.

So the challenge to a budding bowyer is to balance the thickness and length of the limbs to provide the best, most dependable cast possible.

I have found that for the bows I have made, the best ones that were 66 inches in length or shorter have had a taper of 0.006 inch/inch. 66-inch bows seem to be hard to nail down. I have had good ones with tapers of 0.006 inch/inch and good ones with tapers of 0.004 inch/inch. For bows over 66 inches, a taper of 0.004 inch/inch seems to have worked the best.

I give you these tapers so that you will have a starting point in building your bows. I don't give them to you as the last word in what is best.

The reason I mention these tapers now is that choosing the taper will lead to the required core thickness for a given draw force.

As you consider your limb design, I would also like to remind you that they call a longbow a longbow for a reason. It is long. There is a tendency these days to try and make bows as short as possible. I think this tendency has shortchanged the longbow. I believe a longbow works best

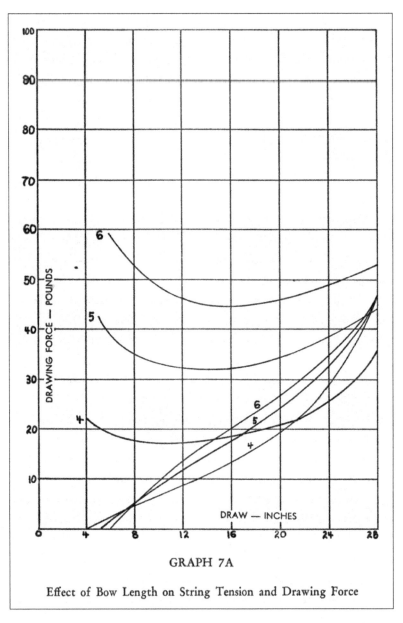

GRAPH 7A

Effect of Bow Length on String Tension and Drawing Force

when it is long. To encourage you to consider making your bow longer than you might normally want to, I will include a graph taken from the book *Archery, The Technical Side.*

This graph shows curves for three bows, all of the same draw force at a 27 1/2-inch draw length. These bows were 4, 5, and 6 feet in length and had a stiff handle section of 8 inches.

The upper three curves show the tension in the string as the bow was drawn. You can see that the tension was greatest at brace height and decreased as the bow was pulled to about 14 inches in draw, at which point the tension began to increase again until the full draw length was reached. You can see that the longest bow had the greatest string tension.

String tension is not such a big deal these days with our modern string materials, like it was in the early part of the 20th century when linen was most commonly used.

The bottom three curves, and the most interesting, show the draw force curves we are all familiar with. What is interesting in these curves is that the curve for the longest bow has the most area under the curve. This area under the curve represents the stored energy in the bow. This energy (less hysteresis) is what is available to cast the arrow. The more stored energy, the faster the arrow will fly.

From these curves we can see that all other things being equal, a longer bow will cast a faster arrow.

<u>String Angle</u>

The importance of string angle was discussed in the tillering chapter. I want to mention here what affects the string angle, but first I would direct your attention to the previous graph one more time.

If you look at the peak area of the draw force curves, that area near the right side of the graph, you will notice that for the shorter bows, the slope of the curve increases at a more rapid rate than the slope of the curves for the longer bows. This is a visual representation of what stacking means: as the bow is drawn to its full draw length, the archer begins to feel the draw force increase at an ever more rapid rate until finally it feels like the bow can be drawn no more.

This stacking sensation is the result, solely, of the increase in string angle. There is no other cause. It is common to think that the sense of stacking felt by the archer is a warning from the bow that it is in danger of breaking, that it cannot take any more stress. This is not true. Neither the wood nor the fiberglass care if you know whether it is approaching its ultimate yield strength. When a bow will fail is always unknown and always a surprise, and it is never related to the sense of stacking.

This condition of increasing string angle and stacking cannot be avoided with an ASL, but it can be minimized.

It should be minimized because the sense of stacking can interfere with the archer's form and concentration. Unless it occurs exactly when the archer reaches full draw or later, it can result in an unwanted stimulus to the archer, which causes the archer to shoot before wanting to.

<u>Minimize String Angle</u>

There are but a few things the bowyer can do to minimize string angle in a bow. They are:

1. <u>Increase limb length</u>. The longer the limbs are, the more gentle their bend. The more gentle their bend, the smaller the string angle. There are two ways to increase limb length.

First and most obvious is to make the overall length of the bow longer. Making a longer bow requires the bowyer to pay special attention to the tillering of the bow. The longer the limbs get, the more uncomfortable a bow is to shoot if the tillering is off. But when the limbs are made to work together well, a longer bow is a more forgiving and faster bow and a pleasure to shoot.

The second is to make the riser shorter. Most ASLs seem to have risers that float around 15 inches in length. Reasons to make the riser longer include making the bow more gentle in the hand. Reasons to make the riser shorter include achieving a smaller string angle. We come back again to the need for good tillering. If we tiller the bow so that the limbs work together well, we can take advantage of a shorter riser while not giving up the advantages of a gentle bow.

2. <u>Discover the correct taper</u>. Finding the perfect thickness taper for the limbs of your ASL can be a challenge. Here, the pros and cons get more difficult to nail down.

If you elect to make your limbs with no taper, otherwise known as parallel taper, you will have a bow that bends more at the fades and less at the tips. This bow will shoot a heavy arrow with the most speed and energy. It will also have the highest stress in the limbs and the highest potential for hand shock.

If you elect to make your bow with a lot of taper, say 0.006 inch/inch or more, you will have a bow that bends more toward the tips and less at the fadeouts. This bow will shoot a lighter arrow well and have the least stress in the limbs with little hand shock. It will also have the greatest string angle and thus the greatest stacking sensation.

Discovering the best taper is an exercise in balance. There is no right answer. There is only this answer: "what works best for me". What I have found works best for me in this department is about 0.006 inch/inch taper for bows of 66 inches or less and about 0.004 inch/inch taper for bows longer than that. These numbers can change somewhat depending on riser length.

3. Incorporate tip wedges. Tip wedges can serve two purposes. Most importantly they can be used to stiffen the tips and move the action of the limbs toward the fadeouts. Second, and more subtly, they can be used to reinforce the tips so that modern string materials with less creep and stretch can be used.

I have run the gamut, I believe, on tip wedges. I have made them from a few inches to a foot in length. When using longer wedges I have used greater limb tapers, and vice versa. I have made the upper and lower limb wedges the same length. I have made them longer in the lower limb, and longer in the upper limb. The results of all these experiments have not been conclusive for me.

What I see in others' bows are shorter tip wedges that are either even in length, or longer in the lower (and shorter) limb. While I cannot explain exactly why, I think I have seen a subtle advantage to having shorter wedges, shallower tapers, and a slightly longer lower limb wedge.

When I make a bow this way, it seems to more easily tiller and come to full draw with both the upper limb and lower limb taking the same bend radius. Is this important? I cannot prove it either way. Does it appeal to my sense of intuition? Yes.

Symmetry, as a default condition, seems most often to prove useful. However, this is not true with regard to overall limb length. As I explained earlier, a longer top limb yields a better-balanced bow. But since we have no argument otherwise, it seems prudent to me to make the limbs bend to the same radius. Short tip wedges, the lower wedge an inch longer than the top wedge, seem to fit the bill.

Asymmetric Riser

To repeat once more, the only two dimensions that affect the character of the bow limb are length and thickness. I have also stated or inferred throughout this book that the riser is symmetric. Here I will make a short argument to violate the symmetry rule again.

When we bowyers acknowledged the fact that an asymmetric bow will answer best the need for a forgiving and accurate bow as a result of having to grasp the bow below the arrow, we opened the door on all sorts of new design problems. Hopefully I have addressed most of these through the chapters of this book. Here is one final adjustment to the design of a bow, the purpose of which is to bring the bow back toward more symmetrical limbs while maintaining the advantages of an overall longer upper limb.

If the fadeout of the lower limb is 1 inch shorter than the fadeout of the upper limb, this will make the lower limb but 1 inch shorter than the upper limb.

By making the limbs closer in length, they will be more closely matched in their natural frequency and thus their dynamic tiller.

When I make a bow of 66 inches with a symmetric riser, I need to make the lower limb 0.020 inch thinner than the upper limb in order to get the bow to tiller correctly.

When I make a bow 68 inches or longer with a symmetric riser, I need to make the lower limb 0.015 inch thinner than the upper limb in order to get the bow to tiller correctly.

When I make a bow of any length with an asymmetric riser, the need for a thinner lower limb is eliminated. The two limbs are now of the same thickness, and the actual working part of the upper limb is but 1 inch longer. This results in a bow that naturally wants to take a 1/8-inch (or a little more) positive tiller.

When I first started making bows with a longer upper limb, I did so while keeping the upper and lower limb equal in thickness. This resulted in an overly stiff lower limb that needed much work to make it statically tiller correctly with the upper limb. What I discovered when I shot the bow, though, was that I could never achieve dynamic tiller. This was evident in the strong hand shock felt during the shot.

When I started to make the lower limb thinner than the upper limb, the bows came into tiller easily and shot well. Their speed increased and the hand shock decreased. It was evident that the limbs were working better together.

When I started to use an asymmetric riser with a 1-inch-longer upper fadeout, I found that the thickness difference could be further reduced (and indeed eliminated), and that the bows became even easier to tiller and shot with the most gentle nature. Happily they were even faster.

None of these improvements were drastic. Just small and incremental improvements letting me know I was on the right path.

Making friends with the American Semi-Longbow means understanding that there is no magical formula that will result in a super-fast bow. The ASL is not about speed. It is about working together to cast an arrow accurately, reliably, quietly, and with satisfaction.

Backset vs. String Follow

The profile of a backset bow shows the limbs gently bending toward the back of the bow, away from the archer, when unstrung. The profile of a string follow bow shows the limbs gently bending toward the belly of the bow, toward the archer, when unstrung.

Before the advent of fiberglass, a discussion of which configuration was most beneficial would have been mostly moot, as most bows without the benefit of fiberglass eventually develop string follow.

Now that fiberglass has been invented and put into use in the manufacture of the American Semi-Longbow, we are faced with the choice of building our bows one way or the other.

What should drive our choice? There seem to be but two design factors.

The primary advantage of an American Semi-Longbow built with backset is increased arrow speed. Increased speed will yield a flatter trajectory, which should help accuracy. It will also yield a better penetrating arrow, which should improve the lethality of the shot.

What is the primary advantage of an American Semi-Longbow built with string follow? I will once again rely on the greater authority of Howard Hill to answer that question:

All other things being equal, a bow with string follow will be more accurate.

This answer from Hill begs further questions. What did he mean by "all other things being equal"? Equal speed? Equal bow draw force? Equal bow length?

If we could make a string follow bow that would shoot an arrow with the same speed as a backset bow of the same draw force, then it would be inherently more accurate?

Isn't accuracy the responsibility of the archer and not the bow?

These questions and more have served to energize many discussions of what makes a good ASL. In fact, if we could know the answer to these questions absolutely, the design of an ASL would become a simpler matter.

As with most things archery, I suspect the answer is specific to the archer. I will attempt to lay out what I have observed about the two designs so that you have a place to start on your own path to answering this question.

One curious observation first. I have noticed that the third option, a straight longbow with neither string follow nor backset, seems to be a mostly ignored configuration. I wonder why?

As to the question of backset or string follow, the first thing to note about the difference between the profiles is their draw force curves. Backset bows have more early draw force and thus approach their full draw force with a lower slope. String follow bows have less early force in their draw and must therefore catch up toward the back of the draw cycle, and thus have a greater slope toward the end of the draw cycle. Consider the graph of two bows, one with 1 1/2-inch backset, one with 5/8-inch string follow:

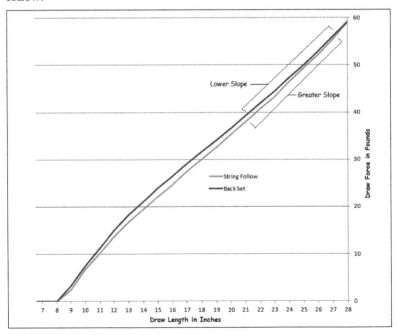

Both bows are 70-inch bows made from the same materials. They differ only in their unstrung profiles.

From this graph, it would be easy to conclude that the backset bow would be easier to draw, would have less sense of stacking, and thus would be inherently more accurate. This conclusion would be based on the gentler, steadier slope of the draw curve for the backset bow.

From this graph it can be seen that the energy stored, the area under the curve, is greater for the backset bow. Thus it will shoot a faster arrow with a flatter trajectory. This is another plus for accuracy.

But something else that needs to be considered is what happens during the early part of the draw. While the backset bow has what could be considered a better curve in the later part of the cycle, it does exhibit a steeper curve at the outset. This is known as "early draw weight."

This is the Achilles heel of the backset bow.

Study the curve again. What you see is that through the first 18 inches or so, the backset bow requires more draw force, up to 2 pounds more than the string follow bow. Could this be a problem?

Everyone is different. But for myself, I find that the quality of the shot is determined most often at the start of the draw, not at the end. I most often sense that the shot will be a good one, or a bad one, before I ever get close to anchor. The momentum of the shot is built as the draw progresses.

Consider the draw. We are most vulnerable to problems at the beginning of the draw, when we are most out of alignment with the forces that must be exerted to bend the bow to its full arc. Our string arm is most out of alignment with the arrow. Our bow arm is most out of alignment with the line that can be drawn between the ball joints of our shoulders.

As we develop the draw from start to finish, our bones and joints move more and more into alignment with the forces in the bow, steadily reducing the need for our muscles to stabilize our form.

To me, at least, it seems reasonable that one of the reasons that the string follow bow is a more forgiving bow to shoot is because it gives us a break when we need it the most. It requires less force to pull the bow when we are least able to provide it. And it makes up for this deficit toward the end of the draw when we can most easily and reliably provide it.

This ergonomic compatibility yields another plus, which allows us to make up for the string follow bow's inherently slower cast. It allows us to shoot a heavier bow more comfortably. I have found that I can shoot up to 10 pounds more draw force in a string follow bow than in a backset bow. By being able to add this additional draw force, I can compensate for the arrow speed that I might have gotten from the lower force bow.

I wonder, too, about shoulder injuries. I wonder if the common rotator cuff injuries archers suffer from might not be relieved by shooting a string follow bow?

Before fiberglass, most all bows were string follow. Wood, asked to work by itself in a bow, cannot help but follow the string. There is no empirical data to support this idea, but I would argue that people who shoot all-wood bows do not suffer from shoulder injuries at the same rate as those of us who shoot bows made with fiberglass.

Fiberglass has given us the choice to shape our bows as we see fit. We can now make a faster, more efficient bow that does not follow the string. This begs the question: Should we?

There are a few things I keep an eye on as I design and build bows. I like to take note of what happens to the string angles as I make changes to my bows. There are three angles to watch: string angle at the lower limb nock, string angle at the upper limb nock, and string angle at the fingers.

As I have mentioned before, the string angle at the limb nocks is responsible for the sense of stacking that archers feel as they draw the bow. As this angle approaches 90 degrees, the sense of stacking, of reaching a wall beyond which the bow cannot be drawn, increases. Thus it behooves us to minimize this angle.

Another sign that a bow will handle well, shoot reliably, and not bother us with too much hand shock, is when the string angles at the upper limb and lower limb are the same, or close to the same. When the angles are the same, it seems to indicate that the limbs will work together in dynamic equilibrium.

When the string angle experienced by the archer's fingers is maximized, the archer has the best chance of getting a clean release. This is no doubt true because the fingers experience less pinch with a larger string angle.

With all these points in mind, I am compelled to try and optimize all these angles, while at the same time trying to keep the bow limb string angles as equal as possible.

I have found that, all other things being equal, I have an easier time building a string follow bow that optimizes these angles.

This can be easily understood when it is observed that the limbs of a string follow bow willingly start to bend more at the fades as the bow is drawn, requiring the rest of the limb to bend less as the bow is drawn.

When I first started building bows, I started with string follow bows. It seemed sensible. Unfortunately, those first bows that I built suffered from low cast and excessive hand shock. In my confidence, born from lack of experience, I decided that this was the nature of such an inefficient configuration as a string follow bow.

I moved on to the more efficient backset bow. More pre-stress built into the limbs, thinner and more efficient limbs, the promise of power. Indeed, my first efforts at this design also yielded thumpers that worried my bow arm and caused me much discomfort. But my experience grew and my bows became more friendly, quieter, and faster.

One of the most important things that I learned through all this was the axiom that has become my anchor: The best bow design will have limbs that bend in the arc of a circle and are thus equally stressed from fadeout to tip.

This axiom may not be true. I cannot prove it, but my intuition and life experience tell me that it is plenty good enough.

My first string follow bows did not follow this axiom. They did most of their bending at the fades so that the outer parts of the limb contributed little to the cast and were left simply to go along for the ride. My most recent string follow bows do follow this axiom and are gentler and faster.

There have been many discussions about why a string follow bow is more forgiving. One explanation that comes up regularly is that string follow bows are more forgiving because the limbs want to come to rest behind the handle, as compared to a backset bow where the limbs want to come to rest in front of the handle. I don't really understand this explanation.

In both the backset and string follow bows, the limbs have a lot of momentum carrying them forward when they come to brace. I do not see why the tendency of the string follow bow to be a bit slower at this point in the shot would contribute the most to its character. Nevertheless, I include this explanation because it has been made, and its truth (one way or the other) is independent of my ability to understand it.

It seems to me that I may have made an argument here that in the end, string follow bows are better bows than backset bows. I don't mean that to be the case.

The bow an archer chooses to shoot is the result of many things, including the archer's physique, temperament, goals, and experience. There is no absolute best bow for everyone. In fact, I think that even when considered on an individual basis, there probably isn't an absolute best bow for any one archer.

One of the things I have learned is that there is no best design. Everyone is different, and as an archer, everyone will benefit from different bows. Adding to this the potential truth that as bowyers, we are more apt to build one bow design better than another, I can see that there can be no specific bow design advice I can give. I cannot explicitly determine the best form of the ASL that will perform the best for everyone.

At first, this seems a disappointment. But after further consideration, it is yet another truth that the ASL has shown to me.

Tolerance. Tolerance for difference, for doing it another way. By embracing the truth that there is no absolute best design, I am free to continue to pursue the best design. How boring would it be to finally arrive at the best design? I cannot imagine it.

As I thought about writing this book, I thought that I would be able to set down exactly how I make bows so that the reader would be able to simply build a good bow by recipe. The uncomfortable truth is that I have probably learned more from writing this book than the reader will learn by reading it.

As I embrace the fact that I will never build the best bow possible, and I look forward to the never-ending road ahead paved with ever "better" bows, my ASL reminds me that, most likely, what is true for the ASL is true in general. Maybe I already knew this, but it's always nice to get a reminder. What is it that makes a good life? Is it the same thing for everyone? Who am I to judge?

I have noticed that we archers and bowhunters can be as judgmental as the worst of them. I have listened to many conversations, read many internet forums, where someone claims to know the best way to shoot, the best equipment to use. I can just imagine what they may think about what makes a good life.

So today, as I draw a line to mark this moment in time, in the sand of what has been my path to the good life, I can say that I am again back to building and shooting string follow bows. But for how long? I cannot say.

Chapter 13
Shooting Tips

As I set to thinking about what I should include in this book, giving advice on shooting the ASL was not on my mind. While I could shoot well enough to kill a deer, that's about all I could claim.

I am sure my shooting troubles were no different from anyone else's. I suffered from the same form problems, consistency problems, and of course, the dread target panic. I won't bore you with the details.

In an effort to improve, I read everything available from all the experts on shooting, and I transitioned closer and closer to the static target form. I tried harder and harder to hold my stance just a moment longer, thinking that if I could do so, I would finally be able to hit that bullseye more often.

The harder I tried, the worse I got.

Between all the experts, and across everything I have read, there is but one thing they all agree on. I believe it is safe to call it a fact as there is unanimous consensus. That fact is that a person can concentrate on only one thing at a time. Applied to archery, that means you can concentrate on your form, or you can concentrate on your target. You cannot concentrate on both at the same time. Violation of this truth accounts, in my case at least, for more misses than any other cause.

The style archers adopt for shooting their bows, I believe, should be determined by their personality and their goals. Part of living the good life is allowing other people to do the same. The good life cannot be defined by one person for another. I believe this truth flows through everything we do, including shooting.

What compelled me to finally include this chapter in the book is, ironically, a violation of this truth. I believe the method of shooting that is outlined here is actually better, and can be proven so, for the archer who chooses to shoot the American Semi-Longbow in the pursuit of hunting.

I offer my apologies to those who prefer the static style of target form. In the case of hunting with the ASL, you are wrong.

The Swing Draw and Why It Works

I believe the dynamic style of the swing draw is the best method for shooting and hunting with the ASL. If you don't believe me, I don't blame you.

In fact, I tried the swing draw several times based on advice given by such people as Howard Hill and John Schulz without success. I was not able to stand on their shoulders. Small wonder.

Then I had the good fortune to strike up a written correspondence, and later phone conversations, with one of the better bowyers of the American Semi-Longbow working today. His name is Nate Steen and he is the bowyer and owner of Sunset Hill Archery. It was upon Nate's shoulders that I was finally able to stand and see the way of the swing draw.

If this chapter has value and truth, the credit for the words and content belong solely to Nate. As I endeavor to communicate the methods and insights that Nate gave to me, I will inevitably mix his words with mine. It cannot be helped.

Before I get into how to learn the swing draw, I want to share some observations about what it is, how it works, and why it works.

The swing draw is a dynamic method of shooting an arrow. By dynamic I mean that the archer never stops moving. This can be better understood by comparing it to the more common target form.

When archers employ target form, they will take their stance, draw their bow to anchor, settle, aim, and release. Target form requires that archers stack their bones to most efficiently resist the compressive forces imposed on their bow arm and back, come to draw, and anchor their string hand for at least a moment at their chosen anchor point. When they reach anchor, they stop. They become static.

When archers employ the swing draw, they will take their stance, draw their bow to anchor, and release. There is no pause at anchor. The archers never stop. They remain dynamic.

This is the most significant difference between target form and the swing draw, and the most significant advantage of the swing draw. The archer never stops moving.

Target form is inherently static. The swing draw is inherently dynamic. Target form depends more upon the bones of the skeleton for stability and consistency. The swing draw depends more upon the muscles for stability and consistency.

There is a reason that target archers use bows with draw forces in the thirties and low forties. There is a reason that hunters use bows with draw forces in the fifties and above.

Shooting a bow is a balancing act. If your intent is to shoot only a target, then you can move the balance toward lighter bows and skeletal stability because your goal is simply to get the arrow to the target. If your intent is to hunt animals, then you should move toward heavier bows and muscular stability because your goal in this case, is to put the arrow completely through the animal.

Our muscles are amazing motors that perform their duty flawlessly. They perform their duty flawlessly for us if we remember their job. Their job is to move.

Muscles move our bodies precisely where we want them to be in time and space. But they are not so good at keeping us in one spot without moving.

For example, pick a spot on the table in front of you, or on the arm rest of the chair you are in. Move your index finger from your nose to that spot, and back again. If you do it several times, you will likely find that you can place your finger precisely in both places repeatedly with consistent results.

Now hold your index finger at arm's length and try to hold your finger on a point in space without moving. Chances are your finger will wobble, just a little bit. You may have noticed that as you extended your arm to locate your finger at that point, there was no wobble. Your arm moved fluidly and perfectly out. The wobble began only when you asked your arm to remain static.

Which brings us to another concept that is universally accepted as paramount to good shooting: muscle memory.

Muscle memory is not just a catch phrase to describe learning how to do a physical task. It is a real thing. Muscle memory is just as real as cognitive memory and gets stored in the brain by the same mechanisms as cognitive memory. Both cognitive memory and muscle memory have their short-term and long-term varieties, and they both get imprinted on the neurons of the brain in much the same way.

Muscle memory is the memory of motion.

Herein lies the fundamental advantage of a dynamic shooting form over a static shooting form, and upon which the method of the swing draw has been developed.

You may have noticed, by some other activity, and you surely will notice if you pursue the swing draw, that if you perform a repetitive task it may not feel natural at the time. But set it aside, sleep on it, and the next day that alien motion will now feel more natural. That is the process of converting short-term muscle memory into long-term muscle memory.

As you become familiar with the power of this knowledge, you will start to see its application in other sports and activities. You will start to understand the power of ingrained muscle memory.

Muscles know exactly where they are, as long as they are moving. As soon as we ask our muscles to stop moving, they forget exactly where they are. This leads to inconsistency.

When we swing a hammer to hit a nail, we don't start with the hammer statically suspended at its highest point, we start by swinging the hammer backwards and then smoothly swinging the hammer forward to the head of the nail.

While this may appear at first as a simple time saver, which indeed it is, its real purpose is to ensure we actually strike the nail on the head.

If you would like to prove to yourself that what I am saying here is true, try it for yourself. Hold the hammer still over your head, then swing it toward the nail. See how successful you are. Then repeat the exercise by the more traditional method of swinging the hammer backward before swinging it forward to the nail.

Other examples of this effect include sports like basketball and baseball. I won't expand on these examples much, as I suck at both. But I will point out that when a person shoots a basketball, the player generally moves the ball backward, away from the goal, and then forward through the shot. In baseball, the batter swings the bat backward and then forward to the ball. All these motions serve the same purpose- to orient the muscles in space and time.

The static form of target archery is best used with a visual orientation cue, like a sight or the point of an arrow. This cue takes the place of eye-hand coordination, based on muscle memory, to get the arrow to the mark.

The dynamic form of the swing draw still depends upon visual cues like the tip of the arrow, but they are not conscious cues. They are subconscious cues that the brain uses as it guides the body through the shot, never stopping.

To recap, the swing draw is a method of shooting an arrow that allows us to draw and shoot the arrow without pause. This method allows us to shoot heavier bows accurately because it is designed around the knowledge that muscles work best when they are moving.

A consequential benefit of this method is that there is no pause at anchor in which the archer can second-guess himself. This benefit alone, for some of us, is well worth the effort, as it removes the moment in which our target panic ruins the shot.

A synonym for the word "method" is the word "system." Another aspect of the swing draw that attracted me to it is that it is a simple system that can be learned in a well defined series of steps and is designed to restore the archer's natural eye-hand motor coordination and tune it to the purpose of casting an arrow to the mark. What could be better?

Required Equipment

The swing draw is, in my opinion, not only easier to learn, less dependent on perfect form, more relaxed, and more fun than the standard target form, it also has a simple list of equipment that allows it to work its best:

- An American Semi-Longbow with a flat to slightly dished grip.
- An arm guard.
- Arrows and a back quiver in which to hold them.
- And a Hill-style glove. Not a tab, not a soft goat skin glove, not any other type of glove but a Hill-style glove.

To impress upon you the value of the Hill-style glove, I will rely on Nate's words almost verbatim:

A Hill glove has a double layer of leather and a stiff insert on the pad of the finger for the express purpose of stiffening the finger stalls so

Hill-style glove

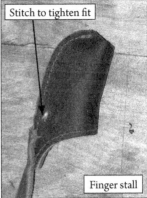

Stitch to tighten fit

Finger stall

that the fingers cannot bend too much at the first joint.

A softer glove can have a tendency to develop a groove in the leather at the area of the first finger joints because the fingers wrap around the string and the fingertips actually face back toward the shooter when the string is gripped with a deep hook.

It's well known that a deep hook allows the hand to be more relaxed, and a better release is the result. So, the double layer leather and stiff inserts of the HH glove allow the fingers to take a deep hook, the hand stays relaxed, but the finger tips will lay more flatly across the string instead of back toward the shooter.

Hill's belief was that this allowed for a smoother release. This was important to him, as he shot targets off the heads of live people and he didn't want a string hanging up on a grooved leather stall.

The Hill glove is a single seam style, so that the seam is on back of the finger where it can't interfere with the placing of the fingers next to each other on the string.

The thin back and straps kept the glove from getting hot and sweaty on his hand. With a properly fitted Hill glove, there is no need for the straps to fit tight to hold the glove stalls on the fingers.

The stalls shouldn't twist either.

As the stall stretches and is fitted to the finger, small stitches can be placed on the top seam to tighten the stall for that particular finger. A leather needle and some stout thread are all that is required.

Baseball rosin or pine pitch can be applied to the finger before inserting the finger into the glove, which will transfer to the interior leather and give a good grip for a good long while.

I actually moisten my finger in my mouth before I slide it into the *stall. As the finger dries out, the glove sticks to my finger with enough tackiness that I have to really firmly twist the stall to get it off my finger when done shooting. This is a trick I learned from Saxton Pope actually.*

A Hill glove is never "broken in" in the sense that the stalls are soft enough to "feel" the string. It wasn't designed that way.

I would suggest that if a person wants to use a Hill glove, get one, rub some pitch blend or baseball glove oil into the leather, and shoot about 1000 shots to form it to the fingers, then adjust the stalls if needed, by individual stitches, to tighten where needed.

Most guys buy one, they shoot about five shots with it, maybe 10 or 20 shots, and they say: "Wow, what a stiff glove, I can't feel the string," and they add it to their collection of "didn't work for me" accessories. Sad. Because if a guy will shoot enough shots to get the glove to fit properly, and gets used to the glove's feel while gripping the string, he will shoot that glove almost forever. The gloves are phenomenal if they are used as they were designed.

I will add additional emphasis to the need to apply pitch blend or other leather lubricants to the inside of the glove. Rub your fingers in it, then put your finger in the stall, twist and seat. You will need to do this for at least the first five or six times you shoot with the glove. This is the secret to success with the Hill-style glove.

I would suggest that you get a glove smaller than you think you might need. Normally I get extra large gloves, and they barely fit. With a Hill-style glove, the large size is right for me. Smaller is better. The leather lubricant will allow you to get the glove on, and the leather will stretch to fit.

Finally, I will add an additional argument in support of the Hill-style glove. This argument shows that, once again, my intuition was wrong, and it is yet another lesson my American Semi-Longbow has taught me in my pursuit of the good life: If we want to know the truth, sometimes we must make our intuition play second fiddle.

While we no doubt survive by our intuition, it can sometimes point us in wrong directions. And if we are willing to accept that our intuition could be wrong, to set it aside while we consider well reasoned arguments, supported by logic and evidence, then we can advance our understanding of the world, and we can, in the process, improve our intuition. We can fine-tune it so that it serves us better in the future. We can improve our awareness of what it is to live the good life.

If we refuse to listen, and stick steadfastly to our flawed intuition, we condemn ourselves to a less enlightened life. On the other hand, if we accept that our intuition is not perfect, accept the possibility that there is a better way, and make a good faith effort to learn it, we improve our intuition, and maybe even our life.

What I learned by setting my intuition aside is that wanting to feel the string with my fingers was actually holding me back. Nate observed that wanting to feel the string is a common desire. I have always believed that feeling the string with my finger was integral to making a good shot. How else can I ensure that I have reached my anchor point?

Let's look a little closer at this desire.

Each person may choose a different anchor point based on individual physiology. It may be the corner of the mouth, it may be a tooth, it may be a point on the jaw bone. Whatever it is, the one thing all these anchor points share is that they are on the face. Another thing all these anchor points share is that there are nerves that respond to touch at each point on the face.

So when we come to anchor and touch our face with our string hand, our brain gets two inputs. It gets a sense of touch from our face, and from our finger- that is, if we use a tab or a soft glove that allows the pressure of contact to be transmitted to our fingers.

Should our brain consider both signals? Which signal takes priority if there is a conflict in the information? How much longer will it take our brain to sort the information delivered from two signals as opposed to one?

Are two signals required to tell the brain that we have reached anchor, and to make a good shot?

The answer is no.

In my job as an engineer, when I designed a device that required sensor input or troubleshot a failure in an existing device, I would always look for conflicting signals that would confuse the system. If I found them, they most often were due to redundant information coming into the processer at slightly different times, or information coming in that should have been redundant but was offset in voltage by a failed sensor. I called these conflicting signals "chatter."

I called it chatter because the most common result of the conflicting input was that a relay would cycle on and off repeatedly and quickly, sounding to me like chatter.

Could this chatter not be analogous to the infamous flinch we archers sometimes suffer when we pause at full draw?

By using a Hill-style glove that keeps our finger tips from actually touching our face or receiving any sort of touch signal, we reduce the inputs our brain must deal with to one. Our brain simply waits for the touch signal received from the nerves in our face, at our anchor point. No dual signal processing, no signal conflicts, results in a more reliable, more repeatable, and more comfortable release.

If you choose to embrace the swing draw, I would encourage you to purchase a Hill-style glove from Howard Hill Archery or E. W. Bateman and Co. as you begin your training. It will add some to the strangeness of how things feel at the beginning, but in the end you will save your brain some effort and have the greatest opportunity to enjoy the relaxed style of the swing draw.

The last piece of equipment you will need is a good target with which you can do some blank bale shooting. In order to ingrain any new muscle memory, you must repeat the motion almost countless times. This is true with the swing draw. A blank bale, used for this purpose, must be able to

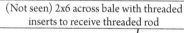

(Not seen) 2x6 across bale with threaded inserts to receive threaded rod

Locked double nuts used to tighten threaded rods

Target face

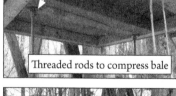

Threaded rods to compress bale

Blank bale with vinyl table cloth rain guard in place

withstand much use.

Almost any target, which can be correctly positioned, will do. How long it will last, and how much maintenance will be required for its up-keep, are questions you will have to consider.

For the purpose of blank bale shooting, I constructed a simple target that is easy to position and utilizes one bale of hay. Behind the bale of hay, I screwed a piece of rubber horse stall mat to the enclosure. This serves to stop arrows when they inevitably penetrate the bale. Adding a vinyl table cloth as a rain shield to the front of the target helps to preserve the hay bale.

I have had the best luck using hay, as opposed to straw. While hay is more expensive, it is also more densely packed and lasts substantially longer, while offering much better arrow-stopping ability.

I have used this type of target for nearly 10 years. In that time, I have replaced the bales after about every three years of daily shooting, and at the same time, I added another layer of stall mat over the shot-out layer.

Another feature which seems to have extended the arrow-stopping capacity of the bale is a system of tie-rods, threaded inserts, and 2x6 boards to compress the bale, as shown in the photo.

While there are countless ways to solve this particular problem, I offer this option to you as it is simple, economical, and has worked well for me.

Finally, there is an optional piece of equipment that I wish I had employed from the beginning- a simple notebook. You will find that as you practice day to day, you will sometimes do something a little different. You may come upon it consciously, you may stumble upon it unconsciously. At the end of the practice you will think about how your draw arm felt really good today. If you do not write it down, by tomorrow you will have forgotten. It's good to write things down to keep track of what works, what doesn't, and how things have improved.

An improvement in your form should not be defined by how the arrow flies. It should be defined by how much more comfortable and fluid your draw is, and how much more relaxed you are about it.

I encourage you to write the previous paragraph on the cover of your notebook, and read it every time you practice.

How to Learn the Swing Draw Method

As Nate instructed me in the skill of shooting with the swing draw method, he did not give me an overview of his instructions. Instead, he fed them to me one step at a time.

This makes sense for a number of reasons, not the least of which is that Nate had no measure of my resolve for learning the process, and thus he had no motivation to spend the time explaining it all to me. If I faded out after the first step or two, then no time was wasted explaining the rest of the process to me.

Another reason, too, might have been to keep me from shortchanging each step in my desire to progress to the next step. This dynamic is not possible when instruction is given and taken in book form. Therefore, I must leave it to you to be honest with yourself about the progress made, and the appropriateness of moving on to the next step. Cheating a step by moving to the next exercise before the last has been mastered will prove fruitless in the end.

You must not shortchange these exercises. In order for this method to work, you must be willing to give up shooting at a mark for a long time. You cannot go into this practice while at the same time shooting with friends, or entering contests, or using any other excuse to hit a target.

Each of these steps has been designed not only to ingrain the muscle memory necessary to shoot in a fluid and relaxed way, it has been designed to build a mental construct of the trajectory of an arrow. Building these two skills together is what results in the reliability and joy of the swing draw. As Nate says, "It's serious fun."

As someone with no particular natural talent who has still benefited from these lessons, I feel qualified at least to advise you to master each step, to the best of your ability, as you go. The more you practice each step, the better you will get, and the more you will see opportunity for improvement. You can spend the rest of your life improving your shot; only you can decide when to progress to the next step.

There are a few things you should keep in mind as you mull over learning the swing draw:

Fits and spurts. You will have good days and bad days. You will be tempted to adjust your form, or try to "figure it out." Don't. Let frustration be your guide to tell you when to stop practicing, but don't let it trick you into "trying something new." Keep steadfastly on course. Time and practice will bring things together.

Learn by miming. When I take my daily walk, I swing draw my imaginary bow and arrow at leaves, birds, stumps, whatever. You will be surprised how much this helps to establish good habits, without getting worn out. There are targets everywhere. Have a few minutes? Take a few swing draws.

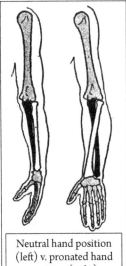

Neutral hand position (left) v. pronated hand position (right)

Smile. There is plenty of scientific evidence that links the act of smiling with a happy attitude and a relaxed body. While we often smile when we feel good, it is also true that we often feel good when we smile. As you take your stance to shoot, take a moment to crack a smile. It will help you shoot better, and it will make your friends wonder what you are thinking about.

Stand up straight. When you take your shooting position, you may be tempted to hunch down over the arrow. Don't. Keep your back comfortably straight and lean your head over the arrow.

Don't be over-bowed. It is tempting to shoot a heavy bow. It is best to shoot a bow that is well within your comfort level. If you feel you can easily draw a 60-pound bow, start with a 50-pound bow. Easy to pull does not mean easy to control.

Thumbs up. What to do with the thumb of your drawing hand can be a challenge for the archer. Normally, folding the thumb across the palm (and maybe holding the pinky finger down with it) is the most common position. If your hands naturally pronate, meaning that when your arms are at rest at your side your palm is not facing your side but is actually facing behind you some, then you may get a more consistent release by keeping your thumb on top of your hand during the draw (as Fred Bear and others do). After you shoot, notice how your palm is oriented. Does it rest against your face, or does it face the ground? If your palm does not stay against your face, this is a clue that your forearm is not relaxed during the draw. A relaxed forearm that does not torque the string at the loose is a challenge.

Take a deep grip. Transitioning to the swing draw required a rethink of every aspect of my shooting. Old habits die hard. One habit that was

Eagle claw grip

particularly hard to change was how I held the bow. The swing draw requires a good and solid grip on the bow. How the bow reacts to the shot can tell you a lot about how to improve your form. Ideally, it should not move much at all. It should not rotate forward, or translate to the side, or rotate to the right. Watching what your bow does at the shot (on video) will inform good troubleshooting.

If the bow rotates forward, that means you are doing something to induce uneven pressure between the top and bottom of the grip. Not heeling the bow, or grabbing the bow with the bottom two fingers at the shot, is common.

If the bow moves to the left at the shot, it can mean that your bow arm elbow is too straight, or your bow shoulder is not pressed down before you begin the draw.

If the top limb rotates to the right at the shot, it means there is a torque between your bow hand and your string hand. This usually results from a string hand and arm that are not relaxed.

Common advice from those who have mastered the swing draw, is to take a deep grip and to hold the bow more tightly with the pinky and ring fingers than with the index and middle fingers. I found this hard to put into practice directly. The Chinese employ a method of gripping the bow that they call the "eagle claw grip." I found that this grip works well for me and that it allows me to hold the bow more with the ring and pinky fingers, as advised. To employ the grip, simply take a deep grip with the bow resting from the middle of the web down to the heel of the hand. Rest your thumb on your ring finger. Then let your index and middle fingers rest on your thumb. While this may feel awkward at first, I found that it really helped me get my bow arm under control and allowed me to grip the bow in a repeatable and reliable way.

Extra-Closed Stance. If you employ an open stance, you will find it hard to control your shot left to right. A closed stance will allow you to maintain a solid bow arm. You may find that even this is not enough to assure a consistent shot. I found that if I imagined a straight line that passed

through both my shoulders and the
bullseye, and if I moved my right
foot back a bit while rotating it so
that my toes pointed away from the
target, I could shoot more consistently.

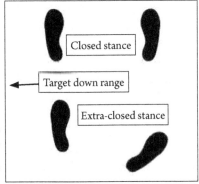

Do not move your head. I
found that I tended to move my
head during the draw so that the
corner of my mouth would meet
my drawing hand as it was coming back and thus achieve anchor. I did
this unconsciously because my form would not allow my hand to meet
my face as it should. As you draw your bow, be sure to keep your head still
and draw to your face.

I spent several months of daily shooting on each step. I would shoot
around 100 shots in a day. Sometimes less, mostly more. Luckily I started
my training after deer season ended. This gave me the room to retrain my
muscles and rebuild my eye-hand coordination to the point where I was
prepared to begin the hunting season the following year. This should give
you some sense of the time frame required to become sufficiently proficient with the swing draw to justify hunting. Plan accordingly. If you keep
with it, you will find that a year's practice is only the beginning.

Let's begin.

Step One - Blank Bale Practice

You will need to place your blank bale target where you will be able to
stand 20 to 25 feet from it. Somewhere on level ground.

Stand close to the target and find a place on the bale that is at the
same height as your bow shoulder; remember that place. Don't put anything there, just know where that area is, because that's the area you will
look at while you are learning your form. Now, from your appointed position between 20 and 25 feet from the bale, you will stand with the body
at right angles to the backstop. Your shoulder should be at right angles
to the target. (The better you can maintain this posture, the better you
will shoot.) Now, swing the bow up as you draw the string, just like John
Schulz shows in his "Straight Shooting" video (available on YouTube),
find an anchor deep into your face, and release.

Make absolutely no effort to hold the bow at full draw. Period.

When your string hand touches your anchor, stop holding the string. You may find this disconcerting at first. Over time it will begin to feel like the natural thing to do. It may help to have a place for your hand to come to rest after releasing the string. I like to have my hand come to rest on my ear. However you do it, your hand should stop shortly after letting the string go.

You should balance your body so that you have more weight on your forward foot, almost enough to lift the heel of the other foot off the ground, just a little.

Look at the area you identified earlier to be at shoulder-height during the entire time you spend drawing the bow and releasing the arrow. DO NOT FOLLOW THE ARROW IN FLIGHT, PERIOD. DO NOT SHIFT YOUR GAZE TO WHERE THE ARROW HITS, PERIOD. Keep looking at the area where you want the arrow to go, and let your peripheral vision see where the arrow hits. Make no conscious adjustment to your aim or form while you shoot. Just swing up, anchor, and release. Do this all in one motion, do it as fluidly and as casually as you can. Take one to two seconds for the entire sequence. It helps to start the swing if you drop your bow hand just a little (as much as 2 inches) at the beginning of the draw and then raise the arm through the swing. Remember how swinging the hammer backward helps us hit the nail on the head.

Don't worry about your release or any other aspect of your shot, but remember to keep your bow hand up and aimed at the target for two to three seconds after the arrow hits. A fluid shot and a relaxed feeling are your goal. Just feel the anchor as your fingers dig deep into your face. Don't just barely touch your anchor. Dig deep. Bury your fingers in your face. Remember that feel every shot.

As you dwell after the shot, observe the mosaic of your bow hand and bow against the background of the target and arrow. Do not worry about where your arrows are hitting. Just keep looking at the area to hit.

I would encourage you to read the previous paragraphs again before you start each blank bale practice, for at least the first week.

As I practiced this first exercise in learning the swing draw, I realized that it includes two very powerful tools.

The first and most powerful tool, the use of which will benefit you even if you never take up the swing draw, and the value of which cannot be overstated, is to focus entirely on the bale while seeing the arrow only in your peripheral vision. If you watch the arrow in flight, how ever can your brain learn the arrow's trajectory?

If your eyes move with the arrow, your brain's point of reference is, by definition, the arrow. Your brain cannot trace, and remember, the parabolic path of the arrow if it never sees it. By watching the arrow in flight, or moving your eyes to the impact point, you are effectively reducing the parabolic flight path of the arrow to a single point: $(0,0)$.

The second powerful tool used in this lesson is the understanding that if we keep our body in motion and allow it to do what it naturally wants to do, it will eventually figure out what's right.

Don't get in a knot about your form, or your anchor point, or your release. Just keep focusing on the spot on the bale and attempting to shoot, smoothly and without pause. Your body will figure out how to do it correctly if you give it the time and practice.

To understand how this can be true, through example, remember what it was like to learn to drive a car. When you first began to drive, you probably sat overly erect in the seat, gripped the steering wheel with white knuckles, failed to heed visual cues, and generally drove poorly.

As you gained experience in driving, you relaxed into it. You became more proficient in every regard until finally it became second nature. You are relaxed in your seat, grasp the wheel in a comfortable manner, unconsciously absorb all the necessary visual cues to drive smoothly and without conscious thought. In fact, you are never aware of keeping the car between the lines while you talk with your fellow passengers about how hard it is to shoot your bow.

When I began this step, I was dreading it. I had shot blank bale before in an attempt to improve my skill. I was never able to stick with it long, and I was bored to death by it.

That's because I was not learning anything.

When you practice bale shooting as described above, you will be learning something on every shot. You will be learning because you are focused on the desired point of impact, not upon the arrow. It makes all the difference. It brings joy to the practice.

I shoot just one arrow into the bale at a time. I walk up, remove it, add it to my quiver, walk back, withdraw the arrow, and shoot again.

By removing the arrow, I maintain the blank bale and avoid the mental clutter that arrows in the bale would bring. This practice ensures my arrows will not be broken, an additional advantage.

This is a good time to practice handling arrows, removing and replacing them in your quiver, and affixing them to your string. If you choose to incorporate the back quiver and fast arrow handling method afforded by it, now's the time.

Grasp the arrow by the nock, withdraw it from your quiver, swing it over your back, affix it to the string, and slide it to the nock set.

To take advantage of this method, it is best to nock your arrow above the nock set. Adjust the nock set on your string accordingly.

Eventually you will be able to carry this motion out without looking. For now, don't worry about it. Look at the string as you affix the arrow. Eventually you will be able to find the nock set on the string with the same ease that you find the buttons on your car radio without looking. How long will it take? It doesn't matter.

This process can be watched in Schulz's "Straight Shooting" video.

I spent a month on this exercise, shooting daily, before adding the next step.

Step Two - Long-Range Practice

How long you have to spend on each step, before moving on, is an individual matter. It is dependent, in large part, on what your shooting habits were before starting to learn the swing draw. If you suffer from target panic, or have other bad habits, it will take longer.

Once you feel like you have ingrained the swing draw into your muscle memory with the blank bale practice, it is time to add some long-range practice to your routine.

The muscle memory you learned in step one will be built upon in this step. This is where you will begin to see the beauty of this system. It is at this point that I began to see how this method works so well to hone our innate eye-hand coordination so that we can learn to be relaxed when we shoot.

When I think of a system, I think of a rigid method that must be followed exactly to result in the desired outcome. This system is different. It is true that, for best results, you must follow the system exactly. But when you have learned what the system has to teach you, you will be free to shoot without the mental clutter so often associated with target form because your shot will be dependent on muscle memory, not a mental checklist.

These steps shouldn't be thought of as discrete exercises through which you proceed in series, but rather layers of exercises upon which you build. You don't "move on" to the next step. You "add" to your routine.

This next lesson is harder, and you will have to return to the blank bale and form shooting often to reinforce the swing draw form. Shooting blank bale at close range allows you to concentrate on the feel of your form without having to worry about where the arrows are going. You may have noticed that your arrow began to hit the bale where you were looking without trying. The arrows are beginning to go where you look even though you aren't thinking about "aiming" the arrow. This next lesson will challenge your progress. Have faith.

You will now start each session with blank bale shooting, maybe 20 or 30 arrows. Then go out to an area where you can shoot long range- at least 50 yards. If you have been adamant about looking at an area on the backstop that was about shoulder height, you have ingrained the full swing draw "level" form. (Basically, without realizing it, you ingrained the proper form for shooting at a target around 30 inches off the ground, and about 40 to 50 yards away.)

This range is defined by the parabolic shape of the arrow's trajectory, the speed of your bow, and your physical height. In most cases it is in the 40 to 50 yard range. What it is exactly, doesn't matter.

It is best to use some sort of blunt on your arrow for this practice so that you don't lose your arrows. You will also want to have a rag to wipe

Bucket on post to store rags or socks for cleaning arrows

the dirt off your arrows before adding them back to your quiver. I use old socks for this purpose, and I leave them where I do my practice so I don't have to remember to bring them each session.

With the bow held so that the bow hand is about level with the shoulder, and because of the work you did to ingrain your form on the blank bale, you will be shooting arrows through an area shoulder-height off the ground at 20 to 30 feet. Because of the parabolic shape of arrow flight, when you shoot, the arrow will continue to rise above shoulder height, and then drop down to shoulder height again at somewhere around 40 yards. The arrow continues on a downward path, depending on how flat it shoots. The arrow will go through an area 30 inches off the ground at around 50 yards- the perfect height to pass through the chest of a deer.

With the basic form you ingrained at 20 feet, you have now ingrained the form necessary to shoot deer-height targets at 50 yards with no adjustments. If you have paid attention to the feel of the shot, you could, in essence, with eyes closed and concentrating on form only, shoot all your arrows into the same area on the ground at 50 to 55 yards just by how the shot felt, because you have ingrained that muscle memory.

Hill told Schulz, "if your form is right, you won't be too far off at 50 yards." Basically, if you have practiced the proper swing draw form at the proper height backstop until it becomes automatic muscle memory, you have ingrained 50-yard form. To shoot an animal standing on the ground at 20 yards or 50 yards, you will have very small adjustments to make in the height of your bow hand, which makes the shot easier to do.

The advantage of these small adjustments can be understood by com-

View down nice, flat, straight alley for long-range practice

paring them to what you would have to do if you practiced your short-range work on a target on the ground. If you were to have ingrained form shooting at a block target on the ground, then to shoot at an animal's chest 30 inches off the ground at 30 yards, you would have to move your bow hand up almost a foot (instead of down an inch). This action takes a lot of mental effort and is subject to a lot more error when compared to practice at shoulder height.

So, now you are going to practice shooting long range, using the same muscle memory that you built at 20 feet. You are going to look at an area on the ground at 50ish yards. THIS IS IMPORTANT! DO NOT TRY TO AIM. Just look at an area on the ground, swing draw, anchor and shoot, just like at the blank backstop.

Chances are, when you begin this practice, it will not go well. No worries, it will come. When I added this long-range form practice to my routine, it took several days to get it going well. Things tend to fall apart, but they will come back together again. Just remember the following goals and each will come back the more you practice:

1. Keep your bow arm up. Keep your bow arm up through the entire shot until the arrow hits the ground.

2. Watch the arrow in your peripheral vision. Do not watch the arrow directly. Just see it, without watching it. This will allow your brain to learn your arrow's trajectory.

3. Maintain form. Make sure you keep the basics right. Weight on the front foot, bow shoulder pressed down, elbow bent, heel bow hand, string hand to anchor.

Your goal should be to shoot at least 100 arrows in a practice session. When I started this, my form did indeed fall apart. As my form went south, my frustration went north. Thus, in the beginning, I did not achieve this goal of 100 arrows of long-range practice. What I failed to do at 50 yards, I made up for on the blank bale. Each day, I had less to make up for as my long-range form improved. As you improve, you will find it easy to shoot 100 arrows at 50 yards.

If you can find a place that will allow it, shoot your quiver of arrows at your spot on the ground, retrieve the arrows, and then shoot them again back toward your starting point. This will save much time and walking.

By this exercise, you are now practicing form shooting with the added visual stimulus of the arrow arc for your brain to see. This is what makes this exercise so difficult. No matter how hard it is, do not start aiming the arrow. Don't. Just look at that area, swing, and shoot. Still concentrate only on the feel of the shot, just like during bale practice. The ground will actually become blurry in your mind's eye. You will find you feel like you are daydreaming because even though you see the area out there on the ground, your mind is focused on the feel of the shot. You are leaving the trajectory and fate of the arrow to those parts of your brain that you are not conscious of.

If you shoot this long range with the same feel of the shot as you did at 20 feet, you will be surprised by how your arrows start grouping out there on the ground at 50 yards. They will start falling into an area around a 36-inch circle on the ground without hardly trying. All you are doing is looking, swinging, and shooting. Your concentration is on the feel and form of the shot, absolutely imitating the form and feel you did at the 20-foot blank bale.

Another reason for the structure of this long-range exercise is that, at this point in time, you don't want anything close enough out there so that you start picking a spot to shoot at. Right now, you are just shooting at an area, kind of a blurry area at that, because you are still ingraining proper form, with some added visual stimuli.

This exercise will be challenging. But for me, as I got better at it, I began to see that I would actually be able to hit a pie plate at 50 yards reliably. Before I began to learn the swing draw, this would never have been possible. I spent two months, shooting daily, on this exercise before adding the next step.

Step Three - Bore a Hole Through It

It's funny how many times I think I understand what someone is telling me when I really don't. The misunderstanding does not result because I am not listening. It happens because I don't have the same experience as the speaker, and thus the words don't create the same image in my mind as they do in the mind of the speaker.

The oft-spoken phrase "bore a hole in it" is a case in point.

Howard Hill spoke these words, oh so long ago, and they have been repeated by many good shooters since. I thought what it meant was to concentrate so hard on the point I want to hit that my sheer focus on that point would melt it away. Superman X-ray vision, if you like.

As it turns out, this is not the meaning at all.

The intent of the previous two lessons was to build muscle memory and form so that the archer would be able to produce the same shot time and time again without thought. To build our autopilot.

As our form improves, another outcome of these exercises is that our brain begins to learn the trajectory of our arrow. If the archer sticks with the same bow and the same arrow throughout these exercises, the outcome of the shot, well executed, will be the same.

The purpose of this third exercise is to learn to place the trajectory of the arrow in space so that it intersects the point we want to hit.

This is where the philosophy upon which the swing draw is built deviates most obviously from other learning methods, and wherein it becomes such a strong method.

Practicing this exercise is where I also learned that I totally misunderstood what Hill and others were trying to tell me.

This exercise will introduce an intended target. But the intended target in this exercise is like no other target you have shot before. It is that way for a reason.

Most likely, every target you have ever shot represented the terminal point of the arrow's journey. When the arrow hits the target, it stops.

This is not the case for this exercise.

In this exercise, you will shoot at a target suspended in the air at shoulder height, the same height you have been shooting since you started practicing. But this target is not solid. It will not stop the arrow. Whether the arrow hits the target or not, the outcome will be the same: the arrow will continue on its path mostly undisturbed.

Let me show you what I do, and then I will explain why. After much fooling around, I came to a target that serves this purpose well and is durable. I took an old bowstring and wrapped it around a stick. Through the loop at the end of the string I tied a small piece of orange surveying tape. I then suspend the target in the air at whatever height and distance I want by simply moving the stick to different holes in my fence.

From time to time, I hit the string which throws my arrow off. But mostly my arrow flies harmlessly by at some point near the survey tape.

I keep the roll of survey tape in my bucket along with my old socks so that I can replace the target as needed. As you improve, you will shoot the tape off the string more often than you might imagine.

Target

Small piece of survey tape tied to end of old bow string and suspended in midair

So what is the point?

The point is to learn to change the way you think about hitting a mark. The point is to learn that the mark doesn't have to represent the end of your mental picture. The point is to learn that the mark should not be, in and of itself, the focus of your focus.

As you practice this exercise, you will come to realize, as I did, what the meaning of "bore a hole in it" really is.

You will not come to understand right away. You must practice this exercise a lot. As with the first two exercises, you will likely feel awkward and your shooting will fall off. Do not fret. You will get better. Do not force it, it will come.

As you practice this exercise, you will begin to get a feel for it. Your aiming will become more instinctive and more three-dimensional in nature.

Other aiming methods such as string walking, secondary vision, gap, etc., all reduce the aiming process to the analysis of a two-dimensional picture intended to model the three-dimensional world. They all require some conscious estimate of distance. As a person gets comfortable with using these methods, they can begin to feel natural. But they are all, at their core, reductionist methods that depends on knowing the boundary conditions of distance, elevation, and shooting angle.

I do not mean to criticize these methods of aiming. I simply want to highlight the differences. These methods have proven not only outstanding for target archery, but superior to the method outlined here, as evidenced by the fact that not a single target archer employs the swing draw.

For the purpose of hunting, though, I believe the ability to know your arrow trajectory, and to be able to make that trajectory intersect the deer, is a more reliable way to kill game. The situation a hunter finds herself in as a deer approaches can never be as predictable as walking up to a static target.

So what is the meaning of "bore a hole through it," then?

As you become skilled in the swing draw, you will begin to see the target as simply a point on the trajectory of the arrow. You will visualize the arrow trajectory both before and after the target. You will begin to focus not on the mark, but on the whole of everything that is in front of you.

The mark will be at the center of your vision, but it will not be the center of your attention. It is just part of the whole shot experience.

As you become skilled in the swing draw, you will begin to see through the target and see where the arrow would go if it passed through the target, just as it does as it flies past your survey tape. You will bore a hole through it.

I think it's safe to say that you will never forget the first time you succeed at this. When your swing draw happens naturally, when you are one hundred percent confident, when your vision is clear and wide, you will see through your target and be genuinely surprised when your arrow actually stops in the target.

So how do you get to that point?

Add this exercise into your routine. Shoot 30 or more arrows at the bale, shoot 20 or more arrows for distance, then set up your hanging target and shoot as much as you can. Proportion your shots for each exercise based on what you can do and what you have time for.

As you become more proficient with this new exercise, vary the distance at which you shoot and the height of the hanging target.

After a month, and if you have the opportunity, take to the woods for a rove. Do not shoot at targets on the ground that will stop your arrows. Instead, shoot at leaves, branches, and snags that are off the ground.

On good days, just go for a rove and don't bother with the hanging target.

Keep at it until everything feels natural. Only then, add in targets that stop the arrow.

<u>Where To From Here?</u>

As I said at the beginning of this chapter, I originally had no intention of including any mention of how to shoot a bow. I came to these exercises after I had started this book. Over the years, I have read just about every shooting instruction book available and tried to put the advice into practice. While some of it seemed to make sense, none of it seemed to fit.

I wish I could tell you that I've been shooting this way for decades, but I can't. This advice that I pass on to you is still mostly advice I have just freshly received myself.

The advice itself is not new. Nor is the method. In fact, the farther you look back in time at those great archers that came before us, the more you will see that they employed a casual swing draw based on but a few fundamentals: solid bow arm, arrows cut just past the back of the bow, a hard glove, and a happy attitude.

I will leave off this discussion of how to shoot the American Semi-Longbow with the words of someone eminently more qualified to speak about it than I am. Here is what Nate Steen had to tell me as I began to understand what it meant to "bore a hole through it":

I guess the last few weeks I've tried to convey the message of not thinking too much during the shot. I hope you see where I'm coming from and learn to trust your hand-eye coordination over a mental checklist type of shot. It takes effort, granted. But to me, it's the best way of shooting in the field at live targets under varied circumstances. When you've done the time, one day it will start to seem effortless and the arrows will start going where you look, or very close to it, all the time, no matter the distance... the "aha" moment if you will. Sure, some days we can't hit our butt with both hands, and you will learn how to hang up the bow on those days...

When I go out... every time... to hunt, I shoot a few long range shots at the fifty to fifty-five'ish yard range. I do it to maintain the level form and to make sure I'm drawing fully, anchoring, and smoothly releasing without thinking about it much... when I see the arrows hit the ground in the area I'm looking, or a lot of the time I actually hit the spot I'm looking at... It gives such a HUGE confidence boost that I get into the "zone" very quickly, and from that moment I feel like I can hit anything I look at. It's all psychological of course, but it works. Then, conversely, if it's one of those off days and my form/eye/hand/mind are all off on their own tangent, I can tell pretty quickly, so I settle for a few short shots into a dirt bank or such to make sure I'm following form and then I know that I will probably only shoot short shots at any animals that come along... that is until I have a chance to stump shoot or warm up some more and the senses sync once again.

Learn to trust this system, as you probably once trusted that you could ride a bike one day... one day... it all came together and now you just jump on the bike and go. If you doubt your own abilities, you will have a longer road. Shoot with utter confidence.

Learn, once and for all, that your form doesn't have to be perfect, the release doesn't have to be perfect to hit the target in the field... your hand eye coordination and subconscious mind will make the necessary allowances to put the arrow on target... If you get out of your own way. These drills and lessons were the way that I was able to get out of my own way.

Chapter 14
The Good Life

There is not enough praise in the world for the American Semi-Longbow, in my opinion anyway. Among all the many lessons my bow has taught me, or because of them, I have finally recognized that there is indeed such a thing as the good life.

I think Maurice Thompson knew this when he wrote:

The bow is the natural weapon of man, and it affords him the most perfect physical and mental exercise that can be conceived. It is to the mind and body what music and poetry are to the soul.

As did E. H. LeBlanc, another archer who speaks to us from the past. LeBlanc, as quoted by Fred Anderson in his book *Toxicated, A Treasury of Archery*, observed that:

"The call of the wild", together with "the call of the longbow", is without question, a revelation, a fascination without equal.

With most things archery, there is little left to discover for the first time. The same must be true of the good life. Whatever the good life is, each generation is left to rediscover it again and again. Despite the trouble we have figuring out exactly what makes a good life, I think it is safe to say that it must, absolutely, involve the land.

As I write this chapter, my children are in the process of growing up, of fledging from our farm. Moving out into the world to discover their own good life.

I have become comfortable in my own good life, as it is now, and as it has been for nearly two decades. Raising my kids, feeding them from the land, warming our home with the sunshine stored in the old oak that finally fell in the back pasture. Teaching them what little I know.

Life goes on, though. As does the good life. Here again comes my trusty American Semi-Longbow to the rescue. If I look around my shop with the same maudlin eye that I use to look back at the flash of time that has elapsed as we raised our children, I see a stack of old bows.

At the time I was building each of those bows, I was under the impression that it would surely be the best version of the ASL that could possibly be made. I shot those bows with enthusiasm, but I eventually learned from them and made another, better bow.

Surely if I shot those old bows now, they would be awful. Wouldn't they?

Surprisingly, no. Each one that I pick up now and shoot, for old time's sake, is a pleasure. What a pleasant surprise, the consequences of which I was not prepared for.

Even my old bows are there to teach me one last lesson, if only I will listen.

It seems that all these bows, conceived in the conceit that I could do it better, turned out alright in spite of me. Maybe there is no perfect bow that can be used to make the perfect shot. There is only a bow and an archer, working together to make the best shot they can.

By extension, I reason that there is no perfect landscape in which to practice archery. I do not need to live in the majestic mountains of the west in order to gain the full effect of hunting with the longbow.

Richard Nelson puts it better than I can in his book *The Island Within*. Nelson says:

> I realized that the particular place I'd chosen was less important than the fact that I'd chosen a place and focused my life around it. Although the island has taken on great significance for me, it's no more inherently beautiful or meaningful than any other place on earth. What makes a place special is the way it buries itself inside the heart, not whether it's flat or rugged, rich or austere, wet or arid, gentle or

harsh, warm or cold, wild or tame. Every place, like every person, is elevated by the love and respect shown toward it, and by the way in which its bounty is received.

I would say this same sentiment applies to our bows as much as it does to the land. I have seen too many people spend too much time and money chasing after the perfect bow.

So is there such a thing as the perfect bow? Yet another question I am not qualified to answer. But I suspect that there may be no one simple answer. Or if the answer does exist, it might be something like: any bow that is not broken, is perfect.

I am pretty confident that that same definition applies to the land and to our relationship with the land. Any land that is not broken, is perfect.

It is the perfect place for those plants and animals that have evolved upon it to live. It is the perfect place for us to live too, if we do so gently and without the conceit that we can make it better.

How many times have we cut a straight path for the meandering stream? We once thought that a straightened stream would mean more bounty from our fields and more places for our homes and businesses. Did we not learn, instead, that in the end a straightened stream leads to erosion, flooding, and biological disaster?

Have we not drained swamps and wetlands only to discover, too late, that they too protected us from flooding and starvation?

We too often think that we are making the land better, more suited to us, when in fact our thinking could be no further from the truth.

I think the same is true with our bows. Instead of trying to make a better faster whiz-bang bow, our time would be better spent giving the bow a fine tiller that results in a gentle and reliable shot.

The nature of a good bow, like the nature of the land, cannot be altered. It can only be destroyed.

The land not only gives us a place to live and the means to do it, it gives us the opportunity for storytelling. Stories may be the single most important form of information we humans share with each other. A story lasts the longest in our minds, and has the greatest effect on our lives.

Whenever we do things we want to share with others, that sharing most often occurs in the form of a story. Everyone likes a good story.

When I mention the "wobbly buck" to my son, it immediately brings to mind the story of the first eight-pointer we shot together, when Liam was but five or six years old...

I came home early from work that day, as the weather promised to be perfect for deer movement. I had intended to grab my gun and sneak out of the house before being noticed. No such luck.

Liam came running up to me, leaned his head way back to look into my eyes, and asked: "Daddy, can we go squirrel hunting?" to which I could have only one answer, grudgingly given nonetheless: "OK, boy. Get your clothes on, and go get your twenty-two."

As we left I grabbed my lever action, just in case. After a slow and tedious walk through the woods with my young son tripping over almost every log and dropping his unloaded gun in the dirt every time, we finally arrived at our appointed knoll and sat down under an oak tree to wait on our squirrels to show themselves.

Our rule in those days was that Liam had to see the squirrel before he could load his gun. I would ask: "Do you see the squirrel?" Liam would reply in the affirmative, and I would reach into my chest pocket, retrieve a cartridge, and hand it to him. Liam would then load the gun, take aim, and hopefully get the squirrel.

So it went on this afternoon. A squirrel came through from our left to our right. Liam saw it, I handed him the shell, he loaded the gun and took aim, but the squirrel made haste and no shot was taken. Liam then withdrew the bullet from the chamber and returned it to me for safekeeping until the next squirrel should appear.

As Liam would point the gun at the squirrel and take aim, I would often hold the barrel to steady the gun. I did this as several squirrels repeated the journey in front of us.

After sitting for about an hour, and much to my surprise, the next critter to travel from our left to our right was a nice eight-point buck. When I noticed him, I asked Liam if he saw the buck and whether he thought we should shoot him. Liam said: "Yeah Dad, shoot him!"

So I raised my gun and took aim. As the sights settled on the deer's side, I noticed an unexplained movement of the gun. When I refocused my eyes to my local environment, I noticed Liam's left hand on the gun barrel, holding it "steady." What a good boy!

I made the best effort I could to accommodate this help, and squeezed the trigger. At which the buck turned and ran out of the woods into the

field, tail spinning in circles as he went. I asked Liam if he thought we might have got him.

Liam said: "We got him all right. He was wobbly!"

We got up, collected ourselves, and walked out of the woods and into the field following the line we watched the deer take. It wasn't long before we found him lying on his side next to a persimmon tree.

What followed was Liam's first lesson in field dressing a deer and seeing everything that is inside the deer, and presumably inside us, that is responsible for life. We had a long lesson that involved opening all the organs to see what was inside:

"Daddy, what's this?"

"It's a kidney, son."

"What does it do, Daddy?"

"It makes pee."

"Do we have a kidney, Daddy?"

"Yes, my boy."

"Daddy, what's this?"

"It's a heart..."

We learned what's inside a deer, what's inside us, how delicate life can be, and how mortal we are.

This story serves to illuminate what has been our good life in several ways. Between my son and me, it has served as a story that has united us in a shared cause, and now that my son has grown up, a shared understanding. We worked together to kill that buck, dress it out, and hang it under the deck to age. The story brings us closer every time it is told.

Between me and you, it also tells the truth that I don't hunt with my American Semi-Longbow alone. My commitment to feeding my family from the good earth of our farm is greater than my commitment to hunting with my ASL. As my family grows older and the children move away, the need for meat will decrease. As the need for meat diminishes, I expect I will have little reason to hunt with anything but my American Semi-Longbow.

For myself, the story reminds me to be flexible. Too often we feel the need to specify what is good in absolute terms. If I had refused to take my boy hunting that day, or refused to carry my gun instead of my bow, we might not have this good story between us.

Which brings me back, one final time, to my American Semi-Longbow.

As I mentioned before, any bow that isn't broken can be considered perfect. If we keep this in mind, and remember to be flexible, we will discover that the bows we make are just fine, and we will be happier for it.

The real value in making our own bows may be that they add to our story, and by adding depth and dimension to our story they add to our lives.

Making our own bow gives us new knowledge and experience, and it teaches us lessons that help us to love and respect the land. As Nelson observed, this elevates the land. I think it helps to elevate us too.

By endeavoring to earn the bounty of the land in the most noble manner possible - that is by our own hand - we write the best stories of our lives, and in so doing, we learn to live the good life.

Appendix A
The Upshot, How I Make Them Now

It took several years to write this book and finally get it edited and published. As I write this appendix, I am making peace with what has been said and what I tried to say. The two don't always match up as well as I had hoped.

Additionally, and obviously, my bow making efforts and my shooting continued during this time as well. The bow/arrow/archer machine works best when all three components are tuned to each other. The more we shoot, the more we evolve as archers. The more we evolve as archers, the more we appreciate how everything works together. The more we evolve as archers, the better we can see opportunities to improve not just our bows, but also ourselves.

Again I see the iterative nature of archery. I make an improvement in the stability of my bow arm, then I see that my string hand needs to change a bit. I change my string hand a bit, and I see that my bow hand needs to move a little. I move my bow hand a little, and I see that my head is a bit out of position. Each little change brings me closer to the perfect shot. Each little change begs another little change somewhere else.

As I make these changes to my form, I see how a few small changes to my bow might be in order. For example, as I get better at the job of heeling my bow grip, I note that a smaller grip would make the task easier.

And so it goes, on and on. And so I will share with you the properties of the last bow I made before handing this manuscript off to be turned into a book. This design is not the best design possible (far from it, I am sure). It is just something that works well for me these days as I work to get better and better at the swing draw method of shooting.

From my notebook, I see that I used a walnut core consisting of two laminations. The root thickness for each lamination was 0.195 inch for a total root core thickness of 0.390 inch. Each lamination had a 0.001 inch/inch taper resulting in a total taper of 0.002 inch/inch. I used 0.050-inch fiberglass on both the back and belly.

For the first time in years, I used no tip wedges.

The bow was made on my string follow form which results in about 5/8 inch of string follow. The bow is 66 inches long, nock to nock.

I used a riser block 12 inches long and 1 1/2 inches thick. The upper fadeout on the riser block was 1 inch longer than the lower fadeout. (Center of the grip to end of top fadeout measures 6.5 inches, center of grip to end of bottom fadeout measures 5.5 inches.)

The core laminations were centered on the form, but the riser was offset 1 inch toward the lower limb.

You can see how I laid the bow out by looking at the plan form figure. You will note that the limb width does not taper uniformly from root to tip.

The limb width at the fades is 1 1/8 inch, which tapers to a width of 3/4 inch 10 inches from the string nock. It then tapers down to a width at the string nock of 3/8 inch. The lines then continue out, at the same slope, another inch to the end of the limb.

I have felt for a long time that the smaller the string angles at the tips of the limbs can be made at full draw, the better the bow will behave and perform. The smaller the string angles at the tips, the bigger the string angle at the fingers. This helps to minimize string pinch.

Thicker limbs, smaller limb taper rates, and shorter risers all contribute

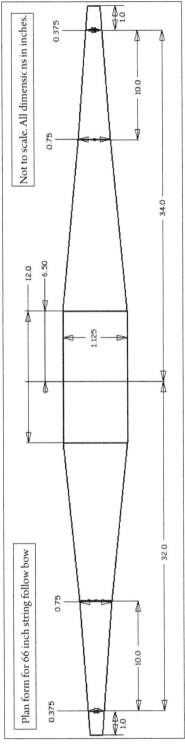

Plan form for 66 inch string follow bow

Not to scale. All dimensions in inches.

to smaller limb tip string angles. These things also contribute to faster, more efficient limbs. Unfortunately, these things, if not done right, are accompanied by excessive hand shock and painful elbows.

By jiggering the length of the riser fadeouts and the position of the riser on the form, I was able to make a bow with a 2-inch-longer top limb that was also dynamically balanced well enough to be gentle in the hand.

I see in my notebook that when I cut this bow just shy of the lines, it came in at 58 pounds of draw force at 27 1/2 inches of draw. When I make a bow, I like it to pull at least 10 pounds more than my desired weight before I start to sand and shape the limbs. In this case my notes say I was trying to get a 50 pound bow in the end. So this initial draw force of 58 pounds is a bit shy. I see that when I finished the bow out, it was 51 pounds at 28 inches. Close, but a bit off my desired weight at 27 1/2 inches, there just was nothing left to sand away, so it will have to do. No worries, next time I'll add 0.010 or 0.015 inch to the core. It looks like this bow shot a 10-grain-per-pound arrow at 170 feet-per-second at my 27 1/2 inch draw length.

When I am sanding a bow to shape, I like to get the sides of the limbs well rounded. That said, I take most of the material off the back side corners of the bow until I get within 5 pounds or so of the desired draw force. Then I pay close attention to the tiller. If I need to adjust the tiller, I do that by sanding the belly side corners of the limbs.

I have found that if you can balance the limbs of the bow on the tillering tree by sanding the belly side corners, the limbs will be better matched in their dynamic response than they would have been had the material been removed from the back side corners only. I think this is so because a bow will only bend as far as the belly will allow it to bend. So no matter how weak you make the back, the limb will only bend so much. By contrast, the bow can only be as strong as the belly and will respond immediately to any weakening of the belly. Cool, eh?

I see that I settled for a positive tiller measured at the fadeouts of 3/16 inch. That's about right for me.

By looking at the figure, you can see that the string angles at each tip are the same at 77 degrees. Nevertheless, to my eye, the top limb looks a bit stiff.

The bow shoots well, and I am happy with it.

If you shoot with a more upright posture, more of a target style where you hold your draw in your back muscles, you may not favor a bow like this too much.

I still favor a shallow dished grip, and so that's what this bow got.

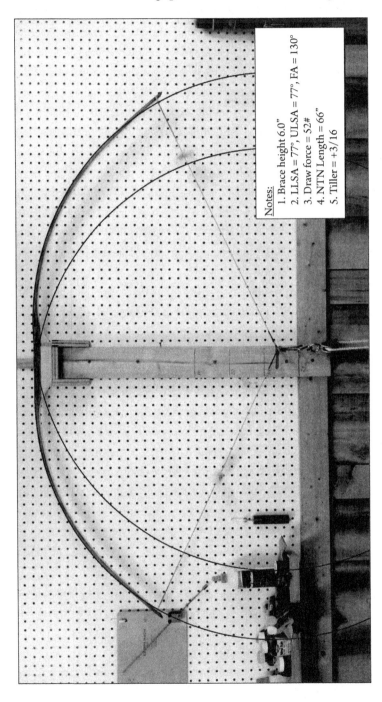

Notes:
1. Brace height 6.0"
2. LLSA = 77°, ULSA = 77°, FA = 130°
3. Draw force = 52#
4. NTN Length = 66"
5. Tiller = +3/16

Appendix B
Glossary of Archery Terms

Action wood - Laminated wood that can be cut across the laminations and used to make the core of a bow.

Arrow shelf - A shelf cut into the handle of a bow designed to accept the arrow and hold it at the same level through the draw and loose of the bow.

Back - The surface of the bow that faces away from the archer and is under tension when the bow is drawn.

Back set - Used to describe the profile of a bow when the tips of the unstrung bow extend past the riser, away from the archer.

Belly - The surface of the bow that faces toward the archer and is under compression when the bow is drawn. Sometimes called the face of the bow.

Bowyer -

    1. A person who makes bows.

    2. One who draws a longbow, a dealer in the marvelous, a teller of improbable stories, a liar (perhaps from the wonderful shots frequently boasted by archers). The word originated in the 12th century, according to Phil Cousineau as recorded in *The Painted Word*.

Brace - To string the bow. A bow at brace is strung and ready to shoot.

Brace height - The measured perpendicular distance from the back of the bow to the inside of the bowstring when the bow is braced.

Cast - A measure of how well a bow can shoot an arrow with respect to its draw force and the arrow's mass weight.

Core - The material, usually wood, in the center of a bow limb between the back and belly fiberglass.

Fadeout - The parts of the riser, located at the top and bottom of the riser, that form the transition between the grip and the limb.

Fistmele - The "fist measure" of the distance from the handle to the string of a braced bow, obtained by placing the base of the fist against the handle and extending the thumb to touch the inside of the string.

Floor tiller - The act of placing the lower limb of the bow on the floor while holding the upper limb in one hand and applying pressure to the grip with the other. Used to roughly judge the action of a bow.

Form - A device used to support and give shape to the laminations of a bow while the glue cures.

Grain - Unit of measure for weight. One ounce equals 480 grains.

Grip - The part of the riser designed to accept the archer's hand. Usually located in the middle of the riser.

Kerf - The width of a saw blade. Also the material removed by the saw blade.

Limb tip - The far end of the limb, past the string nock.

Neutral plane - The plane inside the limb that experiences neither compressive nor tensile stress, usually near the center of the limb between the back and belly surfaces.

Nock set - A bulge on the string, normally made of brass or string, designed to arrest the vertical motion of the arrow at the same point for every shot.

Pin nock - An extremely narrow limb tip wrapped with cord or sinew that provides a lip to retain the string loop instead of notches.

Pre-stress - The effect generated when laminations are glued together around a curve. The resulting cured limb can resist much more force before bending than the individual laminations would have been capable of.

Riser - The handle of the bow, located between the upper and lower limb.

<u>Sistered</u> - Used to describe the relative relationship of boards glued together. Boards that are sistered are glued together along their long dimension. Boards that are butted are glued together at their ends.

<u>Snipe</u> - Uneven thickness on the ends of laminations that have been sanded in a drum sander. Caused by uneven pressure as the drum runs off the end of the lamination.

<u>Stack</u> -

    1. The thickness of all laminations of a bow, usually measured at the middle of the bow.

    2. The sensation felt by the archer as the draw force begins to increase rapidly.

<u>Strain</u> - Material response to an applied force. When a force is applied to a bow, the material in the bow compresses (from compressive stress) or stretches (from tensile stress).

<u>Stress</u> - An applied force. In the case of a bow, there are two principle stresses, compressive (push together) stress and tensile (pull apart) stress.

<u>String</u> - Flexible but inelastic cord connected at each end to opposite ends of the bow.

<u>String follow</u> - Used to describe the profile of a bow when the tips of the unstrung bow extend past the riser, toward the archer.

<u>String nock</u> - Two opposing grooves near the limb tip designed to accept the string and hold it in place.

<u>String silencer</u> - Material added to the string to absorb noise and vibration after the shot.

<u>Tiller</u> -

    1. The act of shaping the bow limbs so that they bend together in harmony.

    2. The shape of the bow limbs when the bow is at brace or drawn.

Appendix C
Bibliography

The following books include those that were quoted directly, as well as those that otherwise informed the writing of this book.

Abbey, Edward. *Desert Solitaire, A Season in the Wilderness*. New York, NY: Ballantine Books, 1968.

Anderson, Fred. *Toxicated, A Treasury of Archery*. Grapeview, WA: Tox Press, 2010.

Axford, Ray. *Archery Anatomy*. London: Souvenir Press, 1995.

Bedau, Mark. *Weak Emergence, Philosophical Perspectives: Mind Causation and World vol 11*. Oxford: Blackwell Publishers, 1999.

Brinkley, Douglas. *The Wilderness Warrior, Theodore Roosevelt and the Crusade for America*. New York, NY: Harper Collins, 2009.

Comstock, Paul. *The Bent Stick*. Delaware, OH: self published, 1988.

Duff, James. *Bows and Arrows - How to Make Them*. New York, NY: The Macmillan Company, 1946.

Hamm, Jim, et al. *The Traditional Bowyers Bible*. Guilford, CT: Bois d'Arc Press, 1992.

Henderson, Al. *Understanding Winning Archery*. Mequon, WI: Target Communications Corp., 2003.

Herrigel, Eugene. *Zen in the Art of Archery*. New York, NY: Random House, 1981.

Hickman, C.N., et al. *Archery: The Technical Side: National Field Archery Association, 1947*.

Hill, Howard. *Hunting the Hard Way*. Lanham, MD: Derrydale Press, 1953.

Leopold, Aldo. *A Sand County Almanac and Sketches Here and There.* New York, NY: Oxford University Press, 1968.

Lewes, George. *Problems of Life and Mind: Third Series, The Study of Psychology, Its Object, Scope and Method.* London: Elibron Classics Series, 1999.

Nelson, Richard. *The Island Within.* New York, NY: Vintage Books, 1991.

Petersen, David. *On the Wild Edge, In Search of a Natural Life.* New York, NY: Henry Holt, 2005.

Pope, Saxton. *Hunting with the Bow and Arrow.* Stilwell, KS: Digireads Publishing, 2007.

Pollan, Michael. *In Defense of Food: An Eater's Manifesto.* New York, NY: Penguin Press, 2008.

Roosevelt, Theodore. *The Wilderness Hunter.* New York, NY: Random House, 1970.

Sigurslid, Dave. *An Archer's Inner Life.* Lincoln, NE: Writers Club Press, 2001.

Schulz, John. *Straight Shooting.* Cody, WY: self published, 2002.

Snyder, Gary. *The Practice of the Wild.* New York, NY: North Point Press, 1990.

Thompson, Maurice. *The Witchery of Archery.* Memphis, TN: General Books, LLC, 2009.

Torges, Dean. *Hunting the Osage Bow, A Chronicle of Craft.* Winfield, KS: Central Plains Books, 1998.

About the Author

One time NASA engineer having worked on some 50 Space Shuttle missions (the only evidence left is the stack of "rocket scientist" T-shirts in the drawer), and one time semi-conductor engineer having worked on equipment and chemical processes used to produce some of the first sub-micron chips (now terribly obsolete), and one time entrepreneur having started an archery company based on a half dozen patents, he now resides on his 50 acre subsistence farm with his family. This book is the result of more than a decade of study, gentle living, and bow building.

CPSIA information can be obtained
at www.ICGtesting.com
Printed in the USA
BVOW03s0838050717
488521BV00015B/45/P

9 780990 782667